First World War
and Army of Occupation
War Diary
France, Belgium and Germany

I0349555

3 CAVALRY DIVISION
Divisional Troops
Royal Army Medical Corps
6 Cavalry Field Ambulance
11 September 1914 - 19 May 1919

WO95/1147/1

The Naval & Military Press Ltd
www.nmarchive.com
Published in association with The National Archives

Published by

The Naval & Military Press Ltd

Unit 10 Ridgewood Industrial Park,

Uckfield, East Sussex,

TN22 5QE England

Tel: +44 (0) 1825 749494

www.naval-military-press.com

www.nmarchive.com

This diary has been reprinted in facsimile from the original. Any imperfections are inevitably reproduced and the quality may fall short of modern type and cartographic standards.

Contents

Document type	Place/Title	Date From	Date To
Heading	WO95/1147/1		
Heading	B.E.F. France & Flanders. 3 Cavalry Div. Troops. 6 Cav Field Ambulance. 1914 Sept To 1919 May. 7 Cav Field Ambulance. 1914 Oct To 1917 June.		
Heading	3rd Cavalry Division No. 6 Cav Field Ambulance Sep. 1914-May 1919		
War Diary	Horse Guards	11/09/1914	11/09/1914
War Diary	Ludgershall	14/09/1914	06/10/1914
War Diary	Southampton	07/10/1914	07/10/1914
War Diary	Fremona	08/10/1914	08/10/1914
War Diary	Ludgershall	03/10/1914	03/10/1914
War Diary	Portsmouth	04/10/1914	05/10/1914
War Diary	Ludgershall	05/10/1914	06/10/1914
War Diary	Ostend	08/10/1914	08/10/1914
War Diary	Meetkerke	09/10/1914	09/10/1914
War Diary	Oost Camp	10/10/1914	10/10/1914
War Diary	Ruddervoorde	10/10/1914	12/10/1914
War Diary	Roulers	12/10/1914	13/10/1914
War Diary	Ypres	13/10/1914	13/10/1914
War Diary	Gheluvelt	13/10/1914	13/10/1914
War Diary	Becelaere	13/10/1914	14/10/1914
War Diary	Iseghem	14/10/1914	14/10/1914
War Diary	Dadizeele	14/10/1914	14/10/1914
War Diary	Ypres	14/10/1914	15/10/1914
War Diary	Wytschaete	15/10/1914	16/10/1914
War Diary	Zonnebeke	16/10/1914	17/10/1914
War Diary	Passchendaele	18/10/1914	18/10/1914
War Diary	Poelcappelle	19/10/1914	20/10/1914
War Diary	Westroosbeke	20/10/1914	20/12/1914
War Diary	Poelcappelle	20/12/1914	20/12/1914
War Diary	Langemarck	20/12/1914	20/12/1914
War Diary	Ypres	20/12/1914	21/12/1914
War Diary	Zandvoorde	21/10/1914	22/10/1914
War Diary	Kleinzillebeke	22/10/1914	25/10/1914
War Diary	Kleinzillebeke	22/10/1914	26/10/1914
War Diary	Zandvoorde	26/10/1914	26/10/1914
War Diary	Kleinzillebeke	26/10/1914	30/10/1914
War Diary	Zillebeke	30/10/1914	31/10/1914
War Diary	Hooge	31/10/1914	31/10/1914
War Diary	Ypres	31/10/1914	31/10/1914
Miscellaneous	Appendix A		
Miscellaneous			
Heading	No 6 Cav. Field Amb		
War Diary	Ypres	01/11/1914	02/11/1914
War Diary	Ypres Menin Rd	02/11/1914	03/11/1914
War Diary	Centre Of The R In Ypres	04/11/1914	07/11/1914
War Diary	Ypres	07/11/1914	07/11/1914
War Diary	Chateau at Level Crossing in Ypres Menin Rd	07/11/1914	07/11/1914
War Diary	Late At Zillebeke	07/11/1914	08/11/1914
War Diary	Ypres	08/11/1914	14/11/1914

War Diary	Groenenjager	15/11/1914	16/11/1914
War Diary	Ypres Menin Rd	16/11/1914	16/11/1914
War Diary	Groenenjager	17/11/1914	17/11/1914
War Diary	Zillebeke	17/11/1914	18/11/1914
War Diary	Groenenjager	18/11/1914	21/11/1914
War Diary	Vieuxberquin	21/11/1914	21/11/1914
War Diary	Steenbecque	21/11/1914	22/11/1914
War Diary	Caudescure	22/11/1914	23/11/1914
Miscellaneous	Appendix B		
Miscellaneous			
Heading	No 6 Cav Field Amb		
War Diary	Caudescure	28/11/1914	14/12/1914
War Diary	Bailleul	14/12/1914	16/12/1914
War Diary	Vierhouck	16/12/1914	31/12/1914
Heading	6th Cavalry Field Ambulance Vol II		
Heading	War Diary of Major W.H.S. Nickerson O.C. No 6 Cav Field Ambulance From 1st Jan 1915 To 31st Jan 1915.		
War Diary	Vierhouck	01/01/1915	28/01/1915
War Diary	Boeseghem	29/01/1915	31/01/1915
War Diary	6th Cavalry Field Ambulance Vol III		
War Diary	Boeseghem	01/02/1915	03/02/1915
War Diary	Hazebrouck	03/02/1915	03/02/1915
War Diary	Ypres	04/02/1915	14/02/1915
War Diary	Boeseghem	15/02/1915	28/02/1915
Heading	No 6 Cavy Field Ambulance Vol IV		
Heading	Lieut Col W.H.S. Nickerson R.A.M.C. Commanding No 6 Cavalry Field Ambulance From 1st March 1915 To 31st March 1915		
War Diary	Boeseghem	01/03/1915	11/03/1915
War Diary	Steenbecque	11/03/1915	11/03/1915
War Diary	La Motte	11/03/1915	11/03/1915
War Diary	Merville	11/03/1915	13/03/1915
War Diary	Boeseghem	13/03/1915	31/03/1915
Heading	No 6 Cavalry Field Ambulance Vol V April 1915		
War Diary	Lt. Col W.H.S. Nickerson D.C. No 6 Cavalry Field Ambulance From 1.4.15 To 30.4.15		
War Diary	Boeseghem	01/04/1915	23/04/1915
War Diary	Hazebrouck	23/04/1915	23/04/1915
War Diary	Abeele	23/04/1915	23/04/1915
War Diary	Eecke	23/04/1915	24/04/1915
War Diary	Boeschepe	25/04/1915	25/04/1915
War Diary	Houtkerke	25/04/1915	26/04/1915
War Diary	St Janster Biezen	26/04/1915	26/04/1915
War Diary	Proven Road	27/04/1915	28/04/1915
War Diary	Forge	29/04/1915	30/04/1915
War Diary	Proven Rd	30/04/1915	30/04/1915
War Diary	Forge	30/04/1915	30/04/1915
War Diary	Proven Rd	30/04/1915	30/04/1915
War Diary	Forge	30/04/1915	30/04/1915
Heading	3rd Cavalry Division 6th Cavalry Field Ambulance Vol VI		
Heading	Lt Col W.H.S. Nickerson D.C. No 6 Cav Field Ambulance From 1st May 1915 To 31st May 1915		
War Diary	Forge	01/05/1915	01/05/1915
War Diary	Proven Rd	01/05/1915	02/05/1915
War Diary	Proven Rd	02/05/1915	02/05/1915

War Diary	Proven	02/05/1915	05/05/1915
War Diary	Level Crossing W of Ypres	05/05/1915	06/05/1915
War Diary	1/2 Mile S.W. of Proven	06/05/1915	07/05/1915
War Diary	Boeseghem	07/05/1915	09/05/1915
War Diary	Camp Rds Near Ypres	09/05/1915	10/05/1915
War Diary	Area Roads	10/05/1915	12/05/1915
War Diary	Hooge	13/05/1915	13/05/1915
War Diary	Camp Rd	13/05/1915	14/05/1915
War Diary	Wittepoorte	14/05/1915	14/05/1915
War Diary	Cain Rds W Of Ypres	14/05/1915	15/05/1915
War Diary	Mehin Rd	15/05/1915	15/05/1915
War Diary	Point 35	16/05/1915	21/05/1915
War Diary	Boeseghem	21/05/1915	29/05/1915
War Diary	Vlamertinghe	29/05/1915	31/05/1915
Miscellaneous	Appendix A		
Miscellaneous			
Heading	3rd Cavalry Division No 6 Cavalry Field Ambulance Vol VII June 1915.		
War Diary	Vlamertinghe	01/06/1915	01/06/1915
War Diary	Ypres	01/06/1915	01/06/1915
War Diary	Woods At Hooge	02/06/1915	02/06/1915
War Diary	Vlamertinghe	02/06/1915	03/06/1915
War Diary	Woods At Hooge	03/06/1915	03/06/1915
War Diary	Ypres	03/06/1915	03/06/1915
War Diary	Vlamertinghe	03/06/1915	03/06/1915
War Diary	Ypres	04/06/1915	04/06/1915
War Diary	Vlamertinghe	04/06/1915	05/06/1915
War Diary	Ypres	05/06/1915	05/06/1915
War Diary	Vlamertinghe	05/06/1915	06/06/1915
War Diary	Point 35	06/06/1915	06/06/1915
War Diary	Boeseghem	06/06/1915	30/06/1915
Miscellaneous	Appendix A		
Miscellaneous			
Heading	3rd Cavalry Division 6th Cav. Field Ambulance Vol VIII From 1st To 31st July 1915		
War Diary	Boeseghem	01/07/1915	31/07/1915
Miscellaneous	3rd Cavalry Division 6th Cav. Field Ambulance Vol IX August 15		
Heading	2nd Col W.H.S. Nickerson R.A.M.C. H. No 6 C.F.A From 1.8.15 To 31.8.15.		
War Diary	Boeseghem	01/08/1915	06/08/1915
War Diary	Flechin	07/08/1915	25/08/1915
War Diary	London	26/08/1915	26/08/1915
War Diary	3rd Cavalry Division No 6 Cavy. Field Ambulance Vol X Aug. Sept. 15		
War Diary	Flechin	25/08/1915	21/09/1915
War Diary	Bois-Des-Dames	22/09/1915	25/09/1915
War Diary	Vermelles	26/09/1915	30/09/1915
Heading	3rd Cavalry Division No 6 Cav. Fd. Amb. Oct & Nov. Vol XI		
War Diary	Ferfay	03/10/1915	03/10/1915
War Diary	Palpart	19/10/1915	20/10/1915
War Diary	St Hilaire	21/10/1915	31/10/1915
War Diary	Livossart	07/11/1915	10/12/1915
Heading	No 6 Cav. Field Ambulance		
Heading	6 Cav Fd Amb Vol. XII XIII XIV XV		

War Diary	Fruges	10/12/1915	31/12/1915
Heading	No 6 Cavalry Field Ambulance For January 1916 February 1916 March 1916		
War Diary	Fruges	01/01/1916	31/03/1916
Heading	3rd Cav. Div. No 6 Cavalry Field Ambulance April 1916.		
War Diary	Fruges	01/04/1916	28/04/1916
Heading	3rd Cavalry Division 6th Cavalry Field Ambulance May 1916		
War Diary	Fruges	01/05/1916	31/05/1916
Heading	3rd Cav. Div. No. 6 Cavalry Field Ambulance June 1916		
War Diary	Fruges	02/06/1916	06/06/1916
War Diary	Offin	11/06/1916	24/06/1916
War Diary	Cornhotte	25/06/1916	25/06/1916
War Diary	St. Leger Les-Domart	26/06/1916	26/06/1916
War Diary	Bonney	27/06/1916	30/06/1916
War Diary	3rd Cav. Div. No. 6 Cav. F Amb. Vol 19		
War Diary	Bonney	01/07/1916	02/07/1916
War Diary	Morlancourt	02/07/1916	03/07/1916
War Diary	Bonney	03/07/1916	04/07/1916
War Diary	Dreuil-Le Hamel	04/07/1916	04/07/1916
War Diary	Hamel	05/07/1916	08/07/1916
War Diary	Corbie	09/07/1916	09/07/1916
War Diary	Vaux-Sur. Somme	09/07/1916	19/07/1916
War Diary	Laneuville	19/07/1916	31/07/1916
Heading	6th Cavalry Field Ambulance Month Of August 1916		
War Diary	Soues	01/08/1916	02/08/1916
War Diary	Millencourt	03/08/1916	04/08/1916
War Diary	Maintenay	04/08/1916	04/08/1916
War Diary	Offin	05/08/1916	25/08/1916
War Diary	Hesmond	26/08/1916	31/08/1916
Heading	6th Cav. Field Amb. Sept 1916		
Heading	6th Cavalry Field Amb. September 1916		
War Diary	Hesmond	01/09/1916	09/09/1916
War Diary	Artoules	10/09/1916	11/09/1916
War Diary	Canchy	11/09/1916	11/09/1916
War Diary	Tirancourt (La Chausee)	12/09/1916	13/09/1916
War Diary	Tirancourt	13/09/1916	13/09/1916
War Diary	Bussy Les Daours	14/09/1916	14/09/1916
War Diary	W. of Bonney	15/09/1916	17/09/1916
War Diary	S. of Pont Noyelle	17/09/1916	21/09/1916
War Diary	Soues	22/09/1916	22/09/1916
War Diary	Drucas (Wavan)	23/09/1916	23/09/1916
War Diary	Douriez	24/09/1916	29/09/1916
War Diary	Rang De Fliers	30/09/1916	30/09/1916
Heading	6th Cav. Field Ambulance Oct 1916		
War Diary	No 6 Cavalry Field Ambulance October 1916		
War Diary	Rang Du Fliers	02/10/1916	19/10/1916
War Diary	Merlimont Plage	21/10/1916	30/10/1916
Heading	3rd Cav. Div. Of No 6 Cavalry Field Ambulance For The Month Of November 1916		
War Diary	Merlimont Plage	01/11/1916	30/11/1916
Heading	3rd Cav. Div. Of 6th Cav. Field Ambulance December 1916		
War Diary	Merlimont Plage	01/12/1916	21/12/1916

War Diary	Hesmond	22/12/1916	31/12/1916
War Diary	3rd Cav Div. Of 6th Cav. Field Ambulance January 1917		
War Diary	Hesmond	01/01/1917	31/01/1917
Heading	6th Cav. Field Ambulance March 1917		
War Diary	Hesmond	01/03/1917	31/03/1917
War Diary	No 6 Cavalry Field Ambulance February 1917		
War Diary	Hesmond	01/02/1917	28/02/1917
Heading	No 6 Cavalry Field Ambulance For April 1917		
Heading	6th Cavalry Field Ambulance 3rd Cav. Div. Cav. Corps. From 8/4/17 3rd Army Till 13/5/17		
Miscellaneous	3rd Cav. Div. Cav. Corps. 3rd Army.		
War Diary	Hesmond	01/04/1917	04/04/1917
War Diary	Contes	05/04/1917	06/04/1917
War Diary	Vacquerie-Le-Boucq	07/04/1917	07/04/1917
War Diary	Fosseux	07/04/1917	09/04/1917
War Diary	Arras	09/04/1917	09/04/1917
War Diary	X Roads By T in Halte on the Arras-St Pol Road 4/1/2 Kilo From Arras (ref of Lens 1/100000)	10/04/1917	10/04/1917
War Diary	H 32d (Ref Maf 51 B & C 1/40,000)	11/04/1917	11/04/1917
War Diary	Arras	12/04/1917	16/04/1917
War Diary	Fosseux	12/04/1917	15/04/1917
War Diary	Le Boisle (Ref Maf Abbeville 1/100,000)	15/04/1917	16/04/1917
Miscellaneous	Le Boisle	18/04/1917	18/04/1917
War Diary	Maintenay	19/04/1917	30/04/1917
Heading	No 6 Cav. Field Ambulance For Month Of May 1917		
Heading	6th Cavalry Field Ambulance 3rd Cav. Div. Cav. Corps. from 8/4/17 3rd Army Till 13/5/17		
Miscellaneous	3rd Cav. Div. Cav. Corps. 3rd Army Till 13/5/17		
War Diary	Maintenay (Ref Maf 1/100,000 Abbeville)	01/05/1917	12/05/1917
War Diary	Maintenay Tortefontaine (Abbeville 1/100,000)	13/05/1917	13/05/1917
War Diary	Frohen-Le-Grand (Lens 1/100000)	14/05/1917	14/05/1917
War Diary	Havernas (Lens 1/100000)	15/05/1917	15/05/1917
War Diary	Bussy-Les-Daours (Amiens 1/100000)	17/05/1917	17/05/1917
War Diary	Bayonvillers (Amiens 1/100000)	18/05/1917	18/05/1917
War Diary	Buire (St-Quentin 1/100000)	21/05/1917	31/05/1917
War Diary	6th C.F.H Month Of June 1917		
War Diary	Buire (St-Quentin 1/100000)	03/06/1917	29/06/1917
Heading	6th. C.F. Ambulance For Month Of July 1917		
War Diary	Buire (St Quentin 1/100000)	01/07/1917	03/07/1917
War Diary	Suzanne (Amiens 1/100000)	04/07/1917	04/07/1917
War Diary	Heilly (Amiens 1/100000)	05/07/1917	05/07/1917
War Diary	Orville (Lens 1/100000)	06/07/1917	07/07/1917
War Diary	Rebreuviette (1/100000 Lens)	07/07/1917	07/07/1917
War Diary	Auchel (Hazebrouck 1/100000)	07/07/1917	16/07/1917
War Diary	Les Lauriers (Hazebrouck 1/100000)	16/07/1917	31/07/1917
War Diary	No 6 Cavalry Field Ambulance For Month Of August 1917		
War Diary	Les Lauriers (Hazebrouck 1/100,000)	02/08/1917	31/08/1917
Heading	No 6 Cav Field Ambulance For Month Of September 1917		
War Diary	Les Lauriers (Hazebrouck 1/100,000)	01/09/1917	30/09/1917
Miscellaneous	No 6 Cav. F.A.		
War Diary	Pont Remy (Abbeville 1/100,000)	03/11/1917	17/11/1917
War Diary	Agnicourt (Amiens F1 1/100,000)	18/11/1917	18/11/1917
War Diary	Cappy (Amiens J1/100,000)	19/11/1917	23/11/1917

War Diary	La Vicogne (Lens D6 1/100,000)	24/11/1917	30/11/1917
Heading	No 6 Cav. Field Ambulance For Month Of October 1917		
War Diary	Les Lauriers Hazebrouck 1/100000	03/10/1917	19/10/1917
War Diary	Huclier (Lens 1/100000)	21/10/1917	22/10/1917
War Diary	Canettemont (Lens 1/100000)	23/10/1917	23/10/1917
War Diary	Donesmont (Lens 1/100000)	24/10/1917	24/10/1917
War Diary	Pont Remy (Abbeville 1/100000)	28/10/1917	30/10/1917
Heading	No 6 Cav. F.A.		
War Diary	La Vicogne (Lens 1/100000)	01/12/1917	01/12/1917
War Diary	Allonville (Amiens NS 1/100000)	02/12/1917	20/12/1917
War Diary	Yaucourt-Bussus (Abbeville 1/100000)	21/12/1917	27/01/1918
War Diary	Belloy-Sur-Somme (Amiens 1/100000)	28/01/1918	28/01/1918
War Diary	Guillaucourt (Amiens 1/100000)	29/01/1918	29/01/1918
War Diary	Meraucourt (62c. V12 G28)	30/01/1918	31/01/1918
Heading	No. 6 Cav. F.A. Feb. 9.8.		
War Diary	Trefcon W (62c10a46)	01/02/1918	10/02/1918
War Diary	Trefcon (62c. W.10a 46)	13/02/1918	28/02/1918
Heading	No. 6 Cav. F.A. Mar. 1918		
War Diary	Trefcon (62 C. W. a 46)	01/03/1918	12/03/1918
War Diary	St.Cren (62 a. p 27a)	13/03/1918	21/03/1918
War Diary	Beaumont-EN-Beine (66d W 6)	21/03/1918	22/03/1918
War Diary	Villequier Aumont (66d X24c59)	22/03/1918	24/03/1918
War Diary	Ugny (66dX20d)	24/03/1918	24/03/1918
War Diary	Chateau D'Estay (702 K 18a11)	24/03/1918	24/03/1918
War Diary	Ollencourt (702 V b65)	25/03/1918	25/03/1918
War Diary	Choisy-Au-Bac (Ref Maf Beauvais 1/100,000)	26/03/1918	28/03/1918
War Diary	Airion (Beauvais 1/100,000)	29/03/1918	29/03/1918
War Diary	La Racineuse Fme (662 A9 C62)	30/03/1918	31/03/1918
Heading	6th Cavalry Field Amb. Apr. 1918.		
War Diary	Bove's (Amiens 1/100000 E2)	01/04/1918	02/04/1918
War Diary	Blangy-Tronville (Amiens 1/10000072)	03/04/1918	03/04/1918
War Diary	Sheet 62d 026 C 94	04/04/1918	04/04/1918
War Diary	Camon (Amiens 1/100000)	06/04/1918	09/04/1918
War Diary	Sheet B z d N 28 d 04	04/04/1918	04/04/1918
War Diary	Camon (Amiens 1/100000)	06/04/1918	06/04/1918
War Diary	Ferfay Hazebrook 1/100000 7.6	13/04/1918	17/04/1918
War Diary	Camon	09/04/1918	10/04/1918
War Diary	Bachimont (Lens B 3 1/100000)	11/04/1918	11/04/1918
War Diary	Conteville Lens D1 1/100000	12/04/1918	13/04/1918
War Diary	Ferfay	17/04/1918	24/04/1918
War Diary	Fontaine-Lez-Hermans (Hazebrouck 1/100000)	25/04/1918	30/04/1918
War Diary	A.D.M.S.		
Heading	No. 6 Cav. F.A. May 1918.		
War Diary	Fontaine-Les-Hermans (Hazebrouck 1/100000)	01/05/1918	04/05/1918
War Diary	Vacquerie Le Boucq (Lens 1/100000 C.3)	05/05/1918	05/05/1918
War Diary	Frohen-Le-Grand (Lens 1/100000 C.3)	06/05/1918	06/05/1918
War Diary	Contay (Lens 1/100000 F 6)	07/05/1918	17/05/1918
War Diary	Belloy-Sur-Somme (Amiens 1/100000 B1)	17/05/1918	31/05/1918
War Diary	Montigny (Amiens 1/100000 F 1)	31/05/1918	31/05/1918
Heading	No. 6 Cav. Fed Amb. Vol 42 June 1918.		
War Diary	Montigny (Amiens 1/100000 F 1)	01/06/1918	09/06/1918
War Diary	Belloy-Sur-Somme (Amiens 1/100000 B1)	14/06/1918	14/06/1918
War Diary	Belloy-Sur-Somme	16/06/1918	30/06/1918
Heading	No 6 Cav Fed Amb July 1918		
Diagram etc			

War Diary	Belloy-Sur-Somme (Amiens 1/100000)	01/07/1918	20/07/1918
War Diary	Riencourt (Amiens 1/100000 A1)	21/07/1918	21/07/1918
Heading	No. 6 Cav. F.A. Aug. 1918		
War Diary	Riencourt (Amiens A1 1/100000)	01/08/1918	01/08/1918
War Diary	Le Mesge (Amiens A1 1/100000)	05/08/1918	06/08/1918
War Diary	Rehancourt (Amiens D2 1/100000)	07/08/1918	07/08/1918
War Diary	N31d (Sheet B2 d 1-40000)	08/08/1918	08/08/1918
War Diary	T 10 d 42 (62d)	08/08/1918	08/08/1918
War Diary	C 11 d (662)	08/08/1918	08/08/1918
War Diary	Maison Blanche (D20e 66E)	08/08/1918	10/08/1918
War Diary	Bouchoir (K23c 61)	10/08/1918	11/08/1918
War Diary	Fouencamps (Amiens 1/100000 23)	12/08/1918	15/08/1918
War Diary	Riencourt (Amiens A1 1/100000)	16/08/1918	21/08/1918
War Diary	Montrelet (Lens 1/100000 C 5)	22/08/1918	25/08/1918
War Diary	Cumonville Lens 1/100,000 A4	26/08/1918	26/08/1918
War Diary	Nuncq Lens 1/1000000 D3	27/08/1918	31/08/1918
Heading	6 Cav. Field Ambce. Sept. 1918		
War Diary	Nuncq (Lens 1/100000 D3)	01/09/1918	04/09/1918
War Diary	Le Parcq (Lens 1/100000)	06/09/1918	18/09/1918
War Diary	Rebreuve (Lens 1/100000)	19/09/1918	21/09/1918
War Diary	Bus-Les-Artois (Lens 1/100000) Meaulte (Amiens 1/100000)	25/09/1918	27/09/1918
War Diary	Hem (Amiens 1/100000)	28/09/1918	29/09/1918
War Diary	Vermand (St. Quentin 1/100000)	30/09/1918	30/09/1918
Heading	No 6 Cav. Field Ambce. Oct. 1918		
War Diary	Vermand (St. Quentin 1/100000)	01/10/1918	02/10/1918
War Diary	Ste Helene (St. Quentine 1/100000)	03/10/1918	04/10/1918
War Diary	Trefcon (St. Quentine 1/100000)	05/10/1918	05/10/1918
War Diary	Bellenglise (St. Quentine 1/100000)	07/10/1918	08/10/1918
War Diary	Maretz (Valencienines.) 1/40,000	09/10/1918	09/10/1918
War Diary	Bertry (Valencienines.) 1/40,000	10/10/1918	10/10/1918
War Diary	Elincourt (Valencienines.)	11/10/1918	11/10/1918
War Diary	Elincourt	12/10/1918	12/10/1918
War Diary	Banteux (Valencienines C 6)	13/10/1918	13/10/1918
War Diary	Bois-De-Hennois (Lens 1/100000)	14/10/1918	31/10/1918
Heading	No 6 C. F. Amb. Nov 1918		
War Diary	Bois de Hennois (Lens 1/100000)	01/11/1918	05/11/1918
War Diary	Marquoin (Valencienines. 1/100000)	06/11/1918	06/11/1918
War Diary	Esquerchin (Valencienines. 1/100000)	07/11/1918	07/11/1918
War Diary	Peronne (Valencienines. B 6 1/100000)	08/11/1918	08/11/1918
War Diary	Ramecroix (Tournai 1/100000)	10/11/1918	11/11/1918
War Diary	Ponenche (Tournai 1/100000)	12/11/1918	17/11/1918
War Diary	Rontant (Tournai 1/100000 L4)	18/11/1918	18/11/1918
War Diary	Bierghes Brussels 1/100000 B4	19/11/1918	21/11/1918
War Diary	Mousty Brussels 1/100000 95	22/11/1918	22/11/1918
War Diary	Long Champs Brussels 1/100000 K 6	24/11/1918	24/11/1918
War Diary	Dhuy Brussels 1/100000	30/11/1918	30/11/1918
Heading	No 6 Cav. F.A. Dec 1918		
War Diary	Dhuy (Brussels 1/100000)	01/12/1918	08/12/1918
War Diary	Abbe (Liege 1/100000 C B)	10/12/1918	11/12/1918
War Diary	La Mallieue Halte (Liege 1/100000)	12/12/1918	31/12/1918
War Diary	Appenidix Court		
Heading	3rd Cav Div Box 853 No 6 Cav. F.A. Jan 1919		
War Diary	La Mallieue Halte (Liege 1/100000)	01/01/1919	31/01/1919
War Diary	No. 6 Cav. F.A. Feb. 1919		
War Diary	La Mallieue Halte Liege 1/100000	01/02/1919	28/02/1919

War Diary	No. 6 Cav. F.A. Mar. 1919		
War Diary	La Mallieue Halte (Liege 1/100000)	01/03/1919	31/03/1919
War Diary	No 6 Cav. F.A. Apr 1919		
War Diary	La Mallieue Halte (Liege 1/100000)	01/04/1919	30/04/1919
War Diary	No 6 Cav. Field Amb. May 1919		
War Diary	La Mallieue Halte (Liege 1/100000)	01/05/1919	12/05/1919
War Diary	Antwerp	12/05/1919	19/05/1919
Diagram etc			

B.E.F. FRANCE & FLANDERS.

3 CAVALRY DIV. TROOPS.

6 CAV FIELD AMBULANCE.

1914 SEPT TO 1919 MAY.

7 CAV FIELD AMBULANCE.

1914 OCT TO 1917 JUNE.

1147.

B.E.F. FRANCE & FLANDERS.

3 CAVALRY DIV. TROOPS.

6 CAV FIELD AMBULANCE.

1914 SEPT TO 1919 MAY.

7 CAV FIELD AMBULANCE.

1914 OCT TO 1917 JUNE.

1147

1914-18

3RD CAVALRY DIVISION

NO.6 CAV FIELD AMBULANCE

SEP. 1914-~~DEC 1918~~ MAY 1919

Instructions regarding War Diaries and Intelligence Summaries are contained in F. S. Regs., Part II. and the Staff Manual respectively. Title pages will be prepared in manuscript.

WAR DIARY
or
~~INTELLIGENCE SUMMARY~~
(*Erase heading not required.*)

Army Form C. 2118.

Hour, Date, Place	Summary of Events and Information	Remarks and references to Appendices
11 a.m. 11-9-14. HORSE GUARDS.	While acting as D.A.D.M.S. to D.D.M.S. Eastern Command, got orders to proceed to LUDGERSHALL & take command of No 6 Cavalry Field Ambulance for service with the Expeditionary Force.	On leave of absence from India.
9 a.m. 14. 9. 14 LUDGERSHALL	Arrived last night. Assumed charge this morning. Only the R.A.M.C. personnel here. No equipment. Some tents, & temporary equipment for them had been drawn.	
20.9.14.	Medical equipment arrived. Deficiencies of N.C.O's & equipment have been pointed out, & the men exercised in Corps drills, exercises, & route marches. Nothing of interest to record during this period. We have been told we will get Ordnance equipment when the 7th Div are equipped.	
10 a.m. 2.10.14	Ordered to draw horses from SALISBURY. Party detailed to go tomorrow. Our A.S.C. drivers have arrived but are camped with other A.S.C. at LUDGERSHALL.	

Instructions regarding War Diaries and Intelligence Summaries are contained in F. S. Regs., Part II. and the Staff Manual respectively. Title pages will be prepared in manuscript.

WAR DIARY
or
~~INTELLIGENCE~~ SUMMARY

(Erase heading not required.)

Army Form C. 2118.

Hour, Date, Place	Summary of Events and Information	Remarks and references to Appendices
3-30 P.m. 6-10-14 LUDGERSHALL	Completed loading of wagons & had horses harnessed.	Horses should have their harness fitted at least a week before starting.
5 P.m.	Marched to Station & loaded up train.	
6 P.m.	Train started for SOUTHAMPTON.	Horses were heavy, too [illegible] harness. Several horses [illegible] bolted, & one wagon was overturned, no damage done.
7.30 P.m. SOUTHAMPTON.	Arrived Docks Station. Unloaded train, & equipment & men were embarked on S.S. FREMONA. Was placed in military charge of ship & given necessary documents.	Entraining & embarkation very rapidly & easily effected.
10 AM. 7.10.14 S.S. FREMONA	Ship left at about 2 a.m. last night was proceeding towards DOVER. Sea smooth. Made out embarkation return.	
6 P.M.	Arrived off DOVER, & ship received orders. Anchored in the DOWNS & waited for Convoy.	
10 a.m. 8.10.14 S.S. FREMONA	Ship arrived at daybreak & anchored off OSTEND. Made out landing return. Ship just entering port.	Handed in returns to Military Landing Officer.
6 P.m.	Waited in dock all day not was then decided to take the ship further in to unload	A pity this was not done earlier. It means unloading after dark

1247 W 3299 200,000 (E) 8/14 J.B.C. & A. Forms/C. 2118/11.

Instructions regarding War Diaries and Intelligence Summaries are contained in F. S. Regs., Part II. and the Staff Manual respectively. Title pages will be prepared in manuscript.

WAR DIARY
~~or~~
~~INTELLIGENCE~~ SUMMARY

(Erase heading not required.)

Army Form C. 2118.

Hour, Date, Place	Summary of Events and Information	Remarks and references to Appendices
7 P.m. 3-10-14 LUDGERSHALL.	Received orders to proceed at once to PORTSMOUTH to draw Ordnance equipment for No. 6 & 7 Cavalry Field Ambulances. Proceeded immediately, arrived PORTSMOUTH 9.20 P.m.	
9 A.M. 4-10-14. PORTSMOUTH	Proceeded to ordnance depot on United Services Mens' recreation ground. Found that Ordnance Officer had already sent off wagons. Met N.C.O. & party of men sent from LUDGERSHALL.	
9-30 P.m.	Have drawn most of equipment. Went to Station & arranged for train in the morning.	
6 a.m. 5-10-14 PORTSMOUTH.	Drew remainder of equipment & had it transferred to the Station. Arranged Special Carriage for the men, & caught train at 10 a.m.	The party sent to draw ordnance equipment was not enough. There should be at least 1 Officer for each F.A. with two N.C.O.s & 15 men apiece.
4-30 P.m. 5-10-14 LUDGERSHALL	Arrived back. Asked how soon we could move, & replied 36 hours. Unloaded train.	
7.30 a.m. 6-10-14. LUDGERSHALL	Started sorting equipment & loading wagons; harness fitted to horses.	
1 P.m. 6-10-14	Rung up on telephone by War Office, & ordered to start at 6 P.m. whether all equipment was ready or not.	

1247 W 3299 200,000 (E) 8/14 J.B.C. & A. Forms/C. 2118/11.

Instructions regarding War Diaries and Intelligence Summaries are contained in F. S. Regs., Part II. and the Staff Manual respectively. Title pages will be prepared in manuscript.

WAR DIARY
or
INTELLIGENCE SUMMARY
(Erase heading not required.)

Army Form C. 2118.

Hour, Date, Place	Summary of Events and Information	Remarks and references to Appendices
	Ref map N.W. EUROPE Sheet 1.	
2 A.M. 8.10.14. OSTEND.	Just completed unloading. Bivouacked on the wharf	No gangways at wharf. We hunted round & found one 1/4 mile away, suitable for horses, then dragged it along & we got horses off. Lt Cree went to town & got hold of the man who works the electric cranes, & he came & cleared the holds for us. Heavy rain last night.
6 a.m. 8.10.14.	Loaded wagons, & eventually got orders to move to near BRUGES at 2 P.m.	
6 P.m. 8.10.14.	Halted at MEETKERKE. Put wagons in a field & billeted men in them & some outhouses of buildings near by.	
9 a.m. 9.10.14 MEETKERKE	Went to BRUGES by myself at 6.30 a.m. for orders, & saw A.D.M.S. 3rd Cav Divn. Returned to 7 a. & opened "B" Sectn for reception of sick. Ordered to evacuate any sick into local hospital, or to entrain them for OSTEND. None admitted.	
1 P.m. 9.10.14.	Marched off through BRUGES to OOSTCAMP.	
4.30 P.m. OOSTCAMP.	Arrived OOSTCAMP. Billeted in school house, & opened "B" Sectn. Took in two cases of injury.	Received orders to march in the morning.
8 AM. 10.10.14.	Marched for RUDDERVOORDE.	
11.30 a.m. RUDDERVOORDE	Arrived here & billeted in the Chateau RUDDERVOORDE. Opened "B" Sectn. Two men detained.	Received orders to march in the morning.

1247 W 3299 200,000 (E) 8/14 J.B.C. & A. Forms/C. 2118/11.

Instructions regarding War Diaries and Intelligence Summaries are contained in F. S. Regs., Part II. and the Staff Manual respectively. Title pages will be prepared in manuscript.

WAR DIARY
or
~~INTELLIGENCE~~ SUMMARY
(Erase heading not required.)

Army Form C. 2118.

Hour, Date, Place	Ref Map N.W. Europe. Sheet I Summary of Events and Information	Remarks and references to Appendices
8 a.m. 12.10.14 RUDDERVOORDE	Marched via THOUROUT to ROULERS. Received orders before starting to attach one section to the 6th Cavalry Brigade.	
1 P.m. 12.10.14 ROULERS	Arrived at ROULERS, Billeted A Section in the house of a merchant, & another house on the opposite side of the street. Took command of this section & sent B Section under Major ELSNER to billets arranged by Divisional Head Quarters.	Received various orders, which were cancelled & at 2 a.m. on 13.10.14 got orders to march with 6th Cavalry Bgde to YPRES
4 A.M. 13.10.14 ROULERS	Got up & turned out the section, joined 6th Cavalry Bgde in the market place. They marched at 7 a.m. Marched via OOSTNIEUWKERKE	
12.45 P.m. 13.10.14 YPRES.	arrived here, & halted an hour. Marched on to GHELUVELT.	
4 P.m. 13.10.14 GHELUVELT.	Got orders to rejoin Divisional Head Quarters at ISEGHEM. Marched at once	Rained hard all this afternoon.
5 P.m. 13.10.14 BECELAERE	Halted for half an hour to feed horses. Marched via DADIZEELE. WINKEL St ELOI to ISEGHEM. Marched 36 miles today. Long delay in DADIZEELE owing to place being blocked with 7th Bgde getting into billets. One horse got both hind legs in a stable in the latter place. 6th Bgde were in touch with enemy & fighting today.	Horses stood the march well despite new harness & being soft. Roads wet, heavy rain all night.
12.5 a.m. 14.10.14 ISEGHEM	Arrived here, & billeted in a large yard near the Station. ~~[illegible]~~	
9.30 a.m. 14.10.14 ISEGHEM.	Marched via WINKEL St ELOI – LEDEGHEM to DADIZEELE.	Got orders at 8 a.m.

1247 W 3299 200,000 (E) 8/14 J.B.C. & A. Forms/C. 2118/11.

Instructions regarding War Diaries and Intelligence Summaries are contained in F. S. Regs., Part II. and the Staff Manual respectively. Title pages will be prepared in manuscript.

WAR DIARY
or
INTELLIGENCE SUMMARY
(Erase heading not required.)

Army Form C. 2118.

Hour, Date, Place	Ref map of N.W. Europe. Sheet 7 Summary of Events and Information	Remarks and references to Appendices
12 midday 14.10.14 DADIZEELE.	Arrived here, & found the place deserted. No sign of troops. Burgomaster knew nothing of any of them.	
10 P.m. 14.10.14. YPRES.	Halted & fed horses. Remained till 5 P.m. & sent cyclist along road to BECELAERE. He found no signs of British troops on any road.	
	Got news at 5 P.m. that enemy was half a mile off, said to be 2000 strong. Immediately afterwards, a patrol of Germans came up the street to within 200 yards of me, & retired. Ordered everyone to mount at once, & marched to BECELAERE, & thence to YPRES. Just avoided several hostile patrols. After starting, picked up a Belgian soldier, & 9 men of 1st Life Guards who had been missing 2 days previously. Also took the horse left behind yesterday with colic; it had now recovered.	
	See Appendix A for full account of today.	
	Reported arrival to Hd Qrs 4th Army Corps. Bivouacked in Market place. Found A.S.C. officer, & succeeded in getting day's rations.	
9.30 AM. 15.10.14. WYTSCHAETE.	Left YPRES at 5.45 a.m. Arrived without incident, though outposts along the road reported that they had been engaged during the night.	
	Picked up a man of the 10th Hussars, who reported that his patrol had been attacked & dispersed.	
10 a.m.	Reported arrival to 3rd Cav. Div. Hd. Qrs. Found we had been put down as missing.	Was told I had been ordered to DADIZEELE in error. See Appendix A
6 P.m.	Ordered to attach a section to 6th Cavalry Bde whose horses were fresher. Detailed "B" section, with myself in command of it.	
9 P.m. 15.10.14	Wounded Germans taken in by the Field Ambulance. Amputated the left arm of a Lt. of German Dragoons. Put other German wounded in Convent.	

1247 W 3299 200,000 (E) 8/14 J.B.C. & A. Forms/C. 2118/11.

Instructions regarding War Diaries and Intelligence Summaries are contained in F. S. Regs., Part II. and the Staff Manual respectively. Title pages will be prepared in manuscript.

WAR DIARY
or
INTELLIGENCE SUMMARY
(Erase heading not required.)

Army Form C. 2118

Key map N.W. Europe Sheet 1.

Hour, Date, Place	Summary of Events and Information	Remarks and references to Appendices
11 P.m. 16.10.14. Cross roads ½ mile N.E. of ZONNEBEKE.	Evacuated wounded & sick by supply motor lorries at 4 a.m. today to DUNKIRK. Marched at 8 a.m. with B Section attached to 6th Cav Bde, to YPRES. Thence to POELCAPPELLE. Brigade engaged all day with enemy's patrols. after dark moved by cross roads near St JULIEN to present position. Billeted men in a barn & officers in a small & very dirty cottage.	No casualties. Very cold. Heavy rain at night.
6 P.m. 17.10.14. ZONNEBEKE.	Patrols encountered Germans during the day. A few casualties which were collected by my wagons, except one, who was within 500 yards of German trenches on ROULERS-MENIN Road, & he was placed in a farm house, wagon being unable to approach him. Moved into the town at 3 P.m. & billeted in farm attached to Chateau.	Ordered at midday to move into ZONNEBEKE.
5 P.m. 18.10.14. PASSCHENDAELE.	Came here this afternoon, by the main road. Billeted in a barn & shop. Lots of straw for men & horses.	Good billets. Orders at 9 P.m. to march in the morning.
10 P.m. 19.10.14. POELCAPPELLE.	Started at 7 a.m. & went to MOORSLEDE. Formed dressing station here. Sent one light wagon down with 6th Bde. This subsequently pushed on to LEDEGHEM. Sent another wagon to cross roads on YPRES-MENIN Rd. Heavy fighting all day. Eventually fell back with wounded to PASSCHENDALE. Went back alone to MOORSLEDE & found rear guard had just left. Evacuated rest of wounded from there on an armoured motor, & rode back myself. Evacuated all wounded by motors to YPRES. Marched here via WESTROOSEBEKE. Billeted in a school house & priest's house.	See Appendix A. Ordered at 5 P.m. to return to POELCAPPELLE. Bad billets. Heavy rain. Orders to move at 6 a.m.

1247 W 3299 200,000 (E) 8/14 J.B.C. & A. Forms/C. 2118/11.

Instructions regarding War Diaries and Intelligence Summaries are contained in F. S. Regs., Part II. and the Staff Manual respectively. Title pages will be prepared in manuscript.

WAR DIARY
or
INTELLIGENCE SUMMARY
(Erase heading not required.)

Army Form C. 2118.

Hour, Date, Place	Ref map N.W. Europe Sheet 7 — Summary of Events and Information	Remarks and references to Appendices
6 a.m. 20.10.14. POELCAPPELLE	Marched along main road towards WESTROOSBEKE & formed dressing station on right hand side of road in two cottages, 1 mile behind above named place. Brigade entrenched themselves on line	
8 A.M. WESTROOSEBEKE	WESTROOSEBEKE–PASSCHENDALE & were heavily attacked. advanced two light wagons to close up to the position under cover of a house. Wounded evacuated from here to dressing station.	
1 P.m. 20.12.14 POELCAPPELLE	Retired here, as ordered, with all wounded in heavy wagons. 6th Bgde fell back to this spot.	12 noon; ordered to retire. 4 P.m. Ordered to billet in LANGEMARCK
5 P.m. 20.12.14 LANGEMARCK.	Just going into billets, when enemy made rapid advance towards this place. Bgde turned out, & fell back on YPRES fighting rear guard action till after dark. Enemy's attack came from POELCAPPELLE.	
8 P.m. 20.12.14. YPRES.	Went back to YPRES by the small road that runs through the X of PILKEM. Billeted in Belgian barracks. Evacuated all wounded into Clearing Hospital here. Brigade had no further casualties in rear guard action.	Could get no orders, so decided to take a small road back to YPRES
9 a.m. 21.12.14 YPRES	Brigade marched along road towards GHELUVELT. Halted at HOOGE.	Found 1st Army Corps entrenching in front of YPRES
2 P.m.	Marched by ZILLEBEKE & level crossings towards VOORMEZEELE. Halted a mile from latter place.	
7 P.m.	Marched towards ZILLEBEKE: several bad blocks in the traffic delayed us. Halted at level crossing as directed.	5 P.m orders to go to level crossing, close to ZILLEBEKE to await orders.

1247 W 3299 200,000 (E) 8/14 J.B.C. & A. Forms/C. 2118/11.

Instructions regarding War Diaries and Intelligence Summaries are contained in F. S. Regs., Part II. and the Staff Manual respectively. Title pages will be prepared in manuscript.

WAR DIARY
or
INTELLIGENCE SUMMARY
(Erase heading not required.)

Army Form C. 2118.

Hour, Date, Place	Ref Map N.W. Europe. Sheet 7. Summary of Events and Information	Remarks and references to Appendices
8.30 P.M. 21.10.14.	Marched through ZILLEBEKE to ZANDVOORDE	
12 midnight ZANDVOORDE	Arrived & reported to Bgde Major, 6th Cav Bgde. Bivouacked in open.	Ordered to fall back a little in the morning, as attack by enemy was certain
4 a.m. 22.10.14. ZANDVOORDE	Went with a wagon to the village to remove some wounded.	
5.30 A.M. KLEINZILLEBEKE	Came here, & formed dressing station. Sent a light wagon forward to the foot of the village of ZANDVOORDE. 6th Bgde occupied the trenches. Went there myself in afternoon, in Motor Ambulance & evacuated some wounded. Sent all wounded to YPRES in Motor Ambulances.	Germans shelled ZANDVOORDE all day.
9 P.M.	Night attack by Germans to S.W. of ZILLEBEKE-ZANDVOORDE road on 7th Division close to us. Turned out section, but not needed.	
11 A.M. 23.10.14. KLEINZILLEBEKE.	Moved about 3/4 mile nearer ZILLEBEKE & shared a dressing station with No 7 Cavalry Field Amb[ulance]. Dressing station shelled before it was moved. Sent light wagons to ZANDVOORDE. Evacuated casualties from the Dressing Station to YPRES in Motor Ambulances.	Shell killed & wounded several in a battery close to place we moved from.
5 P.M.	Went to ZANDVOORDE myself in Motor Ambulance this evening & brought back remainder of wounded. Desultory shelling round us, & heavy shelling on ZANDVOORDE.	6th Cav Bgde were relieved in trenches by 7th Cav Bgde on dark.
8 a.m. 24.10.14 KLEINZILLEBEKE	Billets shelled all last night. 17 horses killed in 7th Cav Bgde	
8 P.M.	7th Cav F.A. was on duty in dressing station. We stood fast.	
8 P.M. 25.10.14 KLEINZILLEBEKE.	We were in Reserve all day. Battle continued in the trenches. Germans shelled whole area day & night	7th Cav F.A. on duty.

1247 W 3299 200,000 (E) 8/14 J.B.C. & A. Forms/C. 2118/11.

Instructions regarding War Diaries and Intelligence Summaries are contained in F. S. Regs., Part II. and the Staff Manual respectively. Title pages will be prepared in manuscript.

WAR DIARY
or
INTELLIGENCE SUMMARY
(Erase heading not required.)

Army Form C. 2118.

Hour, Date, Place	Summary of Events and Information (Reference Map N.W. Europe Sheet 1.)	Remarks and references to Appendices
9 a.m. 26.10.14. ZANDVOORDE.	6th Bgde back in trenches last night. Sent light wagons here early this morning, & came myself to confer with regimental M.O's & arrange for evacuation of wounded.	6th + 7th Bgdes took 48 hour spells in trenches, & relieved one another.
8 P.m. 26.10.14. KLEINZILLEBEKE	All casualties evacuated to YPRES as before.	
9 a.m. 27.10.14. KLEINZILLEBEKE.	Went to Bgde Hd Qrs near ZANDVOORDE, & then again to see regimental M.O's in collecting station. Went up to Hd Qrs of 10th Hussars, at the trenches, & inspected some of latter, as to best means of evacuating wounded from them during the day. Went into ZANDVOORDE itself. It was being heavily shelled by Howitzers, & already largely in ruins. A house had just been knocked down killing 3 men of Hussars & wounding a dozen more. Only a few men were in the village. Saw the dead, & had one wounded man of 10th Hussars removed, & retired back.	
8 P.m.	Light wagons forward as usual, & wounded evacuated to Ypres by motor ambulance.	A good number of wounded of 7th Division found their way to our dressing station.
8 P.m. 28.10.14. KLEINZILLEBEKE.	7th Bgde in trenches. We stood by in same place all day. Usual shelling.	
8 P.m. 29.10.14 KLEINZILLEBEKE.	Stood by all day. 6th Bgde went into the trenches at nightfall.	About 100 casualties from 7th Division ~~[illegible]~~ were taken in at our dressing station.

1247 W 3299 200,000 (E) 8/14 J.B.C. & A. Forms/C. 2118/11.

Army Form C. 2118

WAR DIARY
or
INTELLIGENCE SUMMARY

(Erase heading not required.)

Instructions regarding War Diaries and Intelligence Summaries are contained in F. S. Regs., Part II. and the Staff Manual respectively. Title pages will be prepared in manuscript.

Hour, Date, Place	Summary of Events and Information	Remarks and references to Appendices
	Ref Map N. W. Europe Sheet I	
4 a.m. 30.10.14. KLEINZILLEBEKE.	Enemy attacked at 4 a.m. ~~& again~~ shelled trenches held by a Squadron of the 7th Bgde.	
8 a.m.	7th Bgde shelled out of trenches at ZANDVOORDE. Enemy occupied part of the ridge. 6th Bgde supported 7th. Very heavy fighting started. Road shelled. Shells in front, behind & to sides of my dressing station which was apparently in a good spot, as it was not hit.	Medical units ordered to retire. No orders to me from the 6th Bgde to do so, so decided not to, & remained at dressing station.
9 a.m. 30.10.14.	All other medical units retired, also motors.	
1 p.m. 30.10.14.	The Brigades took up a position below the ZANDVOORDE ridge, & opposed successfully the enemy's advance. Very heavy fighting. Another Cavalry Bgde coming up in support, so my section had to deal with wounded from 3 Bgdes as well as Infantry. M.O. i/c 10th Hussars (Captain Kinkaid) was killed in the afternoon.	See Appendix A
11.30 p.m. 30.10.14. ZILLEBEKE.	Brigade had already retired. Came on with Section F.A. & last of wounded. Halted here for the night.	Orders at 7 p.m. to retire
31.10.14. 7 a.m. ZILLEBEKE.	Took last 3 wounded into YPRES in Motor Ambulance & then went to find my other section. Found it was VOORMEZEELE & ordered it up to level crossing on YPRES-MENIN Rd.	
9 a.m. 31.10.14.	Returned to ZILLEBEKE, which was being shelled by enemy. Dressing station formed under shelter of buildings at North end of village. A few wounded taken in, including 2 Frenchmen. One of the latter subsequently died, & we had to remove a leg from the other, as it was almost severed by a shell.	Orders to rejoin Bgde on YPRES-MENIN Rd

Instructions regarding War Diaries and Intelligence Summaries are contained in F. S. Regs., Part II. and the Staff Manual respectively. Title pages will be prepared in manuscript.

WAR DIARY
or
~~INTELLIGENCE SUMMARY~~
(Erase heading not required.)

Army Form C. 2118

Hour, Date, Place	Summary of Events and Information	Remarks and references to Appendices
	Ref map N.W. Europe Sheet I.	
10 a.m. 31.10.14 HOOGE	Halted just short of this place on YPRES–MENIN Rd. Bde in reserve all day, supporting troops heavily attacked near GHELUVELT. Few casualties.	
7 p.m. 31.10.14 YPRES.	Bivouacked in open field, just south of the vertical stroke of P in YPRES.	

APPENDIX "A"

Ref Map N. W. Europe. Sheet 2.

Narrative of events on the 14th Oct 1914.

While in ISEGHEM got orders at 8 a.m. to proceed to DADIZEELE & to join the 6th Cavalry Bgde at that place.

Marched at 9 a.m. & got to DADIZEELE about midday. Found the place unoccupied by troops. Went to the Burgomaster, who knew nothing of movements of our troops. Ordered poles in the wagons to be let down, & the horses to be watered & fed. Wagons were parked in the market place.

At 1 P.M. sent a cyclist down the road to BECELAERE to reconnoitre in various directions. He returned at 3 P.M. & reported no signs of British troops.

At 5 P.M. I consulted the Burgomaster as to the advisability of staying the night in the village, & was arranging to buy fodder for the horses, when there was a commotion outside. I found a lot of people rushing into the square, crying, shouting, & panic struck. I gathered from them that at least 2000 German Cavalry were half a mile from the village coming from the direction of LEDEGHEM I at once ordered the harness & girths to be tightened up. While this was being done, a lot of people rushed up from a side street & reported that the Germans had arrived. I went to the top of the street, & saw a German patrol of 3 or 4 men, who had dismounted, & were reconnoitring the place. On seeing me, they dismounted & rode back. I surmised that they would report to the main body that the village was held by the British, (they had been unable to see our wagons) & that this would delay the advance of the enemy for at least an hour. Left at once, & moved towards BECELAERE. Just outside DADIZEELE a Belgian soldier riding a bicycle came up & spoke to us in French. He explained that he had lost his regiment & would like to go with us. Almost at the same time 9 men of the 1st Life Guards all on bicycles, rode up to me. They stated that they had been surprised by the Germans when on patrol 2 days ago, & had lost their horses, but had succeeded in hiding, & had commandeered bicycles. Ordered them to accompany me, & sent the Belgian on ahead to scout, & inquire from the people as to the whereabouts of the British when approaching BECELAERE, & whilst going up a rise, a civilian approached us & told us to halt. He said the Belgian soldier had sent him back to warn us that a German patrol was passing. This patrol went the other side of the rise, across our front, & not 100 yards from us, but we were unseen in the dusk.

The Belgian soldier rejoined us a little later, & said that part of the patrol had gone towards ZONNEBEKE, & part up the YPRES road. He followed the latter part & they eventually turned off to the right.

I then proceeded with my wagons into BECELAERE. The Belgian found from various people, that British troops had been seen moving towards YPRES, so I decided to try & reach that place.

Ordered 5 of the 1st Life Guards, & the Belgian to proceed half a mile in front of my wagons, & the other 4 Life Guards half a mile behind the wagons. Each patrol to send back a man every 20 minutes to report to me. The inhabitants of BECELAERE turned out & guided us by an unfrequented way, on to the GHELUVELT road, so that we were enabled to avoid some small patrols of the enemy, who were about. It was now quite dark, & we went along without incident through GHELUVELT towards YPRES. The Belgian soldier, by interrogating the inhabitants, kept us informed of the movements of hostile patrols, & as they all seemed to be going towards ZONNEBEKE we pushed on up the YPRES–MENIN Rd. Our advanced guard eventually came in touch with our Infantry outpost a mile E of YPRES. They had felled a large tree & pulled it across the road. The O.C. outpost informed me that a patrol of about 30 Germans had come & reconnoitred his post an hour previously, & he appeared sceptical as to our having come by the road we mentioned. I can only surmise, that this German patrol, hearing our wagons in the darkness, thought we were a large force, & decamped. My ~~men~~ had to move the tree, & then we got into the Market Square at YPRES, & found Hd Qrs 4th Army there. It was now about 10 P.M. Reported to the Hd Qrs 4th Army, who informed me that the 3d Cav Div. had moved on to WYTSCHAETE. Sent a message to the A.D.M.S. by Motor Cyclist. Bivouacked in the Market Square, got Rations & at 6 a.m. 15.10.14. went on to WYTSCHAETE. Was then told that we were ordered to DADIZEELE in error, & that a cyclist was subsequently sent to warn us, but was fired upon by the enemy, so it was assumed that we were captured. That we were not was chiefly due to our luck in picking up the Belgian soldier.

Delaying action fought by the 3rd Cavalry Division at MOORSLEDE on 19.10.14
Ref Map N.W. Europe Sheet I

The record of the medical arrangements of the 6th Cavalry Bgde may be of interest, as it was a delaying action fought by means of a vigorous offensive at first, & ending in the evening with a retreat.

The Brigade billeted in PASSCHENDAELE the night before, & at 7 a.m. on the 19th Oct, moved into MOORSLEDE. The section Cav Field Ambulance marched immediately in rear of the fighting troops. The Brigade at once pushed on down the road to ROLLEGHEMCAPPELLE. The F.A. was halted in MOORSLEDE, & I ordered one light wagon under the orders of Lt Price, to follow up the Brigade, & halt in the cross roads at the ROULERS-MENIN Rd. Ordered this wagon to push on further, if necessary. About 11.30 A.M. was informed that the Brigade had found the enemy in LEDEGHEM, &, after a smart action, had dislodged them & taken the place.

Sent a second wagon down to the same cross roads. The first wagon had, meanwhile pushed on to LEDEGHEM.

About midday, the 7th Bgde operating on the left of the 6th, encountered such large forces of the enemy that they were obliged to fall back. This left the 6th Bgde rather exposed, & they were ordered to retire

A Dressing Station had, meanwhile, been established in the Convent at MOORSLEDE, & wounded were brought here by light wagons. When the Bgde retired from LEDEGHEM one light wagon which had remained came back with it. It brought the remainder of the casualties, except two or three which occurred in a field close to a house beyond the village, held by the Germans. These had to be left, as the Bgde had no time to advance & clear the house of the enemy. All the heavier part of the F. A. retired about 1.30 P.m. to PASSCHENDAELE, having cleared the dressing station of wounded. Light wagons followed, about 2 P.m. with remainder of wounded. Some motor ambulances had been sent to assist the A.D.M.S. & in them, all wounded were at once evacuated to clearing hospital in YPRES. At 3 P.m. I ordered 2 light ambulance wagons to go back to the level crossing of the railway, on the MOORSLEDE Rd. about 4 P.m. I went to this place myself, & found a wounded officer & some men in a house by the level crossing. Went on from there into MOORSLEDE, & found that the rear guard had just left. An armoured motor was at the far end of the village, holding the road, & the Germans were advancing rapidly. There was one wounded man left. When the armoured car retired it took this man, & I retired also, put another wounded man into the armoured car, & then took the remainder from the road, & house above mentioned in by two light wagons. Thus, with the exception of those men who were wounded beyond LEDEGHEM, all the wounded of the 6th Bgde were picked up & sent to YPRES at once in motors.
The Bgde then went into billets at POELCAPPELLE, & [illegible] F.A. was clear of wounded, by 5 P.m.

Attack by the enemy on the trenches held by the 3rd Cavalry Division at ZANDVOORDE 30.10.14.

The enemy attacked heavily at 4 a.m. & were repulsed, but at 7 a.m. they got the range of some trenches held by the 7th Cav Bgde & blew them up. The 7th Cav Bgde then fell back & the Chateau at HOLLEBEKE had also then to be evacuated.

At the same time the enemy subjected the ZILLEBEKE–ZANDVOORDE Rd to a heavy bombardment, & attacked in great force. The 6th Cav Bgde were at once sent up to support the 7th, & took up a position between KLEINZILLEBEKE & ZANDVOORDE. They held back the enemy successfully for the whole day. The dressing station at this time was in a small house in KLEINZILLEBEKE, & the reserve section of the F.A. & heavy wagons, were in ZILLEBEKE.

At 8 a.m. the ADMS. said that all medical units must retire, but I pointed out that the 6th Bgde had merely notified me that they were going forward & had not ordered me to retire, so I preferred to remain. This was agreed to. Meanwhile another Cavalry Bgde arrived to support us, also some of the 7th Divn but without any medical arrangements. Consequently the one section of the Cavalry Field Ambulance had to take in wounded from 3 Cavalry Bdes & some Infantry.

The only way to cope with this was to keep up a
steady stream of evacuation all day, & not
wait for darkness.
The light wagons worked up & down the
ZANDVOORDE Rd. &, despite the heavy shelling,
escaped without injury. I succeeded in
getting up two of my heavy wagons, but found
that all other medical units had gone.
These heavy wagons took wounded from the
dressing station to YPRES, & once I sent
the two light wagons full of wounded to YPRES
when the dressing station had become too
crowded.
Casualties were very heavy, & several Staff
officers were hit, & to add to the difficulties
the M.O. i/c 10th Hussars was killed.
I borrowed several motor cars belonging to
the Staff, & got wounded away in them, &
dispatched parties of others on foot, if able
to walk well.
At dusk, the A.D.M.S. succeeded in getting
up 5 Motor Ambulances, which rapidly made
journeys to YPRES & back, & by 9 P.M. the
dressing station was clear of wounded.
At 9 P.M. a few were brought in, who had
been lying in places too exposed to be got out
before. At 11 P.M. I fell back to ZILLEBEKE
with these, remained there till 6 a.m. & then
took the last of the wounded into YPRES
& rejoined the Bgde, which had come
on to the YPRES–MENIN Rd.
The point emphasized by the proceedings this
day, is the enormous advantage of motor
ambulances over horse drawn vehicles.

A typical day while the Cavalry were engaged holding a line of trenches.

6.11.14

The 6th Cav Bde on the night of the 5th Nov, took over a line of trenches to the south of the YPRES-MENIN Rd at VELDHOEK about ½ mile from GHELUVELT. The trenches were around a wood, in the midst of which was a Chateau, partially demolished by shell fire of the enemy. During the night of 5th 6th Nov, I kept one light wagon near this wood, & withdrew it at daybreak. Established a dressing station in HOOGE, but very few wounded were received by us during the day. Sent 2 light wagons at dusk (5 P.M.) up to the trenches, & at 6.30 P.M. no wounded had arrived, so I went up myself. Found my two light wagons at the ruined Chateau, on an exceedingly boggy road. There was a thick mist on, & slight rain. Got hold of regimental M.O.s, who said they had been unable to get any wounded away. I subsequently found there were over 60 casualties in 2 regiments. Got them to work with all available men to clear out wounded. Sent walking cases to a spot on the MENIN Rd just clear of the wood, & the light wagons worked backwards & forwards from this spot to the Chateau.

While this was going on, two M.Os from an Infantry Field Ambulance, volunteered to assist. I sent the stretcher squads, (they had 12) down to the trenches, & by this means speedily evacuated all wounded, first taking light wagons, & then to the road. The Motor ambulances never turned up, being in use elsewhere, but there were large numbers of heavy ambulance wagons in the neighbourhood, & all the wounded were taken on by these, to YPRES. All the trenches were clear of wounded by 11 P.M.

I have recorded this days work, to show that if Cavalry are used in the trenches, it is essential that they receive more stretchers, & have men told off as bearers in larger numbers. A Cavalry Field Ambulance has only a few bearers, & relies on light wagons to take their place.

Consequently, it is slow work collecting wounded from trenches under these conditions, & the sudden assistance of the Infantry F. A. on this occasion, showed us that, with lots of stretchers & bearers, the work of clearing trenches is simple.

Narration of the work of the section of the Cavalry Field Ambulance attached to the 6th Bgde, when the latter were engaged in the trenches on the 17.11.14.

The Brigade held two distinct lots of trenches, one in the area ZILLEBEKE - GHELUVELT, & nearer the former place, in support of Lord CAVAN'S Brigade. The 1st Royal Dragoons & 10th Hussars were in these trenches, while the 3rd Dragoon Guards & North Somerset Yeomanry were in the trenches on the KLEINZILLEBEKE ridge.

The section C. F. A. at 3-30 P.m. proceeded to ZILLEBEKE village. On the road, shortly before reaching the village, they came under shell fire, & the horse ridden by one of the Officers was hit by a small fragment of high explosive shell, but the injury was slight.

The section halted in ZILLEBEKE, & I proceeded on foot to the tunnel occupied by the O.C. 3rd D. G. Found that the Brigade had been heavily attacked during the day, & casualties were believed to be large. No attempt had been made, up to then, to collect any, & the number was unknown. At 5 P.m. two light wagons came right up to this tunnel, & the 3rd one was sent to Lord CAVAN'S trenches, where the casualties were believed to have been small.

This turned out to be the case, but, owing to no attempt to collect them having been made during the day, & also that no one knew if there were any at all, & in what place they were, it was 9.30 P.m. before this wagon had got back to ZILLEBEKE. After this, this wagon this wagon was dragged out.

We then made fair progress by way of STRAZEELE to VIEUX BERQUIN, where we arrived at 2 a.m. 21.11.14. We had covered rather more than 20 miles, & had arrived with every wagon & horse, but the horses had had so many falls & such hard work that they were rather done. In this place, we found the 10th Hussars, who stated that the exact situation of the billets was not known, & that they were halting till daylight. Ordered my wagons to outspan in the market square, & watered & fed horses. We sheltered in an estaminet till 6 a.m. & then marched to the Château de La Motte aux Bois. Found that Hd. Qrs of the 3d Cavalry Division had moved to HAZEBROUCK, so we marched to our billeting area S.E of MOORBECQUE, arrived at 10 a.m., sent a cyclist for orders, & got them at 1 P.m. when we moved into our proper billet.

The Section was the only unit of the 6th Bgde to get its wheeled transport through intact on this occasion. Maxim guns & 1st line transport were stuck all along the road. The conclusion to be drawn is, that on bad & difficult roads, only the light Ambulance wagons can be relied on to keep up with a Cavalry Brigade. These wagons above gave us no trouble on the march.

Record of the March of the section of the Field Ambce from YPRES to the HAZEBROUCK district

20.11.14.

Started from GROENENJAGER S.W. of YPRES at 3-30 P.M. It was freezing hard, & there was a foot of snow on the ground. The roads were like a solid sheet of ice. The horses slipped badly, but to OUDERDOM & then to RENINGHELST, the section kept up well with the Brigade though the water cart struggled ~~somewhat~~.

After this, difficulties increased rapidly. At WESTOUTRE, the water cart had fallen far behind. Over the pass here, & by MONT NOIR the greatest difficulty was experienced. The light ambulances were the only ones to get up the long & steep hills without mishap. In all the others, the horses slipped & fell, & it was necessary to lead them up one by one, with all RAMC. men pushing the wheels & body of the cart. Even the forage cart was in difficulties. The water cart came up eventually, its horses having already fallen 6 times. They were taken out, (the cart was empty) & the cart dragged over the hills by the men of the section. Fresh horses were then put in, & a fresh pair in one G.S. wagon that had given great trouble. The cold was intense, & riding impossible, so all had to walk.

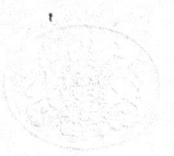

Fair progress was made till near METEREN, when the horses of a G.S. wagon slipped badly, then jibbed, & backed the cart into a ditch. It took 1½ hours digging, & the help of two more horses & all the detachment, before

at the latter place; an Infantry Field Ambulance very kindly took some lying down cases into YPRES in their heavy wagons.

It should be mentioned that, as the last two wagons were loading at the trenches, the enemy once more made an attack, but, as all the wounded had been collected, the work of loading the wagons was proceeded with, no casualties resulted. The Motor Ambulance made several journeys to the Clearing Hospital at YPRES, & at midnight the last of the wounded were removed in my light wagons, & the motor, to the Clearing Hospital. 67 wounded from the two regiments were dealt with in this way, & two wounded Frenchmen.

The point that this action seemed to me to bring out, as regards medical arrangements, that, if Cavalry do work in the trenches, & have only their present number of bearers & stretchers, the light wagons of the Cavalry Field Ambulance must, after dark, push right up to the trenches, & all the unwounded men possible, must be made to clear the trenches of wounded. By adopting this method, the wounded were collected from the two lots of trenches over a wide front, dressed at the dressing station, & in the Clearing Hospl at YPRES 5 hours from the time we commenced operations. This time would have been much shortened but for the fact that the enemy had torn so many holes in the YPRES-ZILLEBEKE road by their shells, that the motor could not come nearer than the level crossing, & also that one of my light wagons was put out of action by a horse going lame.

assisted in evacuating wounded from KLEINZILLEBEKE

The Motor Ambulance was at the level crossing on the YPRES-MENIN Rd.

At KLEINZILLEBEKE, our operations were hampered at the start by the enemy making a night attack about 5-30 P.M. The Collecting station came under heavy fire from two guns, a maxim & rifle fire, & work had to be suspended for half an hour, as the wounded could not be got out of the trenches. I then had an order sent round to all trenches that unwounded men when vacating their trenches were to assist in carrying stretchers, & otherwise assist the wounded.

This was done, & a steady stream soon came in, many of them not dressed.

Stretcher bearers, both regimental & R.A.M.C., were sent to search the trenches of each Squadron, & all outlying places.

Light wagons worked between KLEINZILLEBEKE & the dressing station in ZILLEBEKE.

A horse in one of these wagons went lame at the start, & that wagon was only able to make one journey. It was eventually sent with a load of wounded for the motor wagon at the level crossing, & ordered to remain there.

When the wagon from Lord CAVANS trenches returned it was used to take wounded from the dressing station to the motor.

About 9.30 P.M. we discovered 2 light wagons of No 7 C.F.A. near ZILLEBEKE doing nothing, so used them as well.

Wounded were carried in from the trenches in stretchers & improvised stretchers, by their unwounded comrades, as I had ordered, & at 11 P.M. the last of them were got away from KLEINZILLEBEKE, to ZILLEBEKE.

Nov. 1914

No 6 Cav. Field Amb

8 a.m. 1.11.14. YPRES.	Formed dressing station in a house at HOOGE, about 1¼ miles from our bivouack, on YPRES-MENIN Rd.	No orders or information received by going forward to the Bgde.
12 midday.	Dressing Station shelled; no damage, except broken windows.	
2 P.m. 1.11.14.	6th Bgde ordered to clear the woods south of us, which they did. Sent light wagons south of road to edge of wood.	
5 P.m. 1.11.14.	Went myself to collecting post of 10th Hussars. A few casualties only. Dressing Station shelled again. No damage.	
7 P.m. 1.11.14.	Bivouacked in same place as last night.	
8 a.m. 2.11.14. Railway crossing on YPRES-MENIN Rd.	Formed dressing Station at same place in HOOGE as yesterday.	
5 P.m.	6th Bgde in same woods as yesterday south of HOOGE. Col BARNES & 10th Hussars wounded. Several Infantry collected by my light wagons, including Bgde Genl RUGGLES-BRISE. Sent light wagons to the wood. Dressing Station shelled again; a Zouave in the yard of the house used as our dressing Station was killed by a shell & the horse of one of my officers was wounded. All wounded evacuated by motor ambulances to YPRES as usual.	Did not receive any orders as Bgde was supposed to be in reserve, but acted on my own responsibility.

Instructions regarding War Diaries and Intelligence Summaries are contained in F. S. Regs., Part II. and the Staff Manual respectively. Title pages will be prepared in manuscript.

WAR DIARY

~~or~~

~~INTELLIGENCE~~ SUMMARY

(Erase heading not required.)

Army Form C. 2118.

Hour, Date, Place	Summary of Events and Information (Ref map N.W. Europe Sheet I.)	Remarks and references to Appendices
7 P.m. 2.11.14.	Bivouacked in same place as last 2 nights.	
8 a.m. 3.11.14. YPRES-MENIN Rd	Officers sheltered in a small railway house at the level crossing. Two horses of my reserve section were killed today by a shell. Our house & part of YPRES-MENIN Rd was heavily shelled all last night. 6 men + 5 horses killed at the level crossing in front of house. Houses round us were struck frequently, but we escaped with broken windows. Did not leave the house.	
5 P.m. 3.11.14.	Formed dressing station in the same place as yesterday. YPRES-MENIN Rd heavily shelled all day.	
6 P.m. 3.11.14 Centre of the R in YPRES.	Billeted in a barn at a farm 1 mile N.E. of level crossing where we have been the last 3 days.	Got orders to bivouac at a farm 1 mile N.E. of level crossing
2 a.m. 4.11.14. Centre of R in YPRES	Turned out to support Infantry towards GHELUVELT. Proved to be a false alarm.	
7 P.m. 4.11.14.	Remained here all day. Nothing doing as far as 6th Bgde were concerned.	
11 a.m. 5.11.14. Centre of R in YPRES	3rd Dragoon Guards joined 6th Bgde.	3rd D.G.s arrived from Egypt.
6 P.m.	6th Bgde ordered to take over trenches tonight at VELDHOEK south of YPRES-MENIN Rd about a mile & east of GHELUVELT. Conferred with Brigadier about medical arrangements.	
11 P.m.	Sent a light wagon to remain behind a house close to the trenches, to pull back at daylight. Barn in the farm yard caught alight. 5 men burned to death & a dozen cattle, some sheep, one horse. 8 men burned were dressed & sent to hospital.	Cause of fire unknown, probably a man smoking in the straw.

1247 W 3299 200,000 (E) 8/14 J.B.C. & A. Forms/C. 2118/11.

Instructions regarding War Diaries and Intelligence Summaries are contained in F. S. Regs., Part II. and the Staff Manual respectively. Title pages will be prepared in manuscript.

WAR DIARY
or
~~INTELLIGENCE SUMMARY~~

(Erase heading not required.)

Army Form C. 2118.

Hour, Date, Place	Ref map of N.W. Europe. Sheet 2 — Summary of Events and Information	Remarks and references to Appendices
8 a.m. 6.11.14. Centre of R in YPRES	Had the dead men's remains collected from the burnt building.	
	Formed dressing station in HOOGE	
1 P.m.	Arranged removal of dead men, then went to dressing station	
	Went up to position, but failed to find Bgde Hd Qrs [illegible] on the way.	
5 P.m.	Sent an officer & two light wagons to the trenches.	
6.30 P.m.	No wounded arrived, so went to trenches myself, & found there had been heavy casualties, 600 men & things at a standstill. Started everyone working & remained there. D.D.M.S. did not send motors or heavy wagons asked for. Subsequently found they were required elsewhere.	See Appendix "A"
11 P.m.	Had all wounded clear by [illegible] & retired.	
12.15 a.m. 7.11.14. Centre of R in YPRES	arrived back at billet with wagons etc.	
11 a.m. 7.11.14. Chateau at level crossing on YPRES-MENIN rd.	Moved off with Bgde & halted in the Chateau grounds near the level crossing.	Ordered to proceed to billets near ZILLEBEKE lake
	Sent Bgdr Genl Makins, Commanding 6th Cav Bgde to hospital, sick.	
5 P.m. 7.11.14	Marched to a farm just west of the lake at ZILLEBEKE close to level crossing that is S.W. of the lake.	
7 P.m. Lake at ZILLEBEKE	Billeted in a farm. Men in a barn.	

1247 W 3299 200,000 (E) 8/14 J.B.C. & A. Forms/C. 2118/11.

Instructions regarding War Diaries and Intelligence Summaries are contained in F. S. Regs., Part II. and the Staff Manual respectively. Title pages will be prepared in manuscript.

WAR DIARY

~~or~~

~~INTELLIGENCE SUMMARY~~

(Erase heading not required.)

Army Form C. 2118

Hour, Date, Place	Ref Map of N.W. Europe Sheet 1. Summary of Events and Information	Remarks and references to Appendices
8 a.m. 8.11.14. Lake at ZILLEBEKE	Marched to YPRES-MENIN Rd & halted in a field on north of road 1 kilo from Ypres & close to the Chateau next before the level crossing.	Got orders at 7 a.m. to move.
9 a.m. YPRES.	Reached place noted above.	
1 P.m. YPRES	6th Regt went to the trenches on KLEINZILLEBEKE ridge. We remained in same field, & billeted in a small house. Shelling of this area went on all day.	
4.30 P.m. 9.11.14. YPRES.	Sent light wagons to the trenches, with an officer.	
7 P.m.	Casualties evacuated. Quiet day here, but usual shelling.	No orders.
4 P.m. 10.11.14 YPRES.	Went up to trenches myself, & sent light wagons. Snipers fired at us on the road, but aim very poor.	
6.30 P.m.	The house we were in was damaged by two large Howitzer shells. Windows broken, & we were smothered in mud, but no one hit. All casualties evacuated to clearing hospital in YPRES.	No orders.
1 P.m. ~~[illegible]~~ 11.14. YPRES.	Large Howitzer shell fell among our wagons & men. Fell 5 yards from men sitting in a group, but no one hit. It fell in very soft ground.	

1247 W 3299 200,000 (E) 8/14 J.B.C. & A. Forms/C. 2118/11.

Army Form C. 2118.

Instructions regarding War Diaries and Intelligence Summaries are contained in F. S. Regs., Part II. and the Staff Manual respectively. Title pages will be prepared in manuscript.

WAR DIARY
or
INTELLIGENCE SUMMARY

(Erase heading not required.)

Hour, Date, Place	Ref Map N.W. Europe Sheet 2 — Summary of Events and Information	Remarks and references to Appendices
4.30 P.m. 11.11.14 YPRES.	Sent light wagons to trenches. More casualties than usual.	Got orders to shift bivouack tomorrow, owing to shelling. Rained heavily.
9 P.m. 11.11.14	All casualties evacuated to Clearing Hospital at YPRES	
9 a.m. 12.11.14 YPRES.	Moved up alongside 8th Fld Amb near centre of R in YPRES. Billeted in a farm.	
5 P.m. 12.11.14. near R in YPRES.	Went up to trenches on KLEIN ZILLEBEKE ridge. Shelled on the road by a German Field battery, who were evidently watching it. Found over 30 casualties. Several officers & R.S.M. 10th Hussars killed.	
9 P.m. 12.11.14.	My light wagons came up to trenches after dark. All wounded were evacuated from YPRES by 8 P.m. Area we are in shelled considerably. Our house struck several times by shrapnel bullets. No damage.	Heavy rain
4.30 P.m. 13.11.14. near R in YPRES.	Sent out all light + 2 heavy wagons to the same trenches, under an officer. Ordered heavy wagons to remain in ZILLEBEKE village.	Heavy Rain
10.30 P.m.	The officer returned, having evacuated many wounded, & reported that a heavy ambulance wagon had been lost apparently a shell burst in the village, & the drivers must have bolted, for the wagon galloped off alone. It was empty.	Heavy rain. Orders to move to ~~east~~ of YPRES tomorrow

1247 W 3299 200,000 (E) 8/14 J.B.C. & A. Forms/C. 2118/11.

Instructions regarding War Diaries and Intelligence Summaries are contained in F. S. Regs., Part II. and the Staff Manual respectively. Title pages will be prepared in manuscript.

WAR DIARY
or
~~INTELLIGENCE SUMMARY~~

(Erase heading not required.)

Army Form C. 2118.

Hour, Date, Place	Ref Map N.W. Europe Sheet I. Summary of Events and Information	Remarks and references to Appendices
8 a.m. 14.11.14 Near R in YPRES.	Shelled again last night. 6 casualties amongst horses of R. Dragoons in the field next my horses, but none of latter hit. Sent men mounted on foot to search for wagon, but no trace of it seen.	
2 P.m. 14.11.14	Marched to new billets at Crossroads S.E. of VLAMERTINGHE at GROENENJAGER. Search made for the lost wagon near ZILLEBEKE but without result. Brigade was in reserve today.	Heavy rain
4 P.m.	Reached billets.	
6 a.m. 15.11.14. GROENENJAGER.	Sent Sgt York to search near trenches at KLEINZILLEBEKE for lost wagon.	
4 P.m	Nothing seen of lost wagon. Visited A Section of my F.A. Bgde were back to KLEINZILLEBEKE trenches in the evening.	Very bad weather for the last 14 days pouring rain.
16.11.14. 2 P.m. GROENENJAGER.	Started off with all light & heavy wagons of both sections of the F.A. Shelled passing through YPRES, which was being bombarded.	
4 P.m. 16.11.14 Level crossing on YPRES MENIN Rd	Sent back A Section, less one light wagon. Proceeded to the trenches via ZILLEBEKE. Bgde were holding 2 lines, one between ZILLEBEKE & GHELUVELT & the other on the KLEINZILLEBEKE ridge. Had all wounded in hospital by 7.30 P.m.	On reaching the level crossing heard that casualties were small
9.30 P.m. 16.11.14	Arrived back in billets.	Heavy rain.

Army Form C. 2118.

Instructions regarding War Diaries and Intelligence Summaries are contained in F. S. Regs., Part II. and the Staff Manual respectively. Title pages will be prepared in manuscript.

WAR DIARY
~~or~~
~~INTELLIGENCE SUMMARY~~

(Erase heading not required.)

Hour, Date, Place	Ref Map of N.W. Europe Sheet 1 Summary of Events and Information	Remarks and references to Appendices
2 P.m. 17.11.14. GROENENJAGER	Went via YPRES. to same trenches as yesterday. Took light wagons only.	
3.30 P.m. ZILLEBEKE	Halted in ZILLEBEKE Shelled on the way there. One officer's horse hit by small fragment of Howitzer shell.	
5 P.m.	Went up to trenches, & ordered wagons to follow at dusk. Wagons arrived. Numerous casualties, very scattered. Two attacks on trenches while we were there.	See Appendix A
11.30 P.m.	Got all wounded away to clearing hospital at YPRES.	
2 a.m. 18.11.14 GROENENJAGER.	arrived back in billets	
8 P.m. 18.11.14.	Brigade rested all day, nothing doing	
10 a.m. 19.11.14. GROENENJAGER.	As the result of Court of Inquiry into loss of heavy ambulance wagon, arrested the two drivers, & sentenced each to 28 days field punishment	Snowed. Froze hard.
8 P.m.	Remained here all day.	Snowed & froze hard. See Appendix B
20.11.14. 7 a.m. GROENENJAGER.	Sent an officer to see about billets near HAZEBROUCK.	ordered to march to an area near HAZEBROUCK & rejoin ~~[illegible]~~
3.30 P.m.	Started with the Bgde marched via OUDERDOM - RENINGHELST - WESTOUTRE - MONT NOIRE - METEREN - STRAZEELE to VIEUX BERQUIN.	March took [illegible] with wagons, no slipping [illegible]. See Appendix A
2 a.m. 21.11.14 VIEUX BERQUIN.	arrived & bivouacked in market place.	Froze. Very cold.

1247 W 3299 200,000 (E) 8/14 J.B.C. & A. Forms/C. 2118/11.

Instructions regarding War Diaries and Intelligence Summaries are contained in F. S. Regs., Part II. and the Staff Manual respectively. Title pages will be prepared in manuscript.

WAR DIARY

~~or~~

~~INTELLIGENCE SUMMARY~~

(Erase heading not required.)

Army Form C. 2118.

Hour, Date, Place	Reg Maj R. W. [illegible] Sheet 1. Summary of Events and Information	Remarks and references to Appendices
6 a.m. 21.11.14. VIEUX BERQUIN	Started off for Chateau de la Motte aux Bois.	Froze hard. Cold.
8 a.m.	arrived at Chateau & found that Divisional H.Q. had moved on to HAZEBROUCK. Marched on.	
10 a.m.	Reached a farm 3 miles S.E. of MORBECQUE & halted. Sent cyclist to HAZEBROUCK for orders.	
2 P.m. 21.11.14.	A.D.M.S. arrived & directed me to billets at Level Crossing N.E. of STEENBECQUE. Found A Section already there	Very difficult march on bad & frozen roads.
4 P.m. 21.11.14. STEENBECQUE.	arrived in billets.	
10 a.m. 22.11.14. STEENBECQUE.	Inspected the billets & horses of A Section.	
2.30 P.m. 22.11.14.	Marched through roads of Forêt de NIEPPE to some farms at CAUDESCURE, at a point near the Cross roads S.E. of the E in La MOTTE.	Orders at 1 P.m. to rejoin 6th Bgde on corner of the HAZEBROUCK-MERVILLE Rd
5 P.m. 22.11.14. CAUDESCURE.	Billeted in two farms at this place.	Hard frost. Ground deeply covered in snow.
9 a.m. 23.11.14. CAUDESCURE.	Told that leave will be granted for 72 hours in England. applied for it, & it was granted.	Snowed hard all night.
10.15 P.m. 23.11.14.	Started for BOULOGNE. Handed over charge of the Section to Lt. CREE & of the whole F.A. to Major ELSNER.	Heavy frost.

1247 W 3299 200,000 (E) 8/14 J.B.C.&A. Forms/C. 2118/11.

APPENDIX B. Copy.

Proceedings of a Court of Enquiry held on Service with the British Expeditionary Force on the 17th Nov 1914, by order of the G.O.C. 3rd Cavalry Divn to enquire into the loss of a heavy Ambulance wagon complete with a team of four horses.

President
Major W. H. S. Nickerson
R.A.M.C.
O.C. No 6 Cavalry Field Ambulance.
Member
Lieut R. B. Price
R.A.M.C.

The Court having assembled pursuant to order proceed to take evidence.

1st Evidence. Acty Sergeant R. W. Watchorn R.A.M.C. States:—

On the 13th Nov 1914, I proceeded to ZILLEBEKE in charge of a dressing station party. I established them in a house with the two heavy wagons outside with their drivers. The horses were then facing in the direction of the Cross Roads at HALTE.
I heard the burst of a shell, & saw the flash, & then a sound as though the horses were moving.
I did not go out at first, as I thought the horses were plunging & the drivers holding them.
I then went out, & was only in time to see one wagon going round the corner in the direction of KLEINZILLEBEKE. I did not see the drivers of the lost wagon in the street.

(Signed)
Reginald W. Watchorn.
actg Sgt R.A.M.C.

2nd Evidence. No 26911. Driver R. H. Bristow. A.S.C. States:—

On the evening of the 13th Nov 1914 at about 5 P.M. I was ordered to draw up Heavy heavy Ambulance wagon outside a house in Zillebeke with the horses facing towards the Cross roads at HALTE. I went into the house to get water for the horses. On entering the kitchen I heard a shell strike an adjacent house. I went to the door to attend to the horses, & found that they had gone. I did not see in which direction the wagon went. I saw another wagon disappearing, & pursued that, but found it was not mine.

(Signed) R. H. Bristow.

No 328 Driver H. Gamble. A.S.C. States:—

3rd Evidence.

On the evening of the 13th Nov 1914 at about 5 P.M. I was ordered to draw up my heavy Ambulance wagon outside a house in ZILLEBEKE with the horses facing towards the Cross Roads at HALTE. The other heavy Ambulance was in front of us. I asked the drivers of the other wagon to look after our horses, whilst we went for water for the animals. I went into the house, & almost immediately heard the crash of a shell. I ran out of the house, as I heard the horses moving. I had trouble with the front door bolt, which delayed me. I saw the end of one wagon disappearing, & pursued it, but found that it was not my own.

(Signed) H. Gamble.

No 285 Driver W. V. Bray. A.S.C. States:—

4th Evidence.

On the evening of the 13th Nov 1914 at about 5 P.M. I was standing at my horses' heads in ZILLEBEKE, when a shell burst close by the house. The horses plunged knocked me down, turned right round & bolted in the direction of KLEINZILLEBEKE. The second wagon had already turned & bolted, & my wagon, which had been standing in front of the other wagon, followed it in rear. My wagon was caught higher up the road & brought back.

(Signed) W. V. Bray.

No 319 Driver W. H. Frampton. A.S.C. States:—

5th Evidence.

On the evening of the 13th Nov 1914 at about 5 P.M. I was standing at the heads of the wheel horses of the leading wagon, whilst the drivers of the other wagon went for water for the horses, a shell burst & the horses plunged, turned round, & bolted in the opposite direction towards KLEINZILLEBEKE. The wagon in rear of me, (the one which has been lost) also turned & bolted in rear of ours. My wagon was caught higher up the road & brought back.

(Signed) W. H. Frampton.

Lieut R. E. Cree RAMC. States

1st Evidence.

On the afternoon of the 13th Sept 1914, I was ordered to form a dressing station in ZILLEBEKE.
Having formed one in a house, I kept the two heavy wagons at this spot with the horses facing in the direction of the Cross roads at HALTE.
I then proceeded forward to the trenches about half a mile up the KLEIN ZILLEBEKE road with the two light ambulance wagons.
As I approached the point where I had been ordered to remain, near the reserve trenches, a heavy Ambulance wagon dashed past me at a gallop, & was stopped a short distance further on.
I found no one in charge of the wagon at all.
This turned out to be the wagon driven by Drivers Frampton & Bray. I saw no sign of the other heavy wagon.

On returning to ZILLEBEKE with wounded, I found that the other heavy Ambulance wagon was missing. I caused inquiries to be made in the neighbourhood, but could get no news of it.
I personally searched the neighbourhood next day, mounted; & other men of my Field Ambulance, mounted & on foot, searched also. No news or trace of the missing wagon could be obtained.

(Signed) R. Ewart Cree.
Lt RAMC.

(Signed)

W H S Nickerson. Major
RAMC. President
O.C. No 6 C.F.A.

R. B. Price.
Lt RAMC. Member

P.T.O.

Opinion of the President.

It will be seen that the statements of all witnesses tally, except that one driver of the wagon that was recovered says his wagon was first to bolt & the other followed it, while the other driver of the same wagon states that the lost wagon was first away.

The orders for drivers are, that one is to go for water while the other waits by the horses. This was not obeyed in this case, inasmuch as two drivers of the leading wagon remained & relied on the other wagon being behind their own, to prevent its getting away.

I have had experience of long wagon drivers before, under shell fire, & they have always bolted for the nearest cover, & deserted their wagons, unless prevented by me.

I have no proof against the two men who remained outside, but am convinced in my own mind that they were not knocked down, but ran & hid, for, at first they could not even say which way the wagons had gone. These are quarter lock wagons, & take a long time to turn, ample for the two men to have recovered their feet & seized the horses, had they been there to do so.

(Signed.) W.S. Nickerson. Major.
P.C. No 6 C.F.A.

A. A. & Q. M. G.
3rd Cavalry Division

In my opinion the loss of the wagon was caused by the horses bolting under shell fire, whilst left unattended, & that the two drivers are to blame for having left their horses.

(Signed) R. L. R. Macleod.
Lt Col R.A.M.C.
17th Nov 1914. A. D. M. S. 3rd Cav Div

G. O. C. 3rd Cav Div

Would you please minute enclosed proceedings of Court of Enquiry, stating whether you consider the drivers should be dealt with by C. O. or sent to trial by F. G. C. M.

(Signed) H. S. Davey.
Lt Col.
17/11/14. A. A. & Q. M. G. 3rd Cav Div

To be tried by F. G. C. M.

Ambulance & horses to be struck off charge.

(Signed) J. Byng
M Gen
18. 11. 14. 3rd Cav Div

Note.

It was subsequently found that the wagon turned to the left off the ZILLEBEKE-KLEINZILLEBEKE road, & got behind the trenches in this region. The horses were hit by a shell & killed & the wagon smashed.

DEC. 1914

No 6 CAV FIELD AMB

Army Form C. 2118.

Instructions regarding War Diaries and Intelligence Summaries are contained in F. S. Regs., Part II. and the Staff Manual respectively. Title pages will be prepared in manuscript.

WAR DIARY
~~or~~
~~INTELLIGENCE SUMMARY~~

(Erase heading not required.)

Hour, Date, Place	Ref Map N.W. Europe, Sheet 2. Summary of Events and Information	Remarks and references to Appendices
9 P.m. 28.11.14. CAUDESCURE.	Arrived back from leave & resumed charge of F.A.	
8 P.m. 1.12.14. CAUDESCURE.	Nothing to record since last entry Bgde have been resting	orders received re inspection by H.M. The King tomorrow
8.30 A.M. 2.12.14 CAUDESCURE.	Marched to LA MOTTE with personnel of F.A. & were inspected by H.M. The King. His Majesty stopped & made some complimentary remarks concerning the work done in the war by the R.A.M.C.	
12 noon.	Went to HAZEBROUCK & conferred with A.D.M.S. concerning the reorganization of the F.A.	
4 P.m. CAUDESCURE	Returned to billet.	
9 a.m. 3.12.14. CAUDESCURE.	Went to HAZEBROUCK & officiated for A.D.M.S. 3rd Cav Div who was on leave.	
9 P.m. 3.12.14.	Returned to billet.	
9 a.m. 9.12.14. CAUDESCURE.	Nothing to record in the interval. Brigade Route march, & inspection by Brigadier	
12 noon 9.12.14 CAUDESCURE	Returned to billets.	

1247 W 3299 200,000 (E) 8/14 J.B.C. & A. Forms/C. 2118/11.

Instructions regarding War Diaries and Intelligence Summaries are contained in F. S. Regs., Part II. and the Staff Manual respectively. Title pages will be prepared in manuscript.

WAR DIARY
or
~~INTELLIGENCE~~ SUMMARY
(Erase heading not required.)

Army Form C. 2118.

Hour, Date, Place	Summary of Events and Information	Remarks and references to Appendices
	Reg Maj N. W. Sergt. Sharp	
10 a.m. 10.12.14. CAUDESCURE	Started reorganizing field ambulance into "A" Echelon light, & "B" Echelon, heavy.	Orders for reorganizing arrived this morning. For full details of scheme, see appendix to war diary of D.D.M.S. 3d Cav Divn.
8 P.m. 10.12.14 CAUDESCURE	New Sergeant Major reported arrival. (S.M. Sharpe)	
10 a.m. 11.12.14 CAUDESCURE.	Went over to the reserve section of the F. A. & arranged details of reorganizing, & had necessary changes of personnel & material made at once.	
7 P.m. 11.12.14.	Reported to A.D.M.S. that reorganization was complete.	
13.12.14. 11.30 P.m. CAUDESCURE.	Orders to move at daylight tomorrow.	
6.45 a.m. 14.12.14. CAUDESCURE.	Marched via LACOURONNE & the level crossing near point 45 to BAILLEUL.	
11.30 a.m. BAILLEUL	Went into billets in some greenhouses used for growing fruit.	Ordered to be ready to move at ½ hours notice.
8 P.m. 15.12.14 BAILLEUL	Stood by in reserve all day, but not called out.	Orders to return to old billeting area near CAUDESCURE

1247 W 3299 200,000 (E) 8/14 J.B.C. & A. Forms/C. 2118/11.

Instructions regarding War Diaries and Intelligence Summaries are contained in F. S. Regs., Part II. and the Staff Manual respectively. Title pages will be prepared in manuscript.

WAR DIARY

~~or~~

~~INTELLIGENCE SUMMARY~~

(Erase heading not required.)

Army Form C. 2118.

Hour, Date, Place	Ref Map N.W. Europe Sheet 5 Summary of Events and Information	Remarks and references to Appendices
9.30 a.m. 16.12.14. BAILLEUL	Marched by the same roads as we came to our old billeting area. Billeted in two farms on road from VERTERVE–MERVILLE at halfway point where minor road crosses it, near VIERHOUCK	Orders from A.D.M.S. to find out if any men of recent drafts are unfit for service.
8.30 a.m. VIERHOUCK	Arrived in Billets.	
10 a.m. 17.12.14 VIERHOUCK.	Brigade remains in reserve here.	Orders to be always ready to start at 2 hours notice.
6 p.m. 19.12.14 VIERHOUCK.		Orders to find out if any men in the Regt are unfit for service at the front in any capacity. Sent replies to above queries.
4 p.m. 20.12.14. VIERHOUCK.	All men confined to billets.	Orders to be prepared to move at a moments notice.
7.30 p.m.		Above orders cancelled.
8 p.m. 21.12.14 VIERHOUCK		Orders given that officers & N.C.O's can take 7 days leave. Orders that 2 privates of the F.A. can take 72 hours leave at a time.
8 a.m. 23.12.14 VIERHOUCK.	Sent two privates on leave to England.	

1247 W 3299 200,000 (E) 8/14 J.B.C. & A. Forms/C. 2118/11.

Instructions regarding War Diaries and Intelligence Summaries are contained in F. S. Regs., Part II. and the Staff Manual respectively. Title pages will be prepared in manuscript.

WAR DIARY
or
INTELLIGENCE SUMMARY
(Erase heading not required.)

Army Form C. 2118

Hour, Date, Place	Ref Map N.W. Europe. Sheet I. Summary of Events and Information	Remarks and references to Appendices
8 P.m. 24.12.14. VIERHOUCK.	Received from A.D.M.S. Christmas Cards from the KING for distribution to the F.A.	Froze hard today.
10 A.M. 25.12.14. VIERHOUCK.	Gave out the Christmas Cards received as above.	
1.30 P.m.	Went round A echelon at dinner hour.	
4 P.m.	Went to HAZEBROUCK & received the PRINCESS MARY gifts for distribution to the F.A.	Froze hard all day
6 P.m.	Distributed above gifts.	
7 P.m. 26.12.14. VIERHOUCK.	—	Slight snow this afternoon changing to rain. Now raining hard.
11 A.M. 28.12.14. VIERHOUCK	A.D.M.S. Cavalry Corps inspected the Field Ambulance.	
6 P.m. 31.12.14. VIERHOUCK.	Still in reserve at this place. nothing of importance to record. Officers & N.C.O.s are being given leave. 1 N.C.O. goes at a time. Men get leave for 72 hours, 2 at a time. W.S. Nickerson Major O.C. No 6 C.F.A.	

1247 W 3299 200,000 (E) 8/14 J.B.C. & A. Forms/C. 2118/11.

121/4329

~~Feb.~~ Jan. 1915

6th Cavalry Field ~~Field~~ Ambulance.

Vol II.

Confidential

War Diary

of

Major W. H. S. Nickerson

O.C. No 6 Cav Field Ambulance

From 1st Jan 1915 to 31st Jan 1915

Army Form C. 2118.

WAR DIARY
or
INTELLIGENCE SUMMARY
(Erase heading not required.)

Instructions regarding War Diaries and Intelligence Summaries are contained in F. S. Regs., Part II. and the Staff Manual respectively. Title pages will be prepared in manuscript.

Hour, Date, Place	[illegible] Summary of Events and Information	Remarks and references to Appendices
6 p.m. 1.1.15. VIERHOUCK.	Still in the same billets. Men & horses are exercised by route marches, & drills. Went into HAZEBROUCK to see A.D.M.S.	Weather very bad. Rain almost ceaseless, & frequent gales of wind.
6 p.m. 2.1.15. VIERHOUCK	Another motor ambulance sent to this section, making two in all. Two have also been sent to B echelon. Inspected a farm of 'B' Squadron R.R. Dragoons from which a case of Enteric had been removed.	Very bad weather
2 p.m. 3.1.15. VIERHOUCK.	Went to HAZEBROUCK. Saw A.D.M.S. & then visited the new billets of my B echelon. Inspected the latter, & the horses. F.A. Route marched today.	Rain from [illegible]
9 a.m. 6.1.15.	F.A. went for a Route march.	
6 p.m. 6.1.15 VIERHOUCK	Went to HAZEBROUCK & saw A.D.M.S. Drew pay for F.A.	Very bad weather still; rain & wind.
9 a.m. 8.1.15 VIERHOUCK	F.A. route marched.	
10.30 a.m. 10.1.15 VIERHOUCK.	F.A. route marched. Went to HAZEBROUCK & conferred with A.D.M.S. concerning acting promotions.	Orders from the Bgde to inquire into the prevalence of lice amongst the units. Very bad weather
10.30 a.m. 11.1.15 VIERHOUCK.	D.D.M.S. Cavalry Corps inspected the F.A. F.A. route marched.	Very bad weather still
10.30 a.m. 12.1.15 VIERHOUCK.	Inspected all the billets occupied by 3rd Dragoon Guards.	Orders from Bgde to inspect the billets. Very bad weather. Weather bad as ever. Right..

Instructions regarding War Diaries and Intelligence Summaries are contained in F. S. Regs., Part II. and the Staff Manual respectively. Title pages will be prepared in manuscript.

WAR DIARY
or
~~INTELLIGENCE~~ SUMMARY

(Erase heading not required.)

Army Form C. 2118

Hour, Date, Place	Reg^t^ Leaf^t^ M. W. Europe Sheet 1. Summary of Events and Information	Remarks and references to Appendices
2.30 p.m. 13.1.15 VIERHOUCK.	Went to HAZEBROUCK Saw A.D.M.S. Left motor ambulance (New Hudson Car) to have repairs made.	Heavy rain, especially in the morning & evening.
11 a.m. 14.1.15. VIERHOUCK.	Inspected all billets of 1st Royal Dragoons	Rain in evening.
11 a.m. 15.1.15 VIERHOUCK.	Inspected all billets of N. Somerset Yeomanry. Went to Bgde Hd Qrs	
9 a.m. 16.1.15. VIERHOUCK	F.A. went for route march. Went to HAZEBROUCK, Saw A.D.M.S.	Sent reports in the evening, on the billets, & [illegible] on prevalence of lice to Bgde [illegible]. Rain. Slight rain only
9 a.m. 18.1.15 VIERHOUCK.	F.A. went for route march	Heavy fall of snow. Got orders to find out how many [illegible] in 6th Bgde are not [illegible]
11 a.m. 19.1.15. VIERHOUCK.	A.D.M.S. visited the F.A. & talked of reorganization scheme for Cavalry F.A.'s especially concerning Transport	Rain; not so cold.
9 a.m. 21.1.15 VIERHOUCK.	F.A. went for route march.	Rain & high wind.
11 a.m. 22.1.15. VIERHOUCK	Went to HAZEBROUCK Saw A.D.M.S. & drew pay for F.A.	Fine day. Some frost.
11 a.m. 25.1.15 VIERHOUCK	Went to HAZEBROUCK Saw A.D.M.S. about reorganization of the transport of A echelon. We have now two limbered wagons [illegible] one surgical spring wagon, 4 light ambulances, two motor ambulances	Got orders at B.P. [illegible] cancelling all leave, & asking for an officer to [illegible] tomorrow to find fresh billets
3 p.m. [illegible] 25.1.15	Went to Bgde Office 6th Cav Bgde & was told we are to return to the trenches.	

1247 W 3299 200,000 (E) 8/14 J.B.C. & A. Forms/C. 2118/11.

Instructions regarding War Diaries and Intelligence Summaries are contained in F. S. Regs., Part II. and the Staff Manual respectively. Title pages will be prepared in manuscript.

WAR DIARY
or
~~INTELLIGENCE SUMMARY~~

(Erase heading not required.)

Army Form C. 2118.

Hour, Date, Place	Ref Map N.W. Europe Sheet I Summary of Events and Information	Remarks and references to Appendices
10 a.m. 26.1.15 VIERHOUCK	Sent 2nd Cue to arrange about fresh billets. Went to HAZEBROUCK & saw A.D.M.S. who said the exact date of our move is not yet decided.	Got orders at 6 P.m. to stand by at 7 a.m. tomorrow with all wagons packed. Fine but cold day.
7 a.m. 27.1.15. VIERHOUCK.	Stood by with wagons packed & horses harnessed. Heavy firing heard from the direction of ARMENTIERES.	Frost last night.
9.15 a.m. 27.1.15.	Went to Hd Qrs 6th Bgde	
3 P.m. 27.1.15.	C-in-C inspected 6th Cavalry Bgde. Heard that enemy had attacked but were repulsed, & we were not required.	Ordered to parade at 2 P.m. for inspection by C in C. Fine day, very cold. Orders that night to [illegible] tomorrow
10.30 a.m. 28.1.15. VIERHOUCK	Moved to new billets at BOESEGHEM on the road from HAZEBROUCK to AIRE. Marched via MERVILLE & HAVERSKERQUE	
2.40 P.m. 28.1.15 BOESEGHEM.	Arrived, & billeted in the village.	3rd Cav Div Ordered to go & take over trenches near YPRES [illegible] week.
10 a.m. 29.1.15 BOESEGHEM.	A.D.M.S. visited billets.	Hard frost. Sunshine.
4 P.m. 29.1.15.	Went to HAZEBROUCK & saw A.D.M.S. He told me that only 2 Field Ambulances were to go to YPRES. He had drawn lots, & we are to remain behind, except for the B echelon of No. 6 which is to go.	Hard frost. Fine
6 P.m. 30.1.15. BOESEGHEM	Arranged about further antityphoid inoculation in 6th Cav Bgde. All Hd Qrs of 6th Bgde were inoculated.	Got orders that no further inoculations are to be done after the 10th Feb, for the present.
5 P.m. 31.1.15. BOESEGHEM	Brigadier 6th Bgde informed me that Divisional G.O.C. wishes this Field Ambulance to go to YPRES with the others. Not yet settled & no orders received	

1247 W 3299 200,000 (E) 8/14 J.B.C. & A. Forms/C. 2118/11.

121/4611

~~Jan 1915~~

Feb. 1915

AMD

5th Cavalry Field Ambulance.

Vol III. & II

Note. January Vol II is enclosed herewith. The first 3 sheets of Feby Vol III were sent in as Vol II ✓ (now placed in correct covers)

Instructions regarding War Diaries and Intelligence Summaries are contained in F. S. Regs., Part II. and the Staff Manual respectively. Title pages will be prepared in manuscript.

WAR DIARY
or
INTELLIGENCE SUMMARY
(Erase heading not required.)

Army Form C. 2118.

Hour, Date, Place	Refnop. N.W. Europe Sheet I. Summary of Events and Information	Remarks and references to Appendices
10 a.m. 1.2.15 BOESEGHEM	Sent off monthly returns etc.	No orders to move received.
3 P.m. 2.2.15	Went into AIRE. Met D.D.M.S. Indian Cavalry Corps, who was engaged in a conference with A.D.M.S. 8th Div. Field ambulances. Joined them, & discussed matters concerning cavalry field ambulances.	
5 P.m. 2.2.15 BOESEGHEM	Got orders to march to YPRES tomorrow.	Orders to take 10th Officers & about half A section.
4 a.m. 3.2.15 BOESEGHEM	Reveille.	
6 a.m. 3.2.15.	Marched to HAZEBROUCK.	
7.30 A.M. HAZEBROUCK	Arrived & reported to A.D.M.S.	
8 a.m.	Marched for YPRES via STEENVOORDE – POPERINGHE.	Ordered to send billeting party in lorries, & to be in YPRES by 3 P.M.
2.30 P.m. YPRES.	Arrived YPRES at billets in Rue des CHIENS.	
1 P.M. 4.2.15. YPRES.	Portions of No. 7 & 8 C.F.A.'s. 7th Cav Bgde + half 8th Cav Bgde went to trenches S.E. of ZILLEBEKE. Ordered to send 2 light ambulance wagons for wounded. Took them myself. Went to ZILLEBEKE & then by road to left, a small road then towards round to HOOGE. Left wagons under shelter. Shelled on the way. Went to trenches of 2nd Life Guards & telephoned to R.H.G. about wounded. They said wounded had been taken to HOOGE.	
4 P.m. 4.3.15 YPRES.	Proceeded to HOOGE & collected wounded.	
11 P.m. 4.3.15 YPRES	Town has been shelled during the day. Some shelling still going on tonight. Wagons sent out at 6 P.m. for wounded. [illegible]	

1247 W 3299 200,000 (E) 8/14 J.B.C. & A. Forms/C. 2118/11.

Instructions regarding War Diaries and Intelligence Summaries are contained in F. S. Regs., Part II. and the Staff Manual respectively. Title pages will be prepared in manuscript.

WAR DIARY
or
~~INTELLIGENCE SUMMARY~~

(Erase heading not required.)

Army Form C. 2118.

Hour, Date, Place	Summary of Events and Information	Remarks and references to Appendices
	Ref map N. E. Europe Sheet 1.	
10 a.m. 5.2.15 YPRES.	Went to Divl Hd Qrs & consulted with A.D.M.S. Agreed that two light ambulance wagons are to be sent every night, to be at Lord Cavan's late Hd Qrs, the place east of ZILLEBEKE to which my wagons went yesterday, so as to arrive there at 6-30 P.M. All wounded to be carried from the trenches to this place, & removed to No 837 a in YPRES. M.O.'s at the trenches to keep the A.D.M.S. informed by telephone as to numbers of wounded.	Ordered to send an officer daily at 5 P.M. from one field ambulance to sleep in Divl Hd Qrs to receive messages on the telephone from the trenches. Fine sunny day.
6 P.M. 5.2.15. YPRES.	Wagons from No 7 C.F.A. went out to collect wounded.	
10 a.m. 6.2.15. YPRES.	Went to Divl Hd Qrs consulted with A.D.M.S. & arranged that during the day, any wounded that could be removed should be taken to HOOGE. Telephonic notice of such removals to be given & motor ambulance sent.	
5 P.M. 6.2.15.	Proceeded to ZILLEBEKE with Lt CREE, & two light wagons. Halted in this place till dark. Went to 7th Bde Hd Qrs & consulted with G.O.C. Went on to Lord CAVAN's late Hd Qrs, arrived at 6.30 P.M. Was told that 2nd Life Guards needed a stretcher, so proceeded to the trenches with a party. Found that the message was a mistake. On return to wagons found that all wounded, 9 in all, had been loaded up. Returned to YPRES.	Rained during the time wounded were being collected & while we were returning.
8.35 P.M. 6.2.15. YPRES.	Arrived & sent wounded to No 837 a. Town shelled during the day.	

1247 W 3299 200,000 (E) 8/14 J.B.C. & A. Forms/C. 2118/11.

Instructions regarding War Diaries and Intelligence Summaries are contained in F. S. Regs., Part II. and the Staff Manual respectively. Title pages will be prepared in manuscript.

WAR DIARY

~~or~~

~~INTELLIGENCE SUMMARY~~

(Erase heading not required.)

Army Form C. 2118.

Hour, Date, Place	Summary of Events and Information	Remarks and references to Appendices
	[illegible]	
11.30 a.m. 7.2.15 YPRES.	Proceeded to HOOGE in motor ambulance, arranged for removal of two wounded + one sick men to No 8 C.F.A. On the way back, stopped at Divl. H.Qrs + saw A.D.M.S.	
3 P.m. 7.2.15 YPRES.	Saw O.C. No 8 C.F.A. + gave him orders from A.D.M.S. which were that tonight 3 light wagons are required. Two from No 8 C.F.A. + one from No 7 C.F.A. detailed, also a motor ambulance to be at the junction of MENIN + ZILLEBEKE roads at 7 P.m. to remove Surgn. Major COWIE, [illegible] Life Guards to POPERINGHE. Latter officer apparently shot in chest. Town shelled today by enemy, but no serious damage done, all time Shrapnel.	Orders from A.D.M.S. at 2.30 P.M. Dull cold day, with high wind
6 P.m. 8.2.15 YPRES.	Quiet day. Visited H.Qrs + also place where baths are being erected for men coming out of trenches, also went to 6th Cav Bde H.Qrs + saw G.O.C. 3rd C.F.A. went to trenches + evacuated wounded. Town shelled slightly.	Arranged for daily evacuation of wounded.
10 a.m. 9.2.15 YPRES.	Went to Divl. H.Qrs [illegible] morning + evening. No casualties. Out one light wagon + M.O. from No 8 C.F.A. [illegible] Bde went into trenches last night + 7th Bde came out the relief.	Dull day: no rain.
8.30 P.m. 9.2.15 YPRES.	Went out with two light wagons at 5 P.m. to ZILLEBEKE + after dark to [illegible] H.Qrs [illegible] S.E. of ZILLEBEKE [illegible] saw G.O.C. 6th Cav Bde. Only one wounded man. Removed him + was back in billets by 8 P.m. Some shell fire, but not aimed at us. Town shelled a little during the day.	Rain all day. Ceased at dark.
6 P.m. 10.2.15 YPRES.	Town more heavily shelled this morning. German aviator dropped bomb at my billets, but no casualties. No 8 C.F.A. went out to collect wounded.	Fine day. Some sunshine

Instructions regarding War Diaries and Intelligence Summaries are contained in F. S. Regs., Part II. and the Staff Manual respectively. Title pages will be prepared in manuscript.

WAR DIARY

or

~~INTELLIGENCE SUMMARY~~

(Erase heading not required.)

Army Form C. 2118.

Hour, Date, Place	Ref. map N.W. Europe. Sheet 1. Summary of Events and Information	Remarks and references to Appendices
8-30 a.m. 11.2.15. YPRES.	Got a message that an officer of the N. Somerset Yeomanry was being brought to ZILLEBEKE dangerously wounded. Ordered a light ambulance to proceed to the place & went in motor as far as level crossing on YPRES–MENIN RD, & thence on in the light wagon. Found the officer in ZILLEBEKE, removed him to level crossing & transferred him to motor ambulance, which took him to clearing hospital. ZILLEBEKE road has been shelled again the last two days, but we got back without incident, at 9.30 a.m.	
11 a.m. 11.2.15	Proceeded to [?] 2nd Cav. Div. A.D.M.S. [?]	
8 P.m. 11.2.15 YPRES.	Enemy began shelling YPRES with a 6 inch Howitzer. They shelled the billeting area & dropped shells in many houses.	
9 P.m. 11.2.15.	Was informed that a house in which some 1st Life Guards were billeted had been struck. Went out to the place, & on the way found a wagon of the Territorial R.E. that had been struck by a shell. Two dead men in the wagon, two dead, & two wounded horses. Borrowed revolver & shot one horse, & had the other removed as it was not fatally hit. Went to 1st Life Guards billets. Found that 7 men had been killed & 9 wounded in the house. All 1st Life Guards. They were being attended by M.O. [illegible]. Ordered a stretcher party to go & remove the two dead men from the wagon & took another party to a place where some Belgian civilians were reported wounded. Found 9 women & children all hit by the same shell & all dead.	Orders at 3 P.m. from H.Q.C.F.A. [?] to return to billets at 7.30 a.m. on 13.2.15. Fine day. Some sunshine.
9-30 P.m. 11.2.15 YPRES	Shelling ceased. Returned to billets.	

1247 W 3299 200,000 (E) 8/14 J.B.C. & A. Forms/C. 2118/11.

Instructions regarding War Diaries and Intelligence Summaries are contained in F. S. Regs., Part II. and the Staff Manual respectively. Title pages will be prepared in manuscript.

WAR DIARY ~~or~~ ~~INTELLIGENCE~~ SUMMARY

(*Erase heading not required.*)

Army Form C. 2118.

[illegible]

Hour, Date, Place	Summary of Events and Information	Remarks and references to Appendices
10 a.m. 12.2.15 YPRES	Went to Div HdQrs & saw A.D.M.S. arranged to send the section of No 6 C.F.A. back to their billets tomorrow, but for myself to stay with A.D.M.S. till all 8th Bgde were clear of trenches.	
5 P.m. 12.2.15 YPRES	Proceeded to trenches, & saw Bgde Genl of Cavalry Bgde. Found that two men had been killed.	
6.45 P.m. 12.2.15 YPRES	Took in one sick man & returned to billets. Two officers of No 4 & 5 C.F.A.'s accompanied my [illegible] to the trenches, to see the ground, & method of evacuation of wounded. Very quiet evening & no shelling.	
9 P.m. 12.2.15 YPRES	Enemy shelled the outskirts of the town slightly, with shrapnel from field guns.	Dull day, some sleet & rain. Cold.
7.30 a.m. 13.2.15 YPRES	No 6 C.F.A. marched back to BOESEGHEM, under Lt CREE	
4 P.m. 13.2.15	Went with A.D.M.S. & saw ADMS 2nd Cav Bgde & officers of his Field Ambulances, & conferred on duties of F.A.'s while in YPRES.	
8 P.m. 13.2.15 YPRES	Billeted in a deserted house in YPRES, & gave orders that the 1st Bgde should summon me, if required during evacuation of trenches. Desultory shelling of the town at intervals	Heavy rain [illegible] of the day
9 a.m. 14.2.15 YPRES	Went in motor ambulance to POPERINGHE, [illegible] A.D.M.S. & [illegible] with him to HAZEBROUCK & proceeded on.	
12.15 P.m. 14.2.15 YPRES	arrived at 11.30 a.m. visited 3 [illegible] arrived at BOESEGHEM & resumed Command of F.A.	Heavy rain all day.

Army Form C. 2118.

Instructions regarding War Diaries and Intelligence Summaries are contained in F. S. Regs., Part II. and the Staff Manual respectively. Title pages will be prepared in manuscript.

WAR DIARY
or
INTELLIGENCE SUMMARY

(Erase heading not required.)

Hour, Date, Place	Summary of Events and Information	Remarks and references to Appendices
10.30 P.m. 15.2.15. BOESEGHEM	Proceeded to HAZEBROUCK to start on 7 days leave of absence to England.	
10.30 P.m. 25.2.15. BOESEGHEM.	Arrived back here from base. Arrived at BOULOGNE last night.	
9 a.m. 27.2.15. BOESEGHEM.	F.A. route marched.	
4 P.m. 28.2.15. BOESEGHEM.	D.D.M.S. Cavalry Corps visited these billets	

1247 W 3299 200,000 (E) 8/14 J.B.C. & A. Forms/C. 2118/11.

121/4816

121/4816
March 1915

2o 6. Cavy: Field Ambulance

Vol IV

War Diary

of

Lieut Col W. H. S. Nickerson.

R. A. M. C.

Commanding No 6 Cavalry Field Ambulance.

From 1st March 1915

To 31st March 1915.

Instructions regarding War Diaries and Intelligence Summaries are contained in F. S. Regs., Part II. and the Staff Manual respectively. Title pages will be prepared in manuscript.

WAR DIARY
~~or~~
~~INTELLIGENCE SUMMARY~~
(Erase heading not required.)

Army Form C. 2118.

Hour, Date, Place	Summary of Events and Information	Remarks and references to Appendices
10 a.m. 1.3.15 BOESEGHEM.	A.D.M.S. 3rd Cav Div visited these billets & spoke concerning inoculation of Bgde	
12 midday 1.3.15	Went to 6th Cav Bgde H.Q. Was informed that the 3rd Cav Div are not to go back to trenches at present. F.A. route marched.	High wind & heavy snowstorm in afternoon
10 a.m. 2.3.15 BOESEGHEM.	Saw a case in N. Somerset Yeomanry that may be Cerebro Spinal Fever. Took the case in for observation & gave orders as to isolation of contacts. Very doubtful case in my opinion.	Bad weather still
9 P.M. 3.3.15 BOESEGHEM.	Got a message to say that the above case has been diagnosed Cerebro Spinal Fever. He was removed to HAZEBROUCK this morning. Sent message to M.O. i/c N Somerset Yeomanry & told him to take all precautions.	Weather squally & windy
10 A.M. 4.3.15. BOESEGHEM.	A.D.M.S. D.D.M.S. Cavalry Corps, & Sanitary Officer visited the billet from which the above case came, & issued orders re disinfection etc. Disinfection carried out here also. Saw London Gazette containing my promotion to rank of Lt Col, dated 1.3.15.	High wind, & some rain
3 P.M. 4.3.15. BOESEGHEM.	Went to A.D.M.S.'s Office	
3 P.M. 5.3.15 BOESEGHEM.	Went to HAZEBROUCK visited A.D.M.S.	Bad weather.

1247 W 3299 200,000 (E) 8/14 J.B.C. & A. Forms/C. 2118/11.

Instructions regarding War Diaries and Intelligence Summaries are contained in F. S. Regs., Part II. and the Staff Manual respectively. Title pages will be prepared in manuscript.

WAR DIARY
or
INTELLIGENCE SUMMARY
(Erase heading not required.)

Army Form C. 2118.

Hour, Date, Place	Summary of Events and Information (Ref Map N.W. Europe Sheet I.)	Remarks and references to Appendices
9 a.m. 7.3.15 BOESEGHEM	F.A. route marched.	Weather colder
10 a.m. 8.3.15 BOESEGHEM	A.D.M.S. visited Officers billets. Went to St OMER in motor, returned at 3 P.M.	Snow & frost.
8.30 P.m. 9.3.15 BOESEGHEM	Orders from 6th Cav Bgde to be prepared to start at 1 hours notice.	Frost in morning Rain in evening
9 a.m. 10.3.15 BOESEGHEM	Went to HdQrs 6th Cav Bgde & saw G.O.C. who explained the situation, & gave us a rendezvous at STEENBECQUE, if orders arrived for a move.	Issued orders for F.A. to be partially packed up & ready to move.
8.30 P.m. 10.3.15 BOESEGHEM	Orders came, to be at rendezvous at 6 a.m. tomorrow	Cold & raw. No rain
3.30 a.m. 11.3.15 BOESEGHEM	Reveille.	
5 a.m.	Marched with echelon A of the Field Ambulance.	
6 a.m. STEENBECQUE	Arrived here joined 6th Cav Bgde & marched at once, Marched via STEENBECQUE Station to a point close to the Chateau LAMOTTE au BOIS. Halted here, watered & fed horses.	

1247 W 3299 200,000 (E) 8/14 J.B.C. & A. Forms/C. 2118/11.

Instructions regarding War Diaries and Intelligence Summaries are contained in F. S. Regs., Part II. and the Staff Manual respectively. Title pages will be prepared in manuscript.

WAR DIARY
or
~~INTELLIGENCE SUMMARY~~
(Erase heading not required.)

Army Form C. 2118.

Hour, Date, Place	Ref map N.W. Europe. Sheet 7. Summary of Events and Information	Remarks and references to Appendices
3.30 P.m. 11-3-15. LA MOTTE.	Sent on billeting party.	
4.30 P.m. 11.3.15	Marched on to MERVILLE.	
7 P.m. 11-3-15. MERVILLE.	Billeted on the outskirts, on the road to NEUF BERQUIN.	Orders at 7.30 P.m. to stand to at 5.30 a.m. Fine day, but cold.
4.30 a.m. 12-3-15.	Reveille.	
5.30 a.m. 12-3-15. MERVILLE	Stood to, with horses harnessed & wagons packed.	
3-30 P.m. 12-3-15.	Told to unhook, but to be prepared to march at an hour's notice. Warned that will almost certainly march tonight, towards NEUVE CHAPELLE.	Fine but chill. Rain at night.
4.45 a.m. 13-3-15. MERVILLE	Reveille.	
6 a.m.	Stood to, with wagons packed.	
9 a.m. 13-3-15	Ordered to be ready to move at 2 hours notice.	
3 P.m.	Orders to return to BOESEGHEM.	
6.30 P.m. 13-3-15 MERVILLE	Went to rendezvous.	
9.40 P.m. 13-3-15 BOESEGHEM.	Arrived back in our old billets. Started about 7.15 & went via THIENNES etc.	Fine but chill & cold.

1247 W 3299 200,000 (E) 8/14 J.B.C. & A. Forms/C. 2118/11.

Instructions regarding War Diaries and Intelligence Summaries are contained in F. S. Regs., Part II. and the Staff Manual respectively. Title pages will be prepared in manuscript.

WAR DIARY
~~or~~
~~INTELLIGENCE~~ SUMMARY
(Erase heading not required.)

Army Form C. 2118.

Hour, Date, Place	Summary of Events and Information	Remarks and references to Appendices
	Ref map N.W. Europe Sheet I.	
10.30 a.m. 14.3.15. BOESEGHEM	Went to HAZEBROUCK & reported to A.D.M.S.	Orders to be ready to move at 1 hour 40 mins notice. Fine but dull.
5.40 a.m. 15.3.15 BOESEGHEM	Orders to be ready to move at 45 minutes notice. Turned out men, & had wagons packed.	
8.30 a.m. 15.3.15.	Orders to be at STEENBECQUE half an hour after receipt of orders.	Told we are ready to move up to St ELOI, where an attack by enemy has taken place
2.30 p.m. 15.3.15.	Orders now to be at rendezvous 1½ hours after receipt of orders. Sent horses out for exercise, kept wagons packed.	Morning dull.
10.30 a.m. 16.3.15. BOESEGHEM	A.D.M.S. visited Field Ambulance. Same orders as yesterday hold good all today. Sent horses out for exercise & kept wagons packed.	
8.30 p.m. 16.3.15.	Orders to be ready to move at 3 hours notice.	Fine but dull day.
10.30 a.m. 17.3.15 BOESEGHEM	Went to H.Q. Qrs of 6th Cavalry Bde. Same orders hold good all day. Sent horses for exercise.	Fine early in day, dull later,
3 p.m. 18.3.15. BOESEGHEM.	Went to HAZEBROUCK. Saw A.D.M.S. Orders same as before.	Dull cold, some rain.
6 p.m. 19.3.15 BOESEGHEM.	Resumed the same routine as when we were in these billets before, i.e. exercise for horses, route marches etc for men	Gale, snow & sleet. Cold

1247 W 3299 200,000 (E) 8/14 J.B.C. & A. Forms/C. 2118/11.

Army Form C. 2118.

Instructions regarding War Diaries and Intelligence Summaries are contained in F. S. Regs., Part II. and the Staff Manual respectively. Title pages will be prepared in manuscript.

WAR DIARY
or
~~INTELLIGENCE SUMMARY~~
(Erase heading not required.)

Hour, Date, Place	Refmap N.W. Europe Sheet I. Summary of Events and Information	Remarks and references to Appendices
8 P.m. 20.3.15. BOESEGHEM.	Received report that a man in this Field Ambulance, who had been sent sick, has been diagnosed Cerebro Spinal Meningitis. Div. Sanitary Officer communicated & conferred. Man's clothing etc. had already been disinfected, & the room cleaned.	Fine day
10.30 a.m. 21.3.15. BOESEGHEM.	A.D.M.S. visited billets. Arranged for isolation of contacts of above case, & for inspection, also measures of disinfection.	
4 P.m. 21.3.15	Went to H.d.Qrs Cavalry Corps, at LAMOTTE & saw D.D.M.S.	Fine day
9.30 a.m. 22.3.15. BOESEGHEM.	Route march for Field Ambulance.	
2 P.m. 24.3.15. BOESEGHEM.	Went to HAZEBROUCK & visited A.D.M.S.	Fine day
11 a.m. 25.3.15. BOESEGHEM.	F.G. Court Martial on an A.S.C. man of this Field Ambulance was held here. Charge, Drunkenness.	Rainy day
11.30 a.m. 26.3.15. BOESEGHEM.	O.C. A.S.C. 3rd Cav. Div. inspected all the transport of the Field Ambulance.	Rain
2 P.m. 27.3.15. BOESEGHEM	Went to HAZEBROUCK & visited A.D.M.S. & B echelon H.Q. C.F.A.	Dull & cold.
		Dull & cold.

1247 W 3299 200,000 (E) 8/14 J.B.C. & A. Forms/C. 2118/11.

Instructions regarding War Diaries and Intelligence Summaries are contained in F. S. Regs., Part II. and the Staff Manual respectively. Title pages will be prepared in manuscript.

WAR DIARY

~~or~~

~~INTELLIGENCE SUMMARY~~

(Erase heading not required.)

Army Form C. 2118.

Hour, Date, Place	Summary of Events and Information	Remarks and references to Appendices
	Ref. [illegible] Sheet 7.	
2 P.M. 28.3.15. BOESEGHEM.	Promulgated on parade the sentence of the F.G.C.M. on the [illegible] accused of drunkenness. Finding, guilty. Sentence 10 days Field Punishment No. 1.	Fine but cold.
1 P.M. 31.3.15. BOESEGHEM.	Nothing to record for the past two days. Ordinary routine continues, & no signs of any move on the part of this Div. Lt. Col. Elsmie R.E. [illegible] was ordered to return to England yesterday & report to the War Office.	Fine, but very cold wind for the past 2 days, [illegible]

1247 W 3299 200,000 (E) 8/14 J.B.C. & A. Forms/C. 2118/11.

121/5268
April 1915

121/5268

No 6. Cavalry Field Ambulance

Vol V

[illegible]

WAR DIARY

of

Lt. Col W. H. S. NICKERSON.

O.C. No 6 Cavalry Field Ambulance.

From 1. 4. 15.

To 30. 4. 15.

Instructions regarding War Diaries and Intelligence Summaries are contained in F. S. Regs., Part II. and the Staff Manual respectively. Title pages will be prepared in manuscript.

WAR DIARY

~~or~~

INTELLIGENCE SUMMARY

(Erase heading not required.)

Army Form C. 2118.

Hour, Date, Place	Ref Map N.W. Europe. Sheet I. Summary of Events and Information	Remarks and references to Appendices
9.30 a.m. 1.4.15. BOESEGHEM.	Field Ambulance went for route march.	
2.30 P.m. 1.4.15.	Went to St OMER. returned at 5.30 P.m.	Fine, warm
11.30 a.m. 2.4.15. BOESEGHEM.	Went to Hd Qrs 6th Cav Bde	Fine day.
9.30 a.m. 3.4.15. BOESEGHEM.	Field ambulance went for route march.	Rain, Cold
10.30 a.m. 5.4.15 BOESEGHEM	Went to HAZEBROUCK to see ADMS.	Heavy Rain
11 a.m. 6.4.15. BOESEGHEM.	Inspection of blankets in order to discard surplus, & send them back to Ordnance.	Rain.
11.30 a.m. 7.4.15. BOESEGHEM	Marching order parade for inspection of transport by O.C. Transport 6th Cav Bde	Capt Price ordered to join Command B Echelon.
11 a.m. 8.4.15. BOESEGHEM.	New A.D.M.S. made an informal inspection of the Field Ambce	
2.30 P.m. 9.4.15 BOESEGHEM.	Went to 6th Cav Bde Hd Qrs & sent Lt O'Kelly to N. Somerset Yeomanry	Lt O'Kelly to N. Somerset Yeomanry. Rain. High wind.
	Went to B Echelon. Captain Price joined & took command of B Echelon. Ordered classes in 1st Aid & stretcher drill to start in Bde	Snow & high wind

Instructions regarding War Diaries and Intelligence Summaries are contained in F. S. Regs., Part II. and the Staff Manual respectively. Title pages will be prepared in manuscript.

WAR DIARY
or
INTELLIGENCE SUMMARY
(Erase heading not required.)

Army Form C. 2118.

Hour, Date, Place	Ref map N.W. Europe, Sheet 2 Summary of Events and Information	Remarks and references to Appendices
10 a.m. 10.4.15. BOESEGHEM.	First aid courses started.	Fine.
10 a.m. 12.4.15. BOESEGHEM.	First aid courses etc continued.	
10 a.m. 13.4.15. BOESEGHEM.	A.D.M.S. came & arranged for some moves amongst officers. First aid etc continued. Captain J.H. Richard arrived & took command of B echelon.	Rain
10-30 a.m. 14.4.15. BOESEGHEM.	Went to A.D.M.S's office & arranged about moves. Captain Price proceeded to Bgde of R.H.A. 3rd Cav Div & assumed medical charge. First aid continued.	
12-30 p.m. 15.4.15. BOESEGHEM.	Rev C.S. Ewell left F.A. & proceeded to ABBEVILLE for duty. First aid continued.	Rain. Cold.
10 a.m. 16.4.15. BOESEGHEM.	First aid classes etc completed.	Fine. Dull
10 a.m. 17.4.15. BOESEGHEM.	Examined F.A. in stretcher drill & first aid. 3 cases of measles reported in N. Somerset Yeomanry.	Fine warm
3 p.m. 17.4.15.	Revd F.S. Smithwick joined F.A.	
11 a.m. 18.4.15. BOESEGHEM.	Proceeded to B echelon HAZEBROUCK. Proceeded to STEENBECQUE & conferred with A.D.M.S. & O.C. N. Somerset Yeomanry about measles.	Fine warm
2-30 p.m. 19.4.15. BOESEGHEM.	Paid F.A.	Fine
4 a.m. 20.4.15. BOESEGHEM.	Route march.	Fine

1247 W 3299 200,000 (E) 8/14 J.B.C. & A. Forms/C. 2118/11.

Army Form C. 2118.

Instructions regarding War Diaries and Intelligence Summaries are contained in F. S. Regs., Part II. and the Staff Manual respectively. Title pages will be prepared in manuscript.

WAR DIARY
or
INTELLIGENCE SUMMARY
(Erase heading not required.)

Hour, Date, Place	Ref. map BELGIUM. Sheet 5a. Summary of Events and Information	Remarks and references to Appendices
4 P.m. 21.4.15.	Visited M.O. N. Somerset Yeomanry about Measles. No further cases	Fine.
11 A.M. 22.4.15. BOESEGHEM.	Went to 1st Royal Dragoons & inspected stretcher bearers in drill & 1st Aid. Satisfactory.	
3 P.m. 22.4.15.	Went to B Echelon.	Fine.
6.20 a.m. 23.4.15. BOESEGHEM.	Orders to be ready to move at short notice.	
11.30 a.m.	Ordered to rendezvous at STEENBECQUE at 2 P.m.	
1.15 P.m.	Started. Marched via STEENBECQUE & MORBECQUE to HAZEBROUCK.	Fine but very cold north wind, [illegible] much traffic on roads & clouds of dust
3.30 P.m. HAZEBROUCK	Marched via CAESTRE & GODEWAERSVELDE to ABEELE	
7.15 P.m.	Arrived ABEELE. Ordered to billet in EECKE & sent on a billeting party.	
10 P.m. ABEELE.	Marched via GODEWAERSVELDE to EECKE.	
12.45 a.m. EECKE.	Arrived & billeted.	
2 a.m. 23.4.15. EECKE.	Orders to be ready to move at one hour's notice.	
10 a.m. 24.4.15. EECKE.	Ordered to rendezvous at 10.35 a.m.	
11 a.m. 24.4.15.	Marched to VLAMERTINGHE via GODEWAERSVELDE, MONT des CATS, BOESCHEPE, RENINGHELST.	
2 P.m.	Halted for an hour.	

1247 W 3299 200,000 (E) 8/14 J.B.C. & A. Forms/C. 2118/11.

Instructions regarding War Diaries and Intelligence Summaries are contained in F. S. Regs., Part II. and the Staff Manual respectively. Title pages will be prepared in manuscript.

WAR DIARY
or
INTELLIGENCE SUMMARY

(Erase heading not required.)

Army Form C. 2118.

Hour, Date, Place	Summary of Events and Information (Ref. map of Belgium Sheet 5a)	Remarks and references to Appendices
4.45 P.m. 24.4.15.	Halted at VLAMERTINGHE.	
7 P.m.	Marched to Point 30 S.E. of POPERINGHE.	
8 P.m.	Marched via RENINGHELST. WESTOUTRE to BOESCHEPE	
3 a.m. 25.4.15. BOESCHEPE	Arrived + billeted. G.S. wagon twice got into ditches + was only extracted with difficulty each time, much delay. Very heavy firing all day N.E. of YPRES.	Heavy rain in evening + all night. Hard march. No billets as all the Lahore Div were in the town.
5 a.m. 25.4.15. BOESCHEPE.	Reveille. Ordered to saddle up at 6 a.m.	
9.30 a.m.	Marched to Inn on WESTOUTRE - POPERINGHE Rd.	
11 a.m.	Arrived at Inn + off saddled. Ordered to be ready to move at 12 noon.	
2.15 P.m.	Ordered to move at once. Did so, + marched to Inn on POPERINGHE - Proven Rd. Halted.	
5 P.m.	Moved via PROVEN. WATOU to HOUTKERKE.	POPERINGHE shelled.
7 P.m. 25.4.15. HOUTKERKE.	Billeted.	
10.45 P.m. 25.4.15	Orders to saddle up at 7 a.m.	Fine day, rain in early part of evening. Ordered at 7 P.m. to be ready to move at 1 hours notice.
5.30 a.m. 26.4.15.	Orders to start at once.	
6.15 a.m.	Started + reached rendezvous in HOUTKERKE at 6.30 a.m.	
11.30 a.m. 26.4.15.	Marched via WATOU to near St JANS-TER-BIEZEN. Off saddled.	
12.30 p.m.	Arrived St JANS-TER-BIZEN.	

Instructions regarding War Diaries and Intelligence Summaries are contained in F. S. Regs., Part II. and the Staff Manual respectively. Title pages will be prepared in manuscript.

WAR DIARY
or
INTELLIGENCE SUMMARY

(Erase heading not required.)

Army Form C. 2118.

Hour, Date, Place	Ref Map Belgium Sheet 5a. Summary of Events and Information	Remarks and references to Appendices
8 P.m. 26.4.15. St Jans ter Biezen	Orders for 3/4 of the Bgde to go forward on foot to VLAMERTINGHE. Arranged for light part of F.A. to accompany them.	
8.30 P.m. 26.4.15	Orders from A.D.M.S. that none of F.A. was to go with dismounted men but was all to billet together.	
9.30 P.m.	Moved down POPERINGHE - Proven Rd to a point 1½ miles N.W. of former place. Bivouacked in a field here, with horses of the Bgde remain left with them.	
11 P.m. 26.4.15	Arrived at bivouack. Sent cyclist orderly to Signal post of Divn	POPERINGHE shelled this day
5.45 a.m. 27.4.15. PROVEN Road.	Sent motors to ABEELE for rations. Reveille	
6.30 a.m.	Motors returned with rations	
9 a.m.	Orders came to be ready to move at ½ hours notice. Evacuated sick to POPERINGHE.	
10 P.m. 27.4.15 PROVEN Rd	D.A.D.M.S. came & gave verbal orders that we might be required to move with motors only & leave light wagons behind. Bivouacked in this place. No rations turned up.	
11.30 P.m. 27.4.15.	Orders from A.D.M.S. to send 1 light ambulance, 1 motor, 1 officer, 1 N.C.O. & 2 men to join dismounted part of Bgde at VLAMERTINGHE and go forthwith.	Poperinghe shelled. Cold. Cloudy day
6 a.m. 28.4.15. PROVEN Rd	Reveille	
8.30 a.m.	Went to VLAMERTINGHE to see A.D.M.S. Then went & found Bgde Hd Qrs. Thence to Divl Hd Qrs & reported non-arrival of rations for F.A.	

1247 W 3299 200,000 (E) 8/14 J.B.C. & A. Forms/C. 2118/11.

Instructions regarding War Diaries and Intelligence Summaries are contained in F. S. Regs., Part II. and the Staff Manual respectively. Title pages will be prepared in manuscript.

WAR DIARY
or
INTELLIGENCE SUMMARY
(Erase heading not required.)

Army Form C. 2118.

Hour, Date, Place	Summary of Events and Information	Remarks and references to Appendices
	Reference Belgium Sheet 5A.	
	Brought back with me wagons etc sent out last night.	
12 midday 28.4.15	Got orders to move at 3.30 P.m. Evacuated 4 sick to HAZEBROUCK.	Shelling going on at VLAMERTINGHE which I was there.
3.30 P.m. PROVEN ROAD.	Bgde ordered not to move.	
7.30 P.m.	Bgde moved to billets near FORGE S.W. of St JANSTERBIEZEN.	POPERINGHE shelled.
8.45 P.m. FORGE	Arrived at billets.	Fine day.
9 P.m. 28.4.15	Orders to be ready to move at 2 hours notice.	
2.30 a.m. 29.4.15.	Orders to rendezvous at 8.30 a.m. at the field on PROVEN Rd where we spent the first day. If ordered to move before 8.30, to be ready on ½ hours notice.	
6 a.m. 29.4.15.	Reveille.	
8.15 a.m. FORGE.	Marched to same rendezvous as yesterday via St JANSTERBIEZEN	
3 P.m. 29.4.15. PROVEN Rd	Sent message to ADMS & asked about evacuation of sick. He replied, wounded to BAILLEUL, & sick to HAZEBROUCK, in motors detailed by him.	
5.30 P.m.	Ordered back to last nights billets.	
6 P.m.	Evacuated 2 sick to HAZEBROUCK	Fine warm day.
7 P.m.	Marched.	
7.45 P.m. FORGE	Arrived in same billets as last night.	

1247 W 3299 200,000 (E) 8/14 J.B.C. & A. Forms/C. 2118/11.

Instructions regarding War Diaries and Intelligence Summaries are contained in F. S. Regs., Part II. and the Staff Manual respectively. Title pages will be prepared in manuscript.

WAR DIARY
or
INTELLIGENCE SUMMARY

(Erase heading not required.)

Army Form C. 2118.

Ref Map Belgium Sheet 5A.

Hour, Date, Place	Summary of Events and Information	Remarks and references to Appendices
8 P.m. 29.4.15 FORGE	Orders to be ready to march at 1½ hours notice. Failing further orders, to rendezvous at 8.30 a.m. in same place as today.	
6 a.m. 30.4.15 FORGE	Reveille.	
8.15 a.m.	Marched.	
9 a.m. PROVEN Rd	Arrived at Rendezvous. Orders to be ready to move at ½ hours notice.	
2.30 P.m.	Sent message to A.A.M.S. to evacuate 3 sick.	Very quiet day, & very little gunfire. Fine & warm. Windy morning.
6 P.m.	Motor arrived & evacuated 3 sick to HAZEBROUCK. Orders to return to old billets, & failing further orders, to return here at 8.30 a.m. tomorrow. 1½ hours notice of march.	
6.40 P.m. PROVEN Rd	Marched.	
7.10 P.m. 30.4.15 FORGE	Arrived in billets.	

1247 W 3299 200,000 (E) 8/14 J.B.C. & A. Forms/C. 2118/11.

121/5Y25

May. 1915

3rd Cavalry Division

121/5Y/25

6th Cavalry Field Ambulance

Vol VI

amo

War Diary of

Lt Col W.H.S. Nickerson.

O.C. No 6 Cav Field Ambulance.

From 1st May 1915

To 31st May 1915.

Instructions regarding War Diaries and Intelligence Summaries are contained in F. S. Regs., Part II. and the Staff Manual respectively. Title pages will be prepared in manuscript.

WAR DIARY
or
INTELLIGENCE SUMMARY

(Erase heading not required.)

Army Form C. 2118.

Hour, Date, Place	Refmap Belgium. Sheet 5A. Summary of Events and Information	Remarks and references to Appendices
6 a.m. 1.5.15. FORGE.	Reveille.	
8 a.m. 1.5.15. PROVEN Rd	Returned to same rendezvous as yesterday. The O/C N. Somerset Yeomanry reported 2 officers & one man to be suffering from measles. Inspected their billet & arranged for disinfection.	
8.45 a.m.	Had the cases isolated. Saw A.D.M.S. & arranged to have the cases removed in a special motor.	
11.30 a.m.	Reported to Bgde Hd Qrs the measures taken. Sick removed.	
2 P.m. 1.5.15.	Warned that 6th Cav Bgde are for the trenches tonight.	
3.30 P.m.	Warned that trenches are off.	
6.15 P.m. 1.5.15.	Ordered to return to last night's billets. Proceeded.	Fine dull windy day.
8 P.m. 1.5.15. FORGE.	Orders same as yesterday.	
6 a.m. 2.5.15. FORGE.	Reveille.	
8.45 AM.	Marched to same rendezvous as yesterday.	
11.15 AM. PROVEN Rd	D.A.D.M.S. came & discussed arrangements in the event of the Bde going into the trenches.	
2 P.m. 2.5.15.	Ordered to send a billeting party on	
4 P.m. 2.5.15.	Marched via St JANSTER BIEZEN to billets S.W. of PROVEN	Fine Dull
8 P.m. 2.5.15. S.W. of PROVEN	Degree of readiness given as 2½ hours notice.	

Army Form C. 2118.

Instructions regarding War Diaries and Intelligence Summaries are contained in F. S. Regs., Part II. and the Staff Manual respectively. Title pages will be prepared in manuscript.

WAR DIARY
or
INTELLIGENCE SUMMARY

(Erase heading not required.)

Hour, Date, Place	Refce map Belgium Sheet 5A. Summary of Events and Information	Remarks and references to Appendices
10 AM. 3.5.15. S.W. of PROVEN ½ mile	A.D.M.S. visited billet.	
4.30 P.M.	Orders to rendezvous.	
6.55 P.M.	Arrived at rendezvous ordered to proceed to POPERINGHE & then to point 35 S E of that place.	
9.15 P.M. 3.5.15. Point 35	Arrived & off saddled. Reported position to A.D.M.S.	
10.45 P.M.	Orders to go to billet of A.D.M.S. Proceeded at once. Found that the [illegible] are to go to post beyond VLAMERTINGHE & be in support.	Fine [illegible]
12.45 AM. 4.5.15. Pt 35.	Started off with 4 motor ambulances, 2 M.Os 1 N.C.O. & 24 rank & file, & medical equipment. Went via VLAMERTINGHE to 1st turn on right beyond the level crossing before YPRES.	
1.30 AM.	Arrived at above point, established collecting post in a farm.	
2 AM.	Saw Bgde Major & regimental M.Os & told them of the arrangements.	
6.30 A.M. 4.5.15.	Saw a number of infantry suffering from effects of gas poisoning.	
8.15 A.M. 4.5.15. Point 35.	[illegible] moved back to Pt 35. Withdrew bearers [illegible] & followed them.	Rain all last night. Fine day, rain again in evening.
10.30 a.m. 4.5.15.	Started for same billets as yesterday. Marched via POPERINGHE & PROVEN.	
2 P.M. 4.5.15. ½ mile S.W. of PROVEN	Arrived in billets. Degree of readiness given as 2 hours 20 minutes.	

Instructions regarding War Diaries and Intelligence Summaries are contained in F. S. Regs., Part II. and the Staff Manual respectively. Title pages will be prepared in manuscript.

WAR DIARY
or
INTELLIGENCE SUMMARY
(Erase heading not required.)

Army Form C. 2118.

Ref Map Belgium Sheet 5A.

Hour, Date, Place	Summary of Events and Information	Remarks and references to Appendices
10 a.m. 5.5.15 ½ mile S.W. of PROVEN	Sent horses & men for exercise.	
1.20 p.m.	Proceeded to Bgde Hd Qrs in consequence of orders received. Informed that Bgde will dig trenches tonight at Point 20 south of Y in YPRES. Made necessary arrangements.	
3.30 p.m. 5.5.15	Sent message to A.D.M.S. & asked concerning Motor Convoy position. A.D.M.S. informed me that Motor Convoy are at Pt 25 & that all wounded were to be sent there.	
5.30 p.m.	Started with 2 motor ambulances, 1 M.O. only, 1 N.C.O., 4 men & 6 extra stretchers & necessary surgical equipment. Marched via POPERINGHE to same farm as yesterday just beyond level crossing W. of YPRES.	
6.30 p.m. 5.5.15 Level crossing W of YPRES	Arrived at above place & formed collecting post. Gave out two stretchers to each regiment, & told M.O.s of arrangements.	
7.30 p.m. 5.5.15	Went forward & surveyed the road as far as the YPRES-LILLE Rd.	
9.30 p.m.	Fighting on Hill 60. Terrific shelling all around YPRES. Shelled & set alight. POPERINGHE shelled & a building set alight.	Fine day
1.30 a.m. 6.5.15 Level crossing W of YPRES	Brigade returned. 1 killed & 4 wounded. Evacuated them & also 4 infantry wounded to Pt 25.	
2.30 a.m. 6.5.15	Returned to billet	Fine day
4 a.m. 6.5.15 ½ mile S.W. of PROVEN	Arrived in billet.	

Instructions regarding War Diaries and Intelligence Summaries are contained in F. S. Regs., Part II. and the Staff Manual respectively. Title pages will be prepared in manuscript.

WAR DIARY
or
~~INTELLIGENCE~~ SUMMARY
(Erase heading not required.)

Army Form C. 2118.

Hour, Date, Place	Reference of Belgium Sheet 5A. Summary of Events and Information	Remarks and references to Appendices
9 a.m. 7.5.15. ½ mile S.W. of PROVEN	Orders to be prepared to move back to permanent billets	
1 P.m	ordered to rendezvous at 2.30 P.m.	
2-30 P.m. 7.5.15.	Marched via FORGE - BEAUVOORDE - STEENVOORDE - Crossroads E of St SYLVESTRE - HAZEBROUCK to BOESEGHEM	
9.25 P.m. 7.5.15 BOESEGHEM	arrived in our old billets.	Rain most of afternoon
9 AM. 8.5.15. BOESEGHEM	Degree of readiness given as 3 hours 20 minutes	Fine
6 a.m. 9.5.15 BOESEGHEM	Degree of readiness 1 hour 20 minutes.	
11 a.m. 9.5.15.	ordered to rendezvous with Bgde who were to go north in motor buses at 2.30 P.m. Ordered 2 motor ambulances, 1 M.O. & Staff 1 N.C.O. 5 men, necessary material & extra stretchers to accompany motors & most of 7 a. under Lt CREE to start at 1 P.m.	
2.30 P.m. 9.5.15.	Proceeded via HAZEBROUCK - STEENVOORDE - POPERINGHE to just short of VLAMERTINGHE.	
4 P.m. 9.5.15.	Reached above point. Bgde proceeded on foot to a point just S. of point 20 ½ mile S. of R in BRIELEN. Took my party to the cross roads between 2 & 3 [illegible] milestone on VLAMERTINGHE - YPRES Rd	

1247 W 3299 200,000 (E) 8/14 J.B.C. & A. Forms/C. 2118/11.

Instructions regarding War Diaries and Intelligence Summaries are contained in F. S. Regs., Part II. and the Staff Manual respectively. Title pages will be prepared in manuscript.

WAR DIARY
or
INTELLIGENCE SUMMARY
(Erase heading not required.)

Army Form C. 2118.

Hour, Date, Place	Summary of Events and Information	Remarks and references to Appendices
	Ref. map of Belgium Sheet 5A	
	& established a Collecting post for them in a house.	
8 P.M. 9.5.15. Cross Rds near YPRES.	Message from CREE that at 6.30 P.M. he had arrived at INN 1 mile S of B in St JANSTER BIEZEN. Sent message to ADMS giving my position & arranged with Brigadier as to medical procedure if the Bgde advanced.	Cold N. E. wind.
8 a.m. 10.5.15. Cross Roads	Asked ADMS for another motor ambulance.	
10.30 a.m.	The third motor ambulance asked for arrived. The rest of the F.A. moved to P35.S of 8th milestone on POPERINGHE–YPRES Rd.	
11 a.m. 10.5.15.	Went into YPRES, which was on fire in places, to inspect the roads there.	Fine. Cold.
11.5.15. Cross Roads 8 P.M.	Stood by all day. Issued 500 respirators to Bgde	
10 a.m. 12.5.15. Cross Roads	Orders for Bgde to go into the trenches tonight	
11 A.M 12.5.15.	Saw Brigadier, who showed me the position we are to take up. Saw A.D.M.S. & made medical arrangements.	
P.M. 12.5.15.	Got fresh solution for soaking respirators, & sent it to the Bgde	

Instructions regarding War Diaries and Intelligence Summaries are contained in F. S. Regs., Part II. and the Staff Manual respectively. Title pages will be prepared in manuscript.

WAR DIARY
or
INTELLIGENCE SUMMARY

(Erase heading not required.)

Army Form C. 2118.

Hour, Date, Place	Summary of Events and Information	Remarks and references to Appendices
	Ref Map of Belgium Sheet 5A	
8 P.m. 12.5.15 Cross Roads	Started with 2 bearers, Lt CREE, 1 NCO & 1 man, dressings, stretchers etc. Went through YPRES which was blazing hard, along MENIN Rd to WITTEPOORTE farm on N of road below HOOGE. Established a collecting post in this farm. Left trenches [illegible] N. from HOOGE. Went round trenches & waited while the Bgds took them over. 1 officer killed 1 officer & 2 men wounded all by rifle fire while change was going on. A good deal of rifle fire went on continuously.	Fine
2 a.m. 13-5-15 HOOGE	Left with wounded. Sent the latter to Pt 35 & returned myself to Cross Rds as before. YPRES burning hard.	
8 a.m. 13.5.15 Cross Rds	Informed that enemy were attacking heavily. Some wounded walked in.	
11 a.m. 13-5-15	Went through YPRES with motor Ambulance. Left it near MENIN-ZONNEBEKE Rd junction & walked down MENIN Rd to HALTE. Road under heavy shell & rifle fire & not practicable for wagons. Took the motor up the ZONNEBEKE Rd to Chateau at POTIZE & brought away 2 wounded. Chateau was being shelled, so advised collecting post of 7th & 8th Cav Bgdes to fall back to [illegible]. They did so. Brought in Col [illegible] [illegible] wounded	

Army Form C. 2118.

Instructions regarding War Diaries and Intelligence Summaries are contained in F. S. Regs., Part II. and the Staff Manual respectively. Title pages will be prepared in manuscript.

WAR DIARY
or
INTELLIGENCE SUMMARY
(Erase heading not required.)

Hour, Date, Place	Ref Map Belgium Sheet 5A. Summary of Events and Information	Remarks and references to Appendices
12.30 P.m. 13.5.15 Cross Rds	Message from [illegible] asking for more dressings. Sgt WATCHORN M.C. F.A. had brought this on a motor cycle. Sent dressings.	
8 P.m. 13.5.15	Took 4 motors 1 N.C.O. 10 Privates, 1 Officer, 6 stretchers & dressings etc via YPRES to WITTEPOORTE farm. Shelling mostly stopped now but pretty continuous rifle fire. Found my party safe, & large number of wounded already in farm & dugouts, & more being brought in. For details of evacuation see appendix A.	Heavy rain all day & night.
2 a.m. 14.5.15 WITTEPOORTE	One motor ambulance stuck in a ditch.	
3 a.m. 14.5.15	Daylight but rain & mist rendered us invisible to enemy who were only 300 yards off.	
8 a.m.	Finished evacuation of wounded. Over 200 removed.	See Appendix A.
9 a.m.	Bde moved into trenches in rear of their late position near ZONNEBEKE so withdrew all my personnel etc	
10 A.M. 14.5.15	Went back via YPRES to Cross Rds	
11 A.M. 14.5.15	Went up to Chateau at POTIZE & saw Brigadier. Arranged with him for a new collecting post. Reported arrangements made to A.D.M.S.	

1247 W 3299 200,000 (E) 8/14 J.B.C. & A. Forms/C. 2118/11.

Instructions regarding War Diaries and Intelligence Summaries are contained in F. S. Regs., Part II. and the Staff Manual respectively. Title pages will be prepared in manuscript.

WAR DIARY
or
INTELLIGENCE SUMMARY

(Erase heading not required.)

Army Form C. 2118

Hour, Date, Place	Summary of Events and Information	Remarks and references to Appendices
	Ref. Belgian Sheet 5A	
2 P.m. 14.5.15. Cross Rds W of YPRES	Took Lt O'CALLAGHAN 1 N.C.O. 2 men 1 [illegible] & surgical material & stretchers in a motor. Went through YPRES & down the MENIN Rd to a point on this road just North of S in YPRES. Formed a collecting post here. Walked out N.E. along the railway. Got into the trenches & surveyed the new position of Cavalry Bgde. Returned to Cross roads.	
8 P.m. 14.5.15	Message received from M.O. 1st R Dragoons that Lt Col STEELE & others wounded were now in the farm at WITTEPOORTE where we were last night. Took 2 motors & proceeded at once. Found Col STEELE shot in head. Sent motor with him & others wounded straight through to BAILLEUL. Went thence to collecting post on MENIN Rd.	
12.30 A.M. 15.5.15. MENIN Rd	Found that the 6th Cav Bgde were out of the trenches, so vacated the collecting post & fell back via YPRES to the advanced dressing Stn at Cross Rds W. of YPRES.	Cold day. Rain in morning.
9 a.m. 15.5.15.	Rejoined my unit at main dressing Stn at Point 35 S. of 8th milestone on POPERINGHE-YPRES Rd	
11 a.m.	Gave temporary rank of Corporal to Driver BARKER A.S.C. as Coy Sgt Major YORKE A.S.C. was sent to England yesterday. Saw A.D.M.S. concerning all recent events. Ordered all wagons to be packed.	Fine day

1247 W 3299 200,000 (E) 8/14 J.B.C. & A. Forms/C. 2118/11.

Instructions regarding War Diaries and Intelligence Summaries are contained in F. S. Regs., Part II. and the Staff Manual respectively. Title pages will be prepared in manuscript.

WAR DIARY
or
~~INTELLIGENCE~~ SUMMARY
(Erase heading not required.)

Army Form C. 2118.

Hour, Date, Place	Summary of Events and Information	Remarks and references to Appendices
	Ref Map of Belgium Sheet 5A.	
11 A.M. 16.5.15. Point 35.	Church parade. G.O.C. 6th Cav Bgde addressed the parade & subsequently specially spoke to the Field Ambulance & thanked them.	
6 P.M. 11.5.15. Point 35.	Remained here all day, cleaned up wagons & stretchers. No 6 C.F.A. on duty for Casual sick up to 6 P.M.	Rain. Cold
11.30 A.M. 17.5.15. Point 35.	Sent more respirators to Bgde to make up deficiencies.	
5.30 P.M.	Went to Bgde Hd Qrs & then to funeral of O.C. 10th Hussars & others. – VLAMERTINGHE	Rain. Cold
18.5.15. 11 A.M. Point 35.	Went round Bgde Camps with Divl Sanitary Officer.	
12 noon	Message asking for names of men who did well on the 13th–14th May for publication in Bgde Orders. Sent them	
2.30 P.M.	Went to Bgde Hd Qrs	Rain. Cold
9 P.M. 18.5.15. Point 35.	Divn dug trenches at night.	
6 P.M. 19.5.15. Point 35.	No 6 C.F.A. on duty till 6 P.M. Evacuated sick to HAZEBROUCK.	Rain. Cold

1247 W 3299 200,000 (E) 8/14 J.B.C. & A. Forms/C. 2118/11.

Instructions regarding War Diaries and Intelligence Summaries are contained in F. S. Regs., Part II. and the Staff Manual respectively. Title pages will be prepared in manuscript.

WAR DIARY
or
INTELLIGENCE SUMMARY
(Erase heading not required.)

Army Form C. 2118.

Hour, Date, Place	Summary of Events and Information	Remarks and references to Appendices
	Refering Belgium Sheet 5A	
8 P.m. 20.5.15. Point 35.	6th Cav Bgde went out to dig Trenches. Sent Lt CREGG & small party & 1 motor to a point near the Cemetery on the MENIN Rd	Fine day
3 a.m. 21.5.15. Point 35.	above party returned & reported no casualties	
10 a.m.	Went to RENINGHELST to see ADMS for orders to return to BOESEGHEM.	
11 A.M.	Went to Bgde Hd Qrs & arranged to have one motor with M.O. & dressings to accompany motor buses tonight	
1 P.m. 21.5.15.	Marched to BOESEGHEM via POPERINGHE - STEENVOORDE - HAZEBROUCK. Halted 3/4 hour in latter place at my "B" echelon	
8.30 P.m. 21.5.15. BOESEGHEM.	arrived in our old billets. Good march.	Fine warm day
12.45 a.m. 22.5.15.	Motor & M.O. returned. Bgde all back in billets.	
12.15 P.m. 22.5.15. BOESEGHEM.	Went to B echelon in HAZEBROUCK inspected the hospital there & the horses.	Fine day
11.30 A.M. 23.5.15.	Lt LIGHTSTONE brought our horses from B echelon. Picked out the seven best & exchanged my horses for them.	Fine day. Warm.

1247 W 3299 200,000 (E) 8/14 J.B.C. & A. Forms/C. 2118/11.

Instructions regarding War Diaries and Intelligence Summaries are contained in F. S. Regs., Part II. and the Staff Manual respectively. Title pages will be prepared in manuscript.

WAR DIARY
or
INTELLIGENCE SUMMARY
(Erase heading not required.)

Army Form C. 2118.

Refmap Belgium Sheet 5A.

Hour, Date, Place	Summary of Events and Information	Remarks and references to Appendices
3 P.M. 24.5.15. BOESEGHEM.	Went to AIRE & saw D.D.V.S. 1st Army & D.D.V.S. Indian Cav Corps.	
4.30 P.M.	Orders to send an officer for temporary duty with 1st Cav Div. at YPRES. Sent Lt HALLINAN.	Fine warm
6 P.M. 25.5.15 BOESEGHEM.	Lt HALLINAN returned	Fine day
10 A.M. 26.5.15. BOESEGHEM.	Went to Div Hd Qrs 3d Cav Div now at RENESCURE.	
12.30 A.M.	Told by Lt Col L.H. Lloyd that he had been appointed A.D.V.S. 3d Cav Div. As this officer is junior to myself, proceeded to St. OMER to G.H.Q. & asked Lt Col BIRRELL what was to be my disposal. He informed me that the appointment of Lloyd was a mistake & it would be immediately cancelled.	Fine day
8.30 P.M.	Saw D.D.V.S. Cavalry Corps, who informed me that he had applied for me to be appointed A.D.V.S. 3d Cav Div.	Fine day
10 A.M. 27.5.15. BOESEGHEM.	O'KELLY took over N. Somerset Yeomanry. ROHH returned, & HALLINAN proceeded to B echelon	Windy & cold

1247 W 3299 200,000 (E) 8/14 J.B.C. & A. Forms/C. 2118/11.

Instructions regarding War Diaries and Intelligence Summaries are contained in F. S. Regs., Part II. and the Staff Manual respectively. Title pages will be prepared in manuscript.

Army Form C. 21

WAR DIARY
or
INTELLIGENCE SUMMARY
(Erase heading not required.)

Hour, Date, Place	Ref map BELGIUM Sheet 5A. Summary of Events and Information	Remarks and references to Appendices
11 AM. 28.5.15 BIESEGHEM	Warned that 3rd Cav Div are for trenches tomorrow.	
4.30 P.m.	Went to Bgde HdQrs 6th Cav Bgde & got orders. Returned & issued orders for F.A. to march at 8 a.m. by bus motors, which were to accompany motor buses containing troops	
8.30 P.m.	Went to Cav Corps HdQrs to see D.D.M.S.	Fine cold
8 a.m. 29.5.15 BIESEGHEM	Started off F.A. under Lt CREE. Proceeded in motor to Div HdQrs to see A.D.M.S. & discussed arrangements for respirators for personnel of my F.A.	
10.30 a.m.	Proceeded in motor & caught up F.A. just N.E. of STEENVOORDE at 12 noon. Halted it for one hour.	
1 P.m.	Started off F.A. again & proceeded in motor to VLAMERTINGHE	
2.30 P.m. VLAMERTINGHE	Arrived & arranged for dressing Stn in school at east end of the village.	
4.30 P.m.	Sent to Point 35 & had all men & equipment taken from wagons & brought in motors to the dressing station. Horse transport left at Point 35. Crossley motor Ambulance broke down. Sent it back to Bechelor & asked for another car.	

1247 W 3299 200,000 (E) 8/14 J.B.C. & A. Forms/C. 2118/11.

Instructions regarding War Diaries and Intelligence Summaries are contained in F. S. Regs., Part II. and the Staff Manual respectively. Title pages will be prepared in manuscript.

WAR DIARY
or
INTELLIGENCE SUMMARY
(Erase heading not required.)

Army Form C. 2118.

Hour, Date, Place	Ref Map of BELGIUM Sheet 5A Summary of Events and Information	Remarks and references to Appendices
8 P.m. 29.5.15.	Went out with 1 light wagon + 1 motor to the Ecole Bienfaisance on YPRES-MENIN Rd + established Lt O'CALLAGHAN, 12 O.R. 3 horse + equipment as a Collecting post	
9 P.m. 29.5.15	Went to trenches S of HOOGE, via ZILLEBEKE Rd + track. 3rd Cav Div went into trenches.	Fine Cold
2.30 AM. 30.5.15	Div all in trenches. Took away wounded + provided [illegible]	
4 A.M. 30.5.15 VLAMERTINGHE	Arrived back here	
8 A.M.	Had proper dressing Stn made in the School.	
11.30 A.m. 30.5.15	Sent off Casual sick to HAZEBROUCK	
4 P.m. YPRES.	Went to the City + surveyed the roads by daylight.	
5 P.m. 30.5.15 VLAMERTINGHE	Wounded evacuated by Motor Convoy.	
7.30 P.m.	Heard that we have had some Casualties.	
8 P.m. 30.5.15.	Sent Lt CREE, 6 light wagons + 4 motors with personnel to relieve Collecting post + Collect wounded.	Fine Cold.

1247 W 3299 200,000 (E) 8/14 J.B.C. & A. Forms/C. 2118/11.

Instructions regarding War Diaries and Intelligence Summaries are contained in F. S. Regs., Part II. and the Staff Manual respectively. Title pages will be prepared in manuscript.

WAR DIARY
or
~~INTELLIGENCE SUMMARY~~
(Erase heading not required.)

Army Form C. 2118.

Hour, Date, Place	Summary of Events and Information	Remarks and references to Appendices
	Ref Map BELGIUM Sheet 5A.	
2.30 a.m. 31-5-15. VLAMERTINGHE.	27 wounded brought in	
	Lt O'KELLY M.O. N Somerset Yeomanry wounded. Sent out Lt O'CALLAGHAN at once to replace him.	
3-30 A.M.	Wounded evacuated by Motor Convoy.	
8 P.m. 31-5-15.	Sent out 6 light wagons + 4 motors to collect wounded	[illegible]

1247 W 3299 200,000 (E) 8/14 J.B.C. & A. Forms/C. 2118/11.

Appendix A.

Account of the evacuation of wounded during the German attack on HOOGE 13th 14th May 1915
Ref Map BELGIUM. Sheet 5A.

The 3rd Cavalry Division held a line of trenches running from from the South edge of the BELLEWOORDE lake at HOOGE, north & then east across the ZONNEBEKE-YPRES road near WILTJE. At 3.45 a.m. on the 13th May, the enemy commenced an extremely violent bombardment of these trenches, many of which were blown in. They also bombarded heavily the MENIN Road from YPRES to HOOGE. The 6th Cav Bde who were on the right of the line, had many trenches blown in, but held on to the ground all day, despite heavy losses. The 7th & 8th Bdes lost some trenches & fell back at first on to the trenches in front of POTIJZE. In the afternoon, all the lost ground was recovered by counter attacks & by the evening the whole German attack had failed. Our casualties were 92 officers & 1052 men killed & wounded, out of a total of about 2500 in the trenches.

The three Cavalry Field Ambulances were at Point 35, south of the 8th milestone on the POPERINGHE-YPRES road, & the main dressing station was here. At the BRIELEN-DICKEBUSCH-YPRES-VLAMERTINGHE cross roads was an advanced dressing station.

No. 6 C.F.A. had an advanced post, under an Officer, Lt CREE, at WITTEPOORT farm HOOGE, & Nos 7 & 8 a combined post in the Chateau at POTIJZE.
Each F.A. had 3 Motor Ambulances & 6 light ambulance wagons at its disposal.
At 8 a.m. on the 13th I myself was at the Cross Roads, & a wounded officer arrived with the news that the 6th Cav Bde was heavily engaged. Meanwhile, numerous walking cases had come in from POTIJZE. As the ZONNEBEKE road was fairly safe, motors were sent along it to the Chateau.
At 9 A.M. I proceeded in a motor ambulance to reconnoitre. Went through YPRES & left the wagon under cover at the junction of the MENIN & ZONNEBEKE Roads. Proceeded down the MENIN Road on foot to beyond the level crossing, when a good view could be obtained. Found that the 6th Bde had not fallen back, as I had gone beyond the reserve trenches, & also got a message from Lt CREE, asking for more dressings, saying he had many casualties. The MENIN road was very heavily shelled, & several large trees were struck & brought down, & there was a considerable rifle fire at various parts of it, & it was plainly visible to the enemy. So I decided that no wounded except walking cases could be got away before darkness, & returned to the motor.

Proceeded in the motor to the Chateau at POTIJZE & found that the 7th & 8th Bgde were now back on the reserve trenches, & the Chateau was being heavily shelled. The officers of 20 D & 40 B asked what they should do, so told them to retire half a mile back to another house. Took away wounded in my motor, & the remainder were evacuated by other wagons, & walking, & the post fell back. Subsequently three shells burst in this Chateau.

Proceeded back to the Cross roads & organized arrangements for the evacuation of wounded from HOOGE at night. It appeared to me that it would be advisable to clear the trenches as rapidly as possible, owing to the possibility of the 6th Cav Bgde having to fall back in the night. So arranged that the motors were only to work from the trenches to the Cross roads, & that from there, the light wagons would remove them to the main station at Point 35. At 8 P.m had 18 light wagons at the Cross roads advanced station, & 4 motors, one borrowed from another F.A. The evacuation of wounded from POTIJZE had gone on all day, & some walking cases had got back across the fields from HOOGE, so a large number were already disposed of, & HOOGE itself was the only serious problem left.

Started myself at 8 P.m. with one officer

& about 10 N.C.O's & men, dressings etc, in
the 4 motors. Went via YPRES & the MENIN
road. At the point where the road to the
WILLEPOORT farm leaves the main road is
a house. This we found full of wounded, &
cleared it first. Proceeded to the farm, &
found that during the day upwards of
100 wounded had been transferred to some
dugouts, as the farm was shelled. This
made my task harder, as the dugouts
were narrow, only accessible across a muddy
ditch, & had very small entrances. It was
raining hard, so the cases could not be
brought out long before the wagons were ready
for them. Wounded were still being brought
into the barns & the farm buildings.
Proceeded steadily with evacuation of the
dugouts first, bringing the motors up the
narrow road to the farm, which was only
about 300 yards from the enemy. Motors
had to go on up to the farm & turn there, as
the road was so narrow, & this caused
further delay. Full motors proceeded on
over to the cross roads, unloaded & returned.
There was an exceptionally large number of
lying down cases, to add to the difficulties.
At 3 a.m. 14.5.15 it was daylight but
owing to the mist, the enemy could not
see us. By 5 a.m. all dugouts were clear
& we started on the farm & barns.

Continued the same method as before, but worked more rapidly in the daylight.
At 8 a.m. the last wagon load was sent off & by 9 a.m. the post was evacuated & all my officers & men removed in the last two wagons. The 6th Cav Bde had come out of the trenches in the meanwhile, & gone to their trenches. On arrival at the advanced dressing station at the Cross roads, I found that all wounded had gone on to the main station. From here, the Motor Convoy had been removing wounded all night to BAILLEUL. By 10 a.m. 14.6.15 the main dressing station was also cleared of all wounded.
The main point emphasized is that a Cavalry Field Ambulance is too small to deal rapidly with large numbers of wounded, unless it makes up for lack of size by superior mobility, & the wagons are pushed right up to the trenches.
Another point is that long narrow dug outs should not be used for the collection wounded if possible; the fact that they were, & the rain & mud, were the chief difficulties that night, though the rain undoubtedly saved us from being shelled when daylight broke.

W.B. Dickenson, Lt Col.
O.C. No 6 C.F.A.

4

3rd Cavalry Division

121/5931

June. 1915.

121/5931

No 6. Cavalry Field Ambulance

Vol VII

AWD.

Instructions regarding War Diaries and Intelligence Summaries are contained in F. S. Regs., Part II. and the Staff Manual respectively. Title pages will be prepared in manuscript.

WAR DIARY
or
INTELLIGENCE SUMMARY
(Erase heading not required.)

Army Form C. 2118.

Hour, Date, Place	Ref Map Belgium Sheet 5A Summary of Events and Information	Remarks and references to Appendices
1 A.M. 1.6.15. VLAMERTINGHE	18 wounded & 8 sick arrived at dressing station.	
2 a.m.	Evacuated all wounded by Motor Convoy.	
11 a.m.	Evacuated all sick to HAZEBROUCK. Arranged the detail for tonight	
7 P.m.	Informed that Lt Col F. W. HARDY had been appointed A.D.M.S of this Divn	
8 P.m. 1.6.15.	Heard that there were 12 lying down cases & 35 sitting up for evacuation. Started off with 6 motors & 7 light wagons. Some officers of 1st Ind Cav F.A. accompanied me to see method of evacuation.	
9 P.m. 1.6.15. YPRES.	Started from Collecting post. Took 3 motors & all the light wagons out as usual via the ZILLEBEKE RD & the track to the [illegible] just before reaching ZILLEBEKE. Left the motors just short of the turn off on to this track, & proceeded to trenches with light wagons. Light wagons took wounded from trenches to motors; motors took them to the Collecting post.	Fine day.
1 a.m. 2.6.15. Woods at HOOGE.	All clear, so took remainder of wounded in light wagons & went to Collecting post. Took residue of wounded from there in motors, & returned.	
2.15 a.m. 2.6.15 VLAMERTINGHE	Arrived back at dressing stn. A good many shells came near during wagons. We had no casualties but 3 men of other units were hit alongside of us & were picked up.	

Instructions regarding War Diaries and Intelligence Summaries are contained in F. S. Regs., Part II. and the Staff Manual respectively. Title pages will be prepared in manuscript.

WAR DIARY

or

~~INTELLIGENCE SUMMARY~~

(Erase heading not required.)

Army Form C. 2118.

Hour, Date, Place	Ref Map Belgium. Sheet 5A Summary of Events and Information	Remarks and references to Appendices
8.30 a.m. 2.6.15. VLAMERTINGHE.	Motor Convoy collected all our wounded	
11 a.m.	Sent wagon to "B" echelon with sick.	
12.15 P.m.	A.D.M.S. 1st Indian Cavalry Divn came & asked for information about our methods. Showed him dressing stn etc	
4.30 P.m.	Message from Collecting post – that Lt. O/c K.D.G.s is wounded. Passed it on to 1st Indian Cav Divn	
5.30 P.m.	Went to 1st Hd Qrs on YPRES road. Road shelled, & a howitzer shell landed on it & caused some damage.	
6.30 P.m.	Message from Collecting post that they had been heavily shelled & that a naval M.O. temporarily assisting my F.A. was wounded, also Major HAMMERTON of No 8 C.F.A. Two of my motor drivers killed, another wounded & two motor drivers of No 8 C.F.A. all wounded. Sent another car for wounded.	
7.45 P.m.	Car arrived back with all of the above wounded.	
8 P.m.	Went myself to Collecting post with 6 light wagons & 3 motors. Some shelling of the place still going on.	
9 P.m.	Went on to trenches with 3 motors & 6 light wagons. Left motors in same place as yesterday & took on the light wagons. Found heavy casualties. Light wagons had to make 3 journeys to the motors with lying down cases.	Fine day.
2 a.m. 3.6.15. Works at HOOGE.	All clear. over 120 wounded evacuated by us.	

Instructions regarding War Diaries and Intelligence Summaries are contained in F. S. Regs., Part II. and the Staff Manual respectively. Title pages will be prepared in manuscript.

WAR DIARY
or
INTELLIGENCE SUMMARY
(Erase heading not required.)

Army Form C. 2118.

Hour, Date, Place	Ref Map Belgium Sheet 5A — Summary of Events and Information	Remarks and references to Appendices
2.30 a.m. 3.6.15. YPRES.	Arrived at Collecting post. Evacuated remainder of wounded from here in the motors & returned.	See Appendix A
5.30 a.m. 3.6.15. VLAMERTINGHE	Motor Convoy collected all the wounded	
11 a.m.	D.D.M.S. Cavalry Corps visited us	
12.30 P.m	Buried the motor driver H PAYNE, who was killed yesterday	
2 P.m.	Arranged detail for tonight.	
8 P.m.	Started with 6 light wagons & 3 motors. Went to the Collecting post.	
8.30 P.m. YPRES.	Met an officer of the 9th F.A. & as two regiments of his Brigade are assisting the Cavalry arranged to work with him. He to take up motors, we to take up light wagons.	
9 P.m.	Sent 2 L. Cox on to trenches & remained at Collecting Stn.	See Appendix A
9.30 P.m to 11 P.m	Heavy shelling of Collecting post. Buildings hit, but no casualties	fine day
12.30 a.m. 4.6.15. YPRES	Motors arrived with wounded. Transferred all Cavalry cases from them to our motors, sent off both lots of cars to their respective dressing Stns. My motors ordered to return here.	

1247 W 3299 200,000 (E) 8/14 J.B.C. & A. Forms/C. 2118/11.

Instructions regarding War Diaries and Intelligence Summaries are contained in F. S. Regs., Part II, and the Staff Manual respectively. Title pages will be prepared in manuscript.

WAR DIARY
or
INTELLIGENCE SUMMARY
(Erase heading not required.)

Army Form C. 2118

Hour, Date, Place	Ref. Belgium Sheet 5A. Summary of Events and Information	Remarks and references to Appendices
2.15 A.M. 4.6.15. YPRES	Light wagons arrived, with the rest of the wounded. Sent them straight on to dressing Stn. Retired myself, with motors & remainder of wounded from the post.	
3 a.m. VLAMERTINGHE	Arrived at dressing Stn.	
4.30 A.M.	Motor Convoy collected all our wounded.	
11.30 a.m.	Sent motor with sick to B echelon.	
4 P.m.	Arranged with D.A.D.M.S. & an officer of the 9th F.A. to modify our scheme of last night. Issued orders for tonight.	See Appendix A.
8 P.m.	Started with 6 light wagons & 3 motors. Picked up Infantry F.A. stretcher bearers at their dressing Stn YPRES asylum & proceeded to collecting post.	
9.10 P.m.	Proceeded to trenches, left my motors & the 9th F.A. cars went to ZILLEBEKE Rd. taking light wagons to trenches. Only 30 wounded.	fine day.
1 a.m. 5.6.15. YPRES	Returned to collecting post. Filled my motors with sitting cases & returned to dressing Stn. Reached there 2.15 a.m.	

Instructions regarding War Diaries and Intelligence Summaries are contained in F. S. Regs., Part II. and the Staff Manual respectively. Title pages will be prepared in manuscript.

WAR DIARY
or
~~INTELLIGENCE SUMMARY.~~
(Erase heading not required.)

Army Form C. 2118.

Place	Date	Hour	Summary of Events and Information — Ref map Belgium Sheet 5A.	Remarks and references to Appendices
VLAMERTINGHE	5.6.15.	6 a.m.	Motor Convoy evacuated wounded.	
		11 a.m.	Orders to come out of the trenches tonight. Sent off a motor with sick to 'B' echelon, received orders for tonight.	
		8 P.M.	Sent off 2 motors & 8 light wagons to adopt the same procedure for evacuation as last night.	
		10.30 P.M.	Message from 3rd D.G.'s asking for a wagon for 3 lying down & 5 sitting cases wounded by a shell on the ramparts at YPRES. Sent Motor Ambulance.	
do	6.6.15	2 A.M.	Motors returned. [illegible] few wounded. Two light wagons left until the Div. is out of the trenches.	
		4.30 a.m.	Light wagons returned & reported all Div. out of the trenches.	
		6 a.m.	Motor Convoy evacuated all wounded. Closed dressing Stn. & sent all stuff to	
Point 35	6.6.15	11.30 a.m.	Point 35. Started on march. Went via WESTOUTRE – MONTNOIRE – METEREN – STRAZEELE – HAZEBROUCK to BOESEGHEM. Halted for one hour at 1.30 p.m. & for ½ hour at 5.15 p.m. Sent on [illegible] motor & [illegible] the other to accompany the motor buses.	
BOESEGHEM	6.6.15	7.30 p.m.	Arrived in our old billets. Found both motors had already arrived.	Fine day

Army Form C. 2118.

Instructions regarding War Diaries and Intelligence Summaries are contained in F. S. Regs., Part II. and the Staff Manual respectively. Title pages will be prepared in manuscript.

WAR DIARY
or
~~INTELLIGENCE SUMMARY.~~

(Erase heading not required.)

Place	Date	Hour	Summary of Events and Information	Remarks and references to Appendices
			Ref map Belgium. Sheet 5A.	
BOESEGHEM	7.6.15	11 A.M.	Went to A.D.M.S.'s Office & arranged about leave for the F.A. Went on to B echelon	
		2 P.M.	Message from Bgde Major asking for names of those who did well while at YPRES.	
		3.30 P.M.	Sent list as required, to Bgde Major. 6th Cav Bgde.	Fine day
		4 P.M.	Got pay & paid out.	
	8.6.15	to	13.6.15. On leave.	
do	14.6.15	10 A.M.	Orders to move men & horses into another farm. Went to HQ 2nd to see A.D.M.S.	Fine cold
		6 P.M.	Carried out the move ordered.	
do	15.6.15	A.M.	Went round the new billets	
		3 P.M.	Orders to be at rendezvous on 2 hours notice.	Fine
do	16.6.15	3 P.M.	Went to B echelon.	Fine
do	17.6.15	8 A.M.	Degree of readiness given now as 3½ hours.	
		5 P.M.	Heard that the other motor driver of this F.A. G. HORSFALL wounded at YPRES, has died of wounds.	Fine day
do	18.6.15	12.30 P.M.	C in C inspected the 6th Cav Bgde at STEENBECQUE.	Fine day
do	19.6.15	11 A.M.	Orders for Capt S.A. SMITH to hand over M/c of 3rd D.G.s & proceed to 1st Cav Div for duty, on Monday next.	
do	20.6.15	10 A.M.	Lt O'CALLAGHAN took over M/c 3rd D.Gs from Capt SMITH. Lt WILEY took over M/c	

Instructions regarding War Diaries and Intelligence Summaries are contained in F. S. Regs., Part II. and the Staff Manual respectively. Title pages will be prepared in manuscript.

WAR DIARY
or
INTELLIGENCE SUMMARY.
(Erase heading not required.)

Army Form C. 2118.

Place	Date	Hour	Reference Belgium Sheet 5A. Summary of Events and Information	Remarks and references to Appendices
			N. Somerset Yeomanry.	Fine day
BOESEGHEM	22.6.15	11.30 a.m.	Proceeded to HAZEBROUCK & drew pay for F.A. Went to B echelon & gave them pay.	Slight rain
do	23.6.15		Nil	do
do	24.6.15	11.30 a.m.	A.D.M.S. came, & went round R.H.A. & 1st R Dragoons	Fine day
do	25.6.15	3.30 p.m.	Went to B echelon.	Heavy Rain
do	26.6.15	10.45 a.m.	A.D.M.S. went round 3rd D.G. & N. Somerset Yeomanry.	Fine day
do	27.6.15			Slight rain
do	28.6.15			Slight rain
do	29.6.15	10 a.m.	Digging parties from regiments in the Bde went to NEUVE EGLISE to dig trenches. Medical arrangements made by A.D.M.S. from B echelons.	
		6 p.m.	Orders to send a motor to cross roads by N in NIEPPE, beyond STEENBECQUE station tomorrow at 9 a.m.	Heavy rain in evening.
do	30.6.15	9 a.m.	Brigade practised crossing the canal, swimming horses, etc.	
		5 p.m.	A.D.M.S. visited F.A. & arranged to lecture to Bde on Sanitation.	Fine day

Appendix A.

Observations on the evacuation of wounded during the period 29.5.15 to 6.6.15.

The 3rd Cavalry Division held a line of trenches at HOOGE, on the right of the YPRES-MENIN road, commencing at the Chateau on the left, & going through dense woods on the right. The 6th Cavalry Brigade were in the fire trenches, the 3rd D.G.'s being in the post of danger on the left, the 8th Cav Bgde were mostly in reserve trenches, & the 7th Cav Bgde in reserve in the dugouts under the ramparts at YPRES.

Medical arrangements were as follows.

Horses & horsed wagons kept at Point 35, S. of 8th milestone on YPRES-POPERINGHE road.

Dressing Station & motors, at the east end of VLAMERTINGHE in a school house.

Collecting post in the Industrial school on the YPRES-MENIN Rd.

At the Collecting post, Nos 6 & 8 C.F.A.s each kept one officer, 1 N.C.O. & three men, with the necessary equipment. These two units took it in turns to keep a motor ambulance on duty there for a 24 hours tour.

All the personnel were relieved every 24 hours.

Owing to casualties amongst M.O.s, 4 being wounded, the number at the Collecting post was eventually reduced to one.

Any cases that came in during the day were passed on to the dressing station.
Evacuation at night was done as follows.
At 7.45 P.M. 6 or 8 light Ambulance wagons assembled at the dressing Stn. These were drawn from Nos 6 & 8 C.F.A.'s These were then sent on to the Collecting post & halted there.
At 8 P.M. 3 motors took out the officers & personnel intended for evacuation purposes. The motors were put in a sheltered place at the Industrial school, (making 4 motors there all told) At 9 P.M. the light wagons started off. On the majority of nights I went with them myself, & was thus able to see the good & weak points of our method.
We proceeded down the MENIN road to the level crossing, then down the ZILLEBEKE road to the outskirts of the village of that name & then turned to the left along a track that leads to the trenches. The distance of the ~~track~~ village from the trenches is about 3/4 mile.
Lying down & sitting up cases were removed in the wagons to the Industrial school
We had fixed on a place at the trenches, to which all regimental M.O.'s were to bring their cases after dark.

There were 4 places where the wagons were exposed, the MENIN gate at YPRES (we used to go through the city itself) the MENIN-ZILLEBEKE road junction at the level crossing, the turn off to the left at ZILLEBEKE village, & the place at the trenches where collection took place. There was always a good deal of rifle fire at this latter place, as well as along the road leading to it. But we had no casualty amongst our personnel, though we actually had 3 men of other units hit by shells alongside our wagons going & returning.
The casualties amongst medical personnel occurred, two officers in the trenches, & two officers & 4 motor drivers at the collecting post in the Industrial school.
This system worked well enough for a small number of casualties, but as there was very heavy fighting on the 2nd June I was convinced that it would not do for that day, as there were a large number of casualties, & it was daylight by 2-30 a.m. in those days.
So I ordered 3 motors to accompany the light wagons on the night 2-3rd June, & they proceeded slowly along the Zillebeke road to just short of the turn to the left along the track. The road was full of shell holes

but by going slowly & cautiously the motors reached this point all right. Here, there was slight shelter given by a ruined house. The light wagons went forward on loaded, filled up with lying cases only, proceeded back to the motors, who loaded up, & went right through to the dressing station, & made a second journey. Sent a message also for more motors to go to the Industrial school to pick up walking cases. This was done.

The light wagons had to make 3 journeys, & then about 2 a.m. went off with the last loads & went right through to the dressing station. The motors took us back to the Industrial school, picked up the last of the walking cases, & all proceeded back to the dressing station. In this way over 120 cases were dealt with between 9.45 p.m. & 2 a.m.

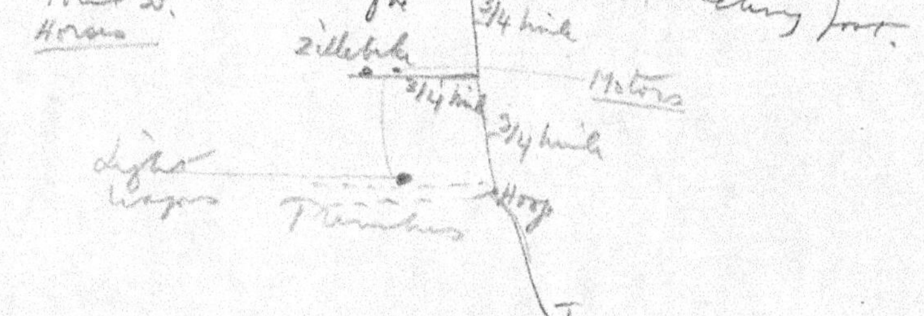

I consider that the weakest point of the scheme was keeping the horses as far away as point 35, which greatly increased their daily work.
The keeping the motors 2½ miles from the trenches was also a weak spot, but this was remedied as shown above.
As rapidity was essential much depended upon whether or not regimental M.O.'s had all their cases collected by the time we arrived. This was mostly done, but one regiment was very bad in this respect & on this occasion delayed us until it was daylight.
The points to be aimed at seem to me to be, light wagons right up to the trenches; motors as close up as possible, & then no more transferring of cases until the dressing station is reached. In this way, there is as little carrying by hand of stretchers as possible, & the horses have only a short stage to work, & this is an advantage, for the light wagons only carry two lying down cases, therefore their stage should be as short as possible to prevent waste of time.

An occasion in which a Cavalry Field Ambulance worked in conjunction with an Infantry F.A.

During the latter part of the period 29.5.15 to 6.6.15 two Infantry regiments were sent to support the Cavalry in the section of the trenches held by the 6th Cav Bgde.
On my way to the trenches I met the officer of the Field Ambulance whose duty it was to collect the wounded from the two Infantry regiments mentioned above.
I arranged with him as an experiment to combine forces. As he had a large number of stretcher bearers & 6 motors, we took the 6 cars to the place on the Zillebeke road to which my motors had gone the night before, & kept them there. The stretcher bearers were conveyed in my light wagons to the trenches. On arrival there, they collected cases rapidly, Cavalry or Infantry & put them into my light wagons. The wagons made their journeys as usual to the motors. The motors stopped at the Industrial school & here all Cavalry cases were taken out & placed in my motors, & so conveyed to the dressing station.
I surmised that the weak part of this arrangement would be the transferring cases

from the Infantry to Cavalry motors, as it proved, for this sorting out entailed much delay.
So later on the Officer from the Infantry F.A. the D.A.D.M.S. & myself discussed the question & evolved the following scheme.
Light Cavalry wagons to call at Infantry dressing station, pick up stretcher bearers & proceed to trenches. 6 motors to go to ~~the~~ Zillebeke road (from Infantry F.A.) as before.
At the trenches, Cavalry & Infantry to be loaded into separate wagons.
Light wagons with Cavalry cases to load into certain motors; Infantry cases into other motors, no mixing up of cases allowed.
On the way back, ~~[illegible]~~ the motors to notify the Industrial School collecting post (where there were 4 Cavalry motors) if more cars were required at the front. In this case, the Cavalry cars to proceed at once to the Zillebeke road. Those Infantry motors full of Cavalry cases, to go on to Cavalry dressing stn, those full of Infantry, to their own dressing stn. Cavalry motors at the trenches to act in the same way as Infantry, i.e. Cavalry & Infantry cases to be in separate cars.
By the time they were full up & had gone, ...

the Infantry bearers would have done their journey & be back again.
A second journey of the Cavalry bearers was hardly likely to be required, so they were to return to the Industrial School & pick up walking cases, Cavalry & Infantry to be in separate cars as before.
When all was clear, the light horse wagons to bring back stretchers bearers etc, & any cases left over.
This plan worked very well & gave no trouble.

W.H.Dickinson. Lt Col.
OC. 6th C.F.A.

3rd Cavalry Division

121/6410

July '15.

121/6410

6th Cavy: Field Ambulance

Vol VIII

From 1st to 31st July 1915

AMD

Instructions regarding War Diaries and Intelligence Summaries are contained in F. S. Regs., Part II. and the Staff Manual respectively. Title pages will be prepared in manuscript.

WAR DIARY
or
~~INTELLIGENCE SUMMARY.~~
(Erase heading not required.)

Army Form C. 2118.

Place	Date	Hour	Summary of Events and Information (Ref Map Belgium. Sheet 5a.)	Remarks and references to Appendices
BOESEGHEM	1.7.15		Brigade practised crossing the Canal. Sent out 1 Motor Ambulance & personnel.	Fine day
do	2.7.15	2.30 pm	Went to HAZEBROUCK & visited "B" Echelon.	Fine day
do	5.7.15		Went on leave of absence.	
do	13.7.15		Returned	Fine day
do	14.7.15	3 P.M.	Visited "B" Echelon.	~~Fine day~~ Rain
do	15.7.15	11 a.m.	Went to Divisional H^d Qrs to see A.D.M.S. about various matters.	Rain
do	16.7.15	1 P.M.	A.D.M.S. visited F.A. & 3rd D.Gds	Fine day
do	17.7.15	11 a.m.	Went with Lt HALLINAN to NEUVE EGLISE to see party of 6th Cav Bde who are digging trenches there. Went forward & viewed MESSINES & German lines. Not much shelling going on. Left HALLINAN & brought Lt BAYLEY back to B Echelon, gave him orders to proceed tomorrow to 1st Cav Div for duty.	Rain
do	18.7.15		Lt WILEY & digging party from near LA BASSEE returned	Fine day
do	19.7.15	11 a.m.	Orders to send 1 M.O. & a party & one Motor Ambulance with a trench digging party that are proceeding N. of YPRES to ELVERDINGHE tomorrow.	
	do	2 P.M.	Went to "B" Echelon & detailed Lt LIGHTSTONE & party for tomorrow.	Fine day
do	20.7.15	9 a.m.	Sent orders to LIGHTSTONE to proceed to ELVERDINGHE at 2.30 P.M.	

1577 Wt. W10791/1773 500,000 1/15 D. D. & L. A.D.S.S./Forms/C. 2118.

Army Form C. 2118.

Instructions regarding War Diaries and Intelligence Summaries are contained in F. S. Regs., Part II. and the Staff Manual respectively. Title pages will be prepared in manuscript.

WAR DIARY
or
INTELLIGENCE SUMMARY.
(Erase heading not required.)

Place	Date	Hour	Summary of Events and Information Ref Map Belgium. Sheet 59	Remarks and references to Appendices
BOESEGHEM.	20.7.15	10.45 6 a.m.	Went to Convalescent hospital at ARQUES & afterwards to St. OMER	Fine
do	21.7.15.	11.45 a.m.	A.D.M.S. visited billets. Case of Enteric Fever reported in 1st R. Dragoons. Sergt. [illegible] reports & ordered necessary precautions.*	Fine. * Case subsequently found not to be Enteric.
do	22.7.15	3.30 p.m.	Went to Brigade H^d Q^rs 6th Cav Bgde saw the Sanitary Corporal & inspected the Sanitary arrangements	Heavy rain.
do	23.7.15	10.30 a.m.	D.D.M.S. Cav Corps visited billets.	
		11.30 a.m.	A.D.M.S. visited billets & 3rd D.G's Vet Officer inspected a horse that had been kicked, & advised shooting the animal.	Fine day.
do	24.7.15	11 a.m.	Vet Officer came & shot the horse	Showery.
do		2.30 p.m.	Went to St. OMER	
do	25.7.15	4 p.m.	Informed by Bgde H^d Q^rs that we will move to fresh billets next week.	Fine.
do	26.7.15.	11 a.m.	A.D.M.S. visited billets. LIGHTSTONE returned to B echelon & 3rd D.G's went to dig trenches at ELVERDINGHE.	Fine day.
do		2.30 p.m.	Visited "B" echelon.	
do	28.7.15	11.30 a.m.	Medical Board on a Warrant Officer & an N.C.O. "C" Batt R.H.A. who have been recommended for Commissions.	Rain early fine later

1577 Wt. W10791/1773 500,000 1/15 D. D. & L. A.D.S.S./Forms/C. 2118.

Army Form C. 2118.

Instructions regarding War Diaries and Intelligence Summaries are contained in F. S. Regs., Part II. and the Staff Manual respectively. Title pages will be prepared in manuscript.

WAR DIARY
or
INTELLIGENCE SUMMARY.

(Erase heading not required.)

Place	Date	Hour	Summary of Events and Information	Remarks and references to Appendices
			Ref Map Belgium Sheet 5a	
BOESEGHEM	29.7.15	10 a.m.	Orders to send away 1 N.C.O. A.S.C. & only have one in future for the whole F.A.? Wrote & objected strongly	[illegible]
	do	3 p.m.	Went to Div Hd Qrs & saw A.D.M.S.	
do	30.7.15	11 a.m.	Went to HAZEBROUCK & then to Cav Corps Hd Qrs. Saw D.D.M.S. about proposed removal of A.S.C. N.C.O. Arranged with him to have 1 N.C.O. & 1 with temporary rank	[illegible]
do	31.7.15	2.30 p.m.	Went to No 4 Stationary Hospital ARQUES	[illegible]
~~do~~				

1577 Wt. W10791/1773 500,000 1/15 D. D. & L. A.D.S.S./Forms/C. 2118.

3rd Cavalry Division

121
6754

Aug '15.

6th Cavy: Field Ambulance

Vol IX

August 15.

Confidential.

War Diary

of

Lt Col W.H.S. Nickerson.

R.A.M.C

re. No 6 C.F.A

From

1.8.15

To

31.8.15.

Army Form C. 2118.

WAR DIARY
or
~~INTELLIGENCE SUMMARY.~~
(Erase heading not required.)

Instructions regarding War Diaries and Intelligence Summaries are contained in F. S. Regs., Part II. and the Staff Manual respectively. Title pages will be prepared in manuscript.

Place	Date	Hour	Summary of Events and Information	Remarks and references to Appendices
			Ref Map Belgium Sheet 5a.	
BOESEGHEM	1.8.15	10a.m.	A.D.M.S. called for me. He went to Cav Corps H.Qrs & thence to B' Echelon. Met D.D.M.S. & discussed proposed change in B' Echelons by which one motor lorry will be substituted for all horse wagons.	
do		12.15pm	Went on to ELVERDINGHE & saw the digging party there. All quiet on that part of the line.	Fine
		4pm	Returned.	
do	2.8.15	10a.m.	Sent in claim for Compensation to Bgde HQ in respect of the owner of the farm in which the F.A. is billeted.	
do		11a.m.	Got notice that we will probably move on the 6th.	Showery
do	3.8.15	9.30 a.m.	O.C. Motor Ambulance workshop came & discussed the proposal to attach his unit to mine. Apparently O.C. A.S.C. objects.	Showery & thundery
do	4.8.15	8pm	Orders to move on the 6.8.15.	Fine
do	5.8.15	2pm	Sent billeting party to FLECHIN to get new billets.	
do	6.8.15	9a.m.	Marched via Port de THIENNES - Cross Roads S.W. of AIRE - ESTREE BLANCHE - CUHEM	
		1.30pm	to FLECHIN. arrived & took up new billets. Notified A.D.M.S. & Bgde HQ of position of billets	Heavy rain
FLECHIN	7.8.15		Settled various affairs in billets & took list of damage already done before our occupation.	Showery.

1577 Wt. W10791/1773 500,000 1/15 D. D. & L. A.D.S.S./Forms/C. 2118.

Instructions regarding War Diaries and Intelligence Summaries are contained in F. S. Regs., Part II. and the Staff Manual respectively. Title pages will be prepared in manuscript.

WAR DIARY
or
INTELLIGENCE SUMMARY.
(Erase heading not required.)

Army Form C. 2118.

Place	Date	Hour	Summary of Events and Information	Remarks and references to Appendices
			Ref Map Belgium Sheet 5a.	
FLECHIN	8.8.15	3P.M.	Went to HQrs 6th Cav Bgde to inquire about the trench digging party	Fine
do	9.8.15	11AM.	A.A.D.M.S. Came to discuss arrangements with me for trench digging party & various other affairs, as A.D.M.S. is on leave.	Showery
do	10.8.15	10.30 a.m.	A.D.M.S. Came & discussed the proposed giving of a motor lorry to 'B' echelon in lieu of other transport.	Showery
do	11.8.15		Arranged for 1 Officer, 1 N.C.O. 2 privates, with surgical equipment & anti-gas solution, & 1 motor Ambulance, to be sent from each Bgde as 600 men from each of the 3 Bgdes are to go & dig trenches at ARMENTIERES.	Fine
do	12.8.15	2P.M.	Warned the party for trench digging. Detailed Lt RONN.	Showery
		8P.M.	Sent notice to Bgde Supply Officer of numbers proceeding from the F.A.	
do	13.8.15	8.30 a.m.	Party proceeded to ARMENTIERES, with orders to report to 6th Cav Bgde.	Showery
do	14.8.15	9.30 a.m.	Sent Lt Orr & interpreter to Bgde HQrs to receive instructions concerning payments to be made for the present billet. Sent Lt Orr to see a Consulting Surgeon (Mr Wallace) as he is not well.	Fine
do	15.8.15	10a.m.	Reported to A.D.M.S. that Lt Orr must be sent sick, & asked for another officer	Showery
do	do	4P.M.	Went to HQrs & saw A.D.M.S. & discussed with him the proposed change in the transport of 'B' Echelon. Visited 'B' echelon on the way back	

1577 Wt. W10791/1773 500,000 1/15 D. D. & L. A.D.S.S./Forms/C. 2118.

Instructions regarding War Diaries and Intelligence Summaries are contained in F. S. Regs., Part II. and the Staff Manual respectively. Title pages will be prepared in manuscript.

WAR DIARY
or
INTELLIGENCE SUMMARY.
(Erase heading not required.)

Army Form C. 2118.

Place	Date	Hour	Summary of Events and Information	Remarks and references to Appendices
			Ry Map Belgium Sheet 5a.	
FLECHIN	16.8.15	1 P.M.	Went to B' Echelon & thence to St OMER. Put Lt CREE in No 10 Stationary Hospital. Returned to B' echelon & thence to FLECHIN	Fine.
do	17.8.15	11.30 A.M.	A.D.M.S. visited the billets.	Showery.
do	18.8.15		Nothing to record. Usual routine carried on.	Showery.
do	19.8.15	4 P.M.	Orders from A.D.M.S. to send another officer to the digging party at ARMENTIERES. Replied that there is none available, as there is only 1 officer here. They already have 5 with a digging party of 1800, so it is difficult to see why another is wanted. Went to Bgde HQ 2nd to discuss various questions.	Fine.
do	20.8.15	9.30 A.M.	Rung up on telephone by ADMS who says he will send an officer from B' Echelon to the digging party. Also he wants me to go to HAZEBROUCK to investigate a claim for damages made against B' Echelon.	Showery.
do	21.8.15	9.30 A.M.	Got word from Bgde H.Q. 2 that BOULOGNE is closed for the present, & leave stopped.	
do		2.30 P.M.	Horses paraded with harness for inspection by O.C. Transport, but he did not turn up.	Fine.
do	22.8.15	10 A.M.	ADMS visited this place. He has sent 2 more officers to the digging party, now making 7 with 1800.	
do	23.8.15	10 A.M.	Went to HAZEBROUCK with a French interpreter, to the farm occupied by the B' Echelons for 8 months. Saw the damage, which is considerable, & for which there are two claims for 1005 francs & 185 francs. Agreed on 800 & 150 francs respectively. Returned to billets at 2.30 P.M.	Fine.
do	24.8.15	10.30 A.M.	ADMS Cav Corps came to billets & told me to send protest to H.Q. & report.	

Army Form C. 2118.

Instructions regarding War Diaries and Intelligence Summaries are contained in F. S. Regs., Part II. and the Staff Manual respectively. Title pages will be prepared in manuscript.

WAR DIARY
or
INTELLIGENCE SUMMARY.
(Erase heading not required.)

Place	Date	Hour	Summary of Events and Information	Remarks and references to Appendices
FLECHIN				
25-8-15.	~~[illegible]~~	11 a.m.	Handed over No. 6 Cav. Field Ambulance to Major S. W. S. Hughes R.A.M.C.	
do		12-30 p.m.	Proceeded to office of A.D.M.S.	
do		2-30 p.m.	Proceeded to BOULOGNE	Fine day.
do		4.30 p.m.	Sailed for England.	
LONDON	26.8.15.	10-30 a.m.	Reported at War Office. Told there was none for charge of a Casualty Clearing Stn. Given leave of absence till 1st Sept.	Fine

3rd Cavalry Division

Aug ~~1st~~ from 28th
Sept 1915

121/6993

No 6. Cavy: Field Ambulance

Vol X

Aug. & Sept. 15

No. 6. Cavalry Field Ambulance

Instructions regarding War Diaries and Intelligence Summaries are contained in F. S. Regs., Part II. and the Staff Manual respectively. Title pages will be prepared in manuscript.

WAR DIARY

~~or~~

~~INTELLIGENCE SUMMARY.~~

(Erase heading not required.)

Army Form C. 2118.

Place	Date	Hour	Summary of Events and Information	Remarks and references to Appendices
FLÉCHIN	25/8/15		Vacated appointment of D.A.D.M.S. Cavalry Corps, to take over the command of No. 6 Cavalry Field Ambulance from Lt. Col. W. H. S. NICKERSON, V.C., R.A.M.C. who has been ordered to proceed to England forthwith and to report himself for duty to the War Office. Lt. Col. NICKERSON handed over the Cav. Fld Ambulance to me and left at 12. noon. The Field Ambulance is divided into an 'A' Echelon which is billeted here and a 'B' Echelon which is grouped with similar 'B' Echelons of the two other Field Ambulances of the 3rd Cavalry Divn. at RADINGHEM, about 10 miles of this place. Including myself there are 4 medical officers with 'A' Echelon but two of them, Lts. H. A. RONN and W. E. HALLIVAN are away at ARMENTIERES with a digging party from the 6th Cav. Brigade. The fourth officer Lt. A. WILEY is here. With 'B' Echelon are Capt. G. H. RICHARD and Lieut. H. LIGHTSTONE. The Field Ambulance is up to strength in personnel, horses & vehicles.	[illegible]
"	5.9.15		Lieuts. RONN & HALLIVAN returned from ARMENTIERES where they had been on duty with a 'digging' detachment from the Brigade.	

Army Form C. 2118.

WAR DIARY
or
INTELLIGENCE SUMMARY.
(Erase heading not required.)

Instructions regarding War Diaries and Intelligence Summaries are contained in F. S. Regs., Part II. and the Staff Manual respectively. Title pages will be prepared in manuscript.

Place	Date	Hour	Summary of Events and Information	Remarks and references to Appendices
FLECHIN	20.9.15	9.00 AM	Message received from 6th Cav. Bde to the effect that the Bde. would probably move on 21st inst. We should be prepared to move at one hour's notice from to-day at 6 p m.	
"	21.9.15	11.30 Am	Orders received as to rendezvous which is to be on the THEROUANNE - FERFAY at 6.30 pm this evening.	
			As Lt. O'CALLAGHAN, Med. Officer of the 3rd Dragoon Gds, has been admitted to hospital and, I ascertained this morning personally, is not likely to be able to return to duty in the near future, I have sent Lieut. HALLINAN to replace him and wired A D H S. accordingly.	
		5.0 pm	Left FLECHIN, reached position at rendezvous 6.20 pm. Arrived at bivouac in BOIS DES DAMES, S.W. of BETHUNE soon after midnight	
BOIS-DES-DAMES	22/9/15	8.30 am	Sent memo to Regt. M.O.'s for all sick to rendezvous at first turning to left after the level crossing, on road running south of BOIS des DAMES (S of the R in Mn ROUGE) Arras Sheet 7, 1:80,000.	
"	24.9.15		Received orders to be prepared to move during the night.	
	25.9.15	1 pm	Left BOIS DES DAMES about 8 a.m. 2 M.O.'s & 2 RAMC orderlies, mounted marched with 'A1 Brigade Echelon' which consisted of the Regtl. limbers. The Cav.	

Instructions regarding War Diaries and Intelligence Summaries are contained in F. S. Regs., Part II. and the Staff Manual respectively. Title pages will be prepared in manuscript.

WAR DIARY
or
INTELLIGENCE SUMMARY.
(Erase heading not required.)

Army Form C. 2118.

Place	Date	Hour	Summary of Events and Information	Remarks and references to Appendices
Continued	25/9/15		Hd. Qrs. marched with 'A 2 Echelon' behind the Ammunition Column, and was about 2 hours behind. The A1 Echelon was about 1 hour behind the Brigade. I myself went with Brigade Hdqrs. and arrived at VERMELLES at 1pm. All the Brigade ~~was~~ spent the night on the open ground W. of the Railway between VERMELLES and the HALTE on the LENS road. The night was very wet.	
VERMELLES	26/9/15	8 am.	Received permission from the Brigadier for 1 G.S. Limbered Wagon & 2 Ambulance Wagons (with covers removed) to march with A1 Echelon. This seemed to be a more useful arrangement than having Ramp Orderlies mounted and as there is a difficulty in supplying vehicles with horses.	
		11. a. m.	Orders received by the Brigade that the Cavalry were to act as Infantry and occupy trenches as far forward as possible. They eventually, by sunset, occupied a line immediately E. of LOOS about $\frac{1}{4}$ mile from the village.	
		9 pm.	Have just returned from LOOS where there are 2 or 3 wounded Cavalry and a large number of Infantry wounded. An Ambulance wagon & a stretcher party removed these. During the whole afternoon wounded Infantry were pouring down the LENS road	

1577 Wt. W10791/1773 500,000 1/15 D. D. & L. A.D.S.S./Forms/C. 2118.

Instructions regarding War Diaries and Intelligence Summaries are contained in F. S. Regs., Part II. and the Staff Manual respectively. Title pages will be prepared in manuscript.

WAR DIARY
or
INTELLIGENCE SUMMARY.
(Erase heading not required.)

Army Form [illegible] 2118.

Place	Date	Hour	Summary of Events and Information	Remarks and references to Appendices
			to VERMELLES. Immediately on hearing that the Brigade was to go into action I arranged for an Advanced Dressing Station at PUITS No 7 about 1 mile E of the HALTE, and for a Main dressing station on the LENS - BETHUNE Road. As there were few Cavalry Casualties the dressing stations were engaged all the afternoon until midnight with Infantry Casualties.	[illegible]
	27.8.15	11am.	Visited Brigade Hdqrs. at LOOS and arranged with the Brigade M.O's for wounded to be collected together near the church about 6.30 pm. when it is safe for wagons to be brought down the road from VERMELLES.	
			This arrangement was carried out with success. All the Cavalry casualties (not more than 20 of the 6th & 8th Brigades were evacuated although the town was being heavily shelled. The 6th & 8th Cavalry Fld Ambulances combined in transport & dressing stations. A large number of Infantry wounded (not less than 250) were taken away from LOOS. There was a difficulty in evacuating these cases to the Clearing Station at BETHUNE as the 5 motor ambulances available were quite insufficient and it was difficult to persuade other cars to take away the cases. However by 1 a.m. all the wounded in our Main Dressing Station were evacuated.	

1577 Wt. W10791/1773 500,000 1/15 D. D. & L. A.D.S.S./Forms/C. 2118.

Army Form C. 2118.

Instructions regarding War Diaries and Intelligence Summaries are contained in F. S. Regs., Part II. and the Staff Manual respectively. Title pages will be prepared in manuscript.

WAR DIARY
or
INTELLIGENCE SUMMARY.
(*Erase heading not required.*)

Place	Date	Hour	Summary of Events and Information	Remarks and references to Appendices
VERMELLES	28/9/15	Noon	Visited Brigade & Regtl. Hdqrs in LOOS and arranged for a similar plan of evacuation as last night, a representative of each regiment to be sent by the M.O. to the LENS road near the town to inform me what wounded there were to evacuate.	
		11 pm	All the Cavalry wounded & some infantry were evacuated by 10 pm. The night was very wet and the road into LOOS congested with traffic.	
	29/9/15		The 6th Cavalry Brigade were relieved about midnight and reached VERMELLES about 2 a.m. The whole Brigade moved off about 5.30 a.m. and marched to their bivouacs in the BOIS DES DAMES that they had occupied before. The Cavalry Field Ambce however has been given billets in the village of LABUISSIÈRE close by. The weather is very bad with continual rain. The men of the regiment had been in the trenches without mackintosh sheets or great-coats. They are suffering too from the fatigue & strain of the last 3 days & to-night have to sleep in the open. I arranged with the M.O.'s of regiments for them to send in any cases that are merely in need of a day or two's rest and they will be sent to 'B' Echelon & not evacuated. The A.D.M.S. was asked to cause arrangements to be made for their reception. I also visited the Brigade Hdqrs. and recommended that a French officer be sent round the district to enquire if any factory or brewery had any sort of room	

1577 Wt. W10791/1773 500,000 1/15 D. D. & L. A.D.S.S./Forms/C. 2118.

Army Form C. 2118.

Instructions regarding War Diaries and Intelligence Summaries are contained in F. S. Regs., Part II. and the Staff Manual respectively. Title pages will be prepared in manuscript.

WAR DIARY
or
INTELLIGENCE SUMMARY.
(Erase heading not required.)

Place	Date	Hour	Summary of Events and Information	Remarks and references to Appendices
	29.9.15	(contd)	where hot pipes could dry the men's clothes & possibly baths be provided and this was agreed to.	
	30.9.15		The Brigade has made arrangements for baths for men of the whole Brigade.	
			Notes. During the period between the evening of 26th & the midnight of the 29th Sept. No 6 Cav Fld. Ambce. evacuated 8 officers & 26 O.R. of the 6th Cavalry Bde and 13 officers & 210 O.R of various Infantry units. No. 8 Cavalry Fld. Ambce. evacuated much the same number. There were no casualties in the Fld Ambce. The behaviour of all ranks was splendid under very trying & dangerous conditions. The need of a suitable type of wheeled stretcher carriage was very evident & the matter has been brought before the notice of the ADMS.	
			[signature] Major RAMC O.C. No. 6 Cav. Fld. Ambce 3rd Cavalry Divn	

3rd Cavalry Division

Oct. } 1915
Nov }

To the
10th Decem.

No. 6 Cav. Fd. Amb.

V

Oct & Nov.

Vol XI

121
7779

WAR DIARY
or
INTELLIGENCE SUMMARY.
(Erase heading not required.)

Army Form C. 2118.

Instructions regarding War Diaries and Intelligence Summaries are contained in F. S. Regs., Part II. and the Staff Manual respectively. Title pages will be prepared in manuscript.

Place	Date	Hour	Summary of Events and Information	Remarks and references to Appendices
FERFAY	3.10.15		Left LABUISSIERE about 4 pm. and arrived at FERFAY at 5.30 pm.	
PALFART	19.10.15		Left FERFAY at 11.30 a.m. with Brigade & arrived at PALFART at 3 pm.	
" "	20.10.15		As PALFART is on the extreme southern edge of the area allotted to the Brigade and very far from any place to which sick can be evacuated, Captain LIGHTSTONE was sent to ascertain if a better position could be allotted. He obtained permission from Divisional Hdqrs to look for a place on the western outskirts of ST. HILAIRE if permission could be obtained from the General in command of the Infantry now billeted there. A very suitable place at COTTES (which is in the 6th Cav. Bde. area) was found but it will not be available until the present troops leave, a move which is expected shortly. Meanwhile permission was obtained to occupy a field & some buildings in ST. HILAIRE.	
ST. HILAIRE	21.10.15		Left PALFART at 8.40 am & arrived at ST. HILAIRE at 10.40 am.	
	31.10.15		Major G H RICHARD left the unit to report to the War Office for duty.	
LIVOSSART	7.11.15		As there was a possibility of the unit being turned out of the billet at ST. HILAIRE the Field Ambulance was moved to-day to LIVOSSART which is in the Brigade Area. Although by no means an ideal situation for the Field Ambulance it is the only place available.	

1577 Wt. W10791/1773 500,000 1/15 D. D. & L. A.D.S.S./Forms/C. 2118.

Instructions regarding War Diaries and Intelligence Summaries are contained in F. S. Regs., Part II. and the Staff Manual respectively. Title pages will be prepared in manuscript.

WAR DIARY
or
INTELLIGENCE SUMMARY.
(Erase heading not required.)

Army Form C. 2118.

Place	Date	Hour	Summary of Events and Information	Remarks and references to Appendices
17.11.15.			Left LIVOSSART and billetted at TORCY.	
6.12.15.			As TORCY was required for billets and there was no suitable place for the Fld Ambce in the 6th Cav. Bde area the Fld Ambce. moved into billets at FRUGES with the permission of the 3rd Cav. Div. Hdqrs.	
10.12.15.			Handed over command of No 6 CFA to Major. G.H.L. HAMMERTON, RAMC (T) as I have been appointed DADMS. 33rd Div.	
			[illegible signature] Major RAMC	

1577 Wt. W10791/1773 500,000 1/15 D. D. & L. A.D.S.S./Forms/C. 2118.

No. ~~28~~ 6 Cav. Field Ambulance

Dec/15

3 C

6 Cav Fd Amb

Vol. XII

XIII

XIV

XV

Instructions regarding War Diaries and Intelligence Summaries are contained in F. S. Regs., Part II. and the Staff Manual respectively. Title pages will be prepared in manuscript.

WAR DIARY
or
~~INTELLIGENCE SUMMARY.~~
(Erase heading not required.)

Army Form C. 2118.

Place	Date	Hour	Summary of Events and Information	Remarks and references to Appendices
FRUGES	10/12/15		MAJOR G.H.L HAMMERTON. RAMCT. took over the command of No 6 CAV. FLD. AMB. from MAJOR G.W. HUGHES ~~[illegible]~~ DSO RAMC. G.H.L.H.	
"	11/12/15		Inspected Personnel, Equipment and Billets. The Field Ambulance is divided into A and B' Echelons. The 'B' Echelon has charge of the Divisional Rest Station situated in a building in this Town. The Field Ambulance is complete in Officers, Men, Horses & Vehicles. The Officers are 'A' Echelon MAJOR HAMMERTON, CAPTAIN HALLINAN, LIEUT. WILEY and LIEUT. GRANT. 'B' Echelon CAPTAIN LIGHTSTONE and LIEUT. Mc LAY. LIEUT. GRANT is attached to 'B' for temporary duty. G.H.L.H.	
"	12/12/15 to 20/12/15		General Routine. G.H.L.H.	
"	20/12/15		The Field Ambulance was inspected by the A D M S. 3 CAV. DIV. LIEUT. WILEY sent to NORTH SOMERSET YEOMANRY for Temp. Duty G.H.L.H.	
"	20/12/15 to 27/12/15		General Routine G.H.L.H.	

Instructions regarding War Diaries and Intelligence Summaries are contained in F. S. Regs., Part II. and the Staff Manual respectively. Title pages will be prepared in manuscript.

WAR DIARY
or
~~INTELLIGENCE SUMMARY.~~
(Erase heading not required.)

Army Form C. 2118.

Place	Date	Hour	Summary of Events and Information	Remarks and references to Appendices
FRUGES	27/12/15		Received orders that the 3rd COMP. CAV. FLD AMB. would be mobilized on the 28/12/15. Had all equipment packed and ready to move. G.S.H.	
"	28/12/15		Received orders that 3rd Comp Cav. Field Ambulance would mobilize on the 1/1/16 and not on the 28/12/15. G.S.H.	
"	29/12/15		LIEUT. WILEY relieved from temp duty with N.S. YEOMANRY. G.S.H.	
"	30/12/15		General Routine G.S.H.	
"	31/12/15		Received orders to send 1 Motor Ambulance with 4 Stretcher Bearers to BETHUNE to act as an advance party of 3rd Comp Cav Fld Amb. CAPTAIN LIGHTSTONE on leave to England. [illegible] Received orders that 3 Comp Cav Fld Amb would mobilize at MARESQUEL (Ref Map ARRAS) at 2 pm on the 1/1/16.	
			[illegible] Hamilton Major O.C. 6 Cav. Fld Amb.	

1577 Wt. W10791/1773 500,000 1/15 D. D. & L. A.D.S.S./Forms/C. 2118.

War Diary

of

No. 6. Cavalry. Field Ambulance.

For

~~December 1915.~~

January 1916

February 1916

March 1916

Jan-March/16

Instructions regarding War Diaries and Intelligence Summaries are contained in F. S. Regs., Part II. and the Staff Manual respectively. Title pages will be prepared in manuscript.

WAR DIARY
or
~~INTELLIGENCE SUMMARY.~~
(Erase heading not required.)

Army Form C. 2118.

Place	Date	Hour	Summary of Events and Information	Remarks and references to Appendices
FRUGES.	1/1/16.		Detachment of Personnel, RAMC and ASC consisting of 1 OFFICER. NCOs and MEN with 2 Light Ambulance Wagons, 2 G. S. Wagons and 1 Motor Ambulance left to mobilize with the 3 Corps Cav. Fld Amb. 4 extra Stretcher Bearers were sent by orders of DDMS Cav. Corps. [illegible]. CAPTAIN LIGHTSTONE assumes Command temporarily of 6 C.F.A. G.S.H.	
FRUGES.	2/1/16		General Routine. G.S.H.	
FRUGES	3/1/16		CAPTAIN HALLINAN left to take up duties as M.O. to 6th Dismounted Battalion. LIEUT GRANT left to take up duties (temporary) as M.O. 1st Life Guards. G.S.H.	
FRUGES.	4/1/16		Surprise Visit by SURG GEN. O'KEEFE DDMS CAV. CORPS who expressed himself pleased with all he saw. G.S.H.	
"	7/1/16		Telephone fitted in Head Qrs Office [illegible]. No. of Sick admitted to D.R.S. 1 Officer and 48 men G.S.H.	
"	11/1/16		CAPT. LIGHTSTONE inspected billets of both men and horses everything satisfactory G.S.H.	
"	11/1/16 to 15/1/16		General Routine [illegible] No of Sick for week ending 14th admitted to DRS 1 Officer and 37 men. G.S.H.	
"	15/1/16		CAPTAIN H. LIGHTSTONE awarded Military Cross. SERGT MAJOR SHARPE awarded D.C.M. G.S.H.	

Army Form C. 2118.

Instructions regarding War Diaries and Intelligence Summaries are contained in F. S. Regs., Part II. and the Staff Manual respectively. Title pages will be prepared in manuscript.

WAR DIARY

or

~~INTELLIGENCE SUMMARY.~~

(Erase heading not required.)

Place	Date	Hour	Summary of Events and Information	Remarks and references to Appendices
FRUGES.	17/1/16		LIEUT. McLAY sent for duty to 3rd D. Guards to relieve CAPT. RONN on leave. [initials]	
"	18/1/16		LIEUT GRANT returned from duty with 1st LIFEGUARDS. [initials]	
"	21/1/16		Driver ELWIN ASC to proceed to 22 VET. H. for course in shoeing authority A.D.V.S. CAV. CORPS. No. of sick admitted to D.R.S. for week ending 21/1/16. 52. O.R. [initials]	
"	23/1/16		LIEUT. WILEY on leave to ENGLAND [initials]	
"	24/1/16		Received orders from A.D.M.S. 3rd CAV. DIV. to send 1 NCO RAMC 1 light ambulance 4 horses and 2 Drivers to be attached to M.O. i/c 3rd D. Gds. to bring sick to TORCY (Ref Map. ARRAS) each morning. [initials] Received orders from A.D.M.S. to send a light Ambulance to TORCY to meet Ambulance from 3rd D. Gds. and bring sick to D.R.S. [initials] No of sick admitted to D.R.S. for week ending 28/1/16 51. O.R. [initials]	
"	24/1/16 to 31/1/16		General Routine. No of sick admitted to D.R.S. during month 2 Officers and 206 men. [initials]	

[signature] Lieut. Col. ...
O.C. 6 C.F.A.

1577 Wt. W10791/1773 500,000 1/15 D. D. & L. A.D.S.S./Forms/C. 2118.

Instructions regarding War Diaries and Intelligence Summaries are contained in F. S. Regs., Part II. and the Staff Manual respectively. Title pages will be prepared in manuscript.

Army Form C. 2118.

WAR DIARY

or

~~INTELLIGENCE SUMMARY.~~

(Erase heading not required.)

Place	Date	Hour	Summary of Events and Information	Remarks and references to Appendices
FRUGES.	1 2/16.		Sent. 1 N.C.O. RAMC. 2 Drivers A.S.C. 1 Light Ambulance and 2 horses to M.O. i/c 3rd D. Gds with instructions to collect sick from that part of Brigade area and bring them to TORCY ref map ARRAS. where a Light Ambulance from FRUGES would be waiting to bring them to the D.R.S. this is a procedure to obviate the use of Motor Ambulances. GSHB	
"	1 2/16 to 8 2/16.		General Routine. No of Sick admitted to D.R.S. during weekending 7 2/16 - 68 men GSHB.	
"	11 2/16		French Interpreter transferred to HAVRE GSHB.	
"	12 2/16		Detachment of 6 C.F.A. returned from 3rd C.C.F.A. at 9-30 A.M. after 6 weeks work with the Dismounted Division	
"	16 2/16.		MAJOR HAMMERTON proceeded on leave to ENGLAND. CAPT. HALLILAN assumes command. No of Sick admitted to D.R.S. for weekending 14 2/16 74 men GSHB.	
"	20 2/16		CAPTAIN. H. LIGHTSTONE. ordered to proceed to 4th ARMY as M.O. to GENl O'KEEFE took with him his Batman and 1 Riding Horse. GSHB.	
"	22 2/16		No. of Sick admitted to D.R.S. for week ending 21 2/16. 136 men GSHB.	

Army Form C. 2118.

Instructions regarding War Diaries and Intelligence Summaries are contained in F. S. Regs., Part II. and the Staff Manual respectively. Title pages will be prepared in manuscript.

WAR DIARY

or

~~INTELLIGENCE~~ SUMMARY.

(*Erase heading not required.*)

Place	Date	Hour	Summary of Events and Information	Remarks and references to Appendices
FRUGES	27/2/16		MAJOR HAMMERTON returned from leave assumes command. [illegible]	
"	29/2/16		No. of sick admitted to D.R.S. for week ending 28/2/16 = 95 men. Total for month = 378 men	[illegible]
			[illegible] Major R.A.M.C. T.F. O.C. 6 C.F.A	

Army Form C. 2118.

Instructions regarding War Diaries and Intelligence Summaries are contained in F. S. Regs., Part II. and the Staff Manual respectively. Title pages will be prepared in manuscript.

WAR DIARY
or
~~INTELLIGENCE SUMMARY.~~
(Erase heading not required.)

Place	Date	Hour	Summary of Events and Information	Remarks and references to Appendices
FRUGES.	2 3/16		CAPTAIN E.F. HEAP. RAMC. detailed from 7 CFA for duty with this unit. arrived for duty with 1 Batman and 1 Riding Horse. GSHH.	
"	8 2/16		Received instructions from G.O.C. 6th CAV. BDE to make an inspection of the Sanitary arrangements of all the units in the Bde. No of sick admitted to D.R.S. for week ending 7 3/16. = 100 GSHH.	
"	12 2/16		Inspected 1st ROYAL DRAGOONS and found their sanitary arrangements very good incinerators and soakage pits not used as they should be. GSHH	
"	13 3/16		Inspected 'C' Battery R.H.A. and BDE HdQtrs found sanitary arrangements very bad. ordered this to be improved. GSHH.	
"	15 3/16		The FIELD AMBULANCE was inspected on parade by the G.O.C 6th CAV. BDE who expressed himself very pleased with all he saw. No of sick admitted to D.R.S. for weekending 14 3/16 = 90. GSHH.	
"	18 3/16		CAPTAIN W.E. HALLINAN and 1 N.C.O. and 2 men with a sufficiency of medical Equipment detailed by order of A.D.M.S. were sent to Divisional Training School at TRAMCOURT ref. Map ARRAS for duty. GSHH.	
"	19 3/16		LIEUT. A. WILEY having completed 12 months service was granted 14 days leave to ENGLAND GSHH.	

1577 Wt. W10791/1773 500,000 1/15 D. D. & L. A.D.S.S./Forms/C. 2118.

Instructions regarding War Diaries and Intelligence Summaries are contained in F. S. Regs., Part II. and the Staff Manual respectively. Title pages will be prepared in manuscript.

WAR DIARY
or
~~INTELLIGENCE SUMMARY.~~
(Erase heading not required.)

Army Form C. 2118.

Place	Date	Hour	Summary of Events and Information	Remarks and references to Appendices
FRUGES	21/3/16		The FIELD AMBULANCE consisting of Personnel, ~~wagons~~ Horses, Wagons & Motor Ambulances was inspected on Parade by the A.D.M.S. he afterwards inspected the Office Billets of Horses and men, he also inspected the D.R.S. and Scabies Hospital. he expressed himself pleased with all he saw. No. of sick admitted to D.R.S. for week ending 21/3/16 = 131	G.H.H.
"	25/3/16		1 N.C.O. and 4 men arrived as reinforcements G.H.H.	
"	26/3/16		Inspected the sanitary arrangements of the 3rd D.G.ds and 6th MACHINE GUN SQD.	G.H.H.
"	27/3/16		Inspected the sanitary arrangements of the NORTH SOMERSET YEOMANRY	G.H.H.
"	31/3/16		1 N.C.O arrived as reinforcement. No. of sick admitted to D.R.S. for week ending 28/3/16 = 144 Total for month = 523. G.H.H.	

G Stew L Hamilton Major RAMC T.F.
O.C. 6 C.F.A.

1577 Wt. W10791/1773 500,000 1/15 D. D. & L. A.D.S.S./Forms/C. 2118.

3rd Cav Div.

No. 6 Cavalry Field Ambulance.

April 1916.

6 Cav 7th Amb 3C

Army Form C. 2118.

Instructions regarding War Diaries and Intelligence Summaries are contained in F. S. Regs., Part II. and the Staff Manual respectively. Title pages will be prepared in manuscript.

WAR DIARY
or
~~INTELLIGENCE SUMMARY.~~

(*Erase heading not required.*)

Vol 16

Place	Date	Hour	Summary of Events and Information	Remarks and references to Appendices
FRUGES	1/4/16		Capt. W.E. HALLINAN returned from leave; resumed duty as M.O. i/c Divis. Schools TRAMECOURT.	
			Lieut. J.F. McKay rejoined unit from temp. duty as M.O. i/c Div. Schools, & takes over duty as M.O. i/c Div. Rest Station FRUGES.	
			Lieut. GRANT granted leave to U.K. from 3rd to 19th inst. on completion of 12 months service, & signing new contract. S.A.H.	
"	2/4/16		Lieut. A. WILEY promoted to rank of Capt. (London Gazette of Mch 10th 1916.) S.A.H.	
"	3/4/16		Capt. A. WILEY having returned from leave takes over duties as M.O. i/c D.R.S. S.A.H.	
"	4/4/16		Pte. C.A. FIGGINS No. 50369 has been appointed Regtl. Barber to the unit. S.A.H.	
"	6/4/16		Capt (Rev) W.P. HANKS - Batman - 2 horses & Grf proceeded to N.S.Y. Lieut J.F. McKay granted leave to U.K. from 7th to 16th inst. S.A.H.	
"	7/4/16		Two drivers A.S.C. rejoined unit from No 22. Vet. H.P. after completing	

1577 Wt. W10791/1773 500,000 1/15 D. D. & L. A.D.S.S./Forms/C. 2118.

Army Form C. 2118.

Instructions regarding War Diaries and Intelligence Summaries are contained in F. S. Regs., Part II. and the Staff Manual respectively. Title pages will be prepared in manuscript.

WAR DIARY
or
~~INTELLIGENCE SUMMARY.~~
(Erase heading not required.)

Place	Date	Hour	Summary of Events and Information	Remarks and references to Appendices
FRUGES	7/4/16		Course in Cold Shoeing.	
"	8/4/16 to 16/4/16		General Routine	
"	17/4/16		Lieut J.M. GRANT rejoined from leave, having been recalled by wire.	
"	23/4/16		Capt R. MARSHALL R.A.M.C. arrived at 6 C.F.A. for duty.	
"	24/4/16		Detachment of 2 Officers (Capt R SLANEY & Lt PRINGLE) & 28 N.C.O's & men of No 8 C.F.A. arrived for temporary duty at R.R.S. FRUGES.	
"	25/4/16		Lieut P.A. McCULLUM R.A.M.C. arrived at 6 C.F.A. for duty. Lieut J.F. McCAY R.A.M.C. proceeded to No 19 Gen H. ETAPLES for duty. Capt A. WILEY detached for temp. duty as M.O. i/c 19th Divisional Cavalry & Cyclist Coy. (FRESSIN) & also of C Battery R.H.A. (SAINS-LE-FRESSIN)	

1577 Wt. W10791/1773 500,000 1/15 D. D. & L. A.D.S.S./Forms/C. 2118.

Instructions regarding War Diaries and Intelligence Summaries are contained in F. S. Regs., Part II. and the Staff Manual respectively. Title pages will be prepared in manuscript.

WAR DIARY

or

~~INTELLIGENCE~~ SUMMARY.

(Erase heading not required.)

Army Form C. 2118.

Place	Date	Hour	Summary of Events and Information	Remarks and references to Appendices
FRUGES.	26/4/16		Lieut J.M. GRANT granted leave to U.K. from 27/4/16 to 4/5/16. SAH	
"	27/4/16		Capt R MARSHALL detached for Temp duty as MO i/c Divis. Schools at TRAMECOURT.	
"	"		Capt. W.E. HALLINAN proceeded to No 7 C.F.A. for duty. SAH	
"	28/4/16		1 Light Ambulance Wagon with driver & orderly were detailed to report to MO i/c NSY at HESDOND at 4PM. for Temp. duty. SAH	
			G Stewart Hamilton Major OC 6 C.F.A.	

1577 Wt. W10791/1773 500,000 1/15 D. D. & L. A.D.S.S./Forms/C. 2118.

3rd Cavalry Division

6th Cavalry Field Ambulance

May 1916

Instructions regarding War Diaries and Intelligence Summaries are contained in F. S. Regs., Part II. and the Staff Manual respectively. Title pages will be prepared in manuscript.

WAR DIARY
or
INTELLIGENCE SUMMARY.
(Erase heading not required.)

Army Form C. 2118.

6 Cav Fd Amb
Vol 17

Place	Date	Hour	Summary of Events and Information	Remarks and references to Appendices
FRUGES	1/5/16		General Routine. Lieut. I.M GRANT promoted Captain (London Gazette Apl 1st) GSHBt.	
"	5/5/16		Party of 1 N.C.O. and 3 men attached to 3rd Signal Squadron for 7 days instruction in Semaphore Signalling. Major HAMMERTON on leave to ENGLAND. Two reinforcements RAMC G.D.O's received GSHBt.	
"	7/5/16		Party of 1 N.C.O. and 6 men sent to No 2 Cav. Cas. Clear. Station for 14 days instruction in Nursing Duties. Capt. GRANT attached to 3 D Gds. for Temp. Duty. Patients admitted to D.R.S. for weekending 6/5/16 = 91 GSHBt.	
"	9/5/16		Capt. WILEY rejoined unit. GSHBt	
"	13/5/16		Capt. GRANT rejoined unit. Capt. MARSHALL and 4 other Ranks rejoined unit from duty with Divisional Training School. Patients admitted to D.R.S for week ending 13/5/16 = 92. GSHBt	
"	14/5/16		Ordered to send a Detachment of 3 Officers and 32 other Ranks together with 3 Light Ambulances and 1 Motor Ambulance to the Divisional Training Ground at St. RIQUIER (ref map ABBEVILLE) for duty with the Brigade. Sent off 1 Officer and 4 other Ranks in Motor Ambulance to procure Billets, the remainder to move ~~[illegible]~~ to OFFIN for the night. GSHBt.	

1577 Wt. W10791/1773 500,000 1/15 D. D. & L. A.D.S.S./Forms/C. 2118.

Instructions regarding War Diaries and Intelligence Summaries are contained in F. S. Regs., Part II. and the Staff Manual respectively. Title pages will be prepared in manuscript.

WAR DIARY
or
~~INTELLIGENCE SUMMARY.~~
(Erase heading not required.)

Army Form C. 2118.

Place	Date	Hour	Summary of Events and Information	Remarks and references to Appendices
FRUGES	15 5/16		Detachment left OFFIN at 7-0 AM. for Brigade rendezvous at BEAURAINVILLE. left there at 7-30 AM. arrived at Billets at 3 p.m. Opened Temporary Hospital in empty House South of the Church. No. of Sick admitted = 6. Detachment not required to take part in Tactical exercises of Brigade. 28 cases of sickness were admitted including 19 measles.	GStH
FRUGES	21 5/16		Detachment arrived at 1-15 pm No of sick admitted to D.R.S = 94. GStH.	
"	23 5/16		Two O.Rs. together with 1 light Horsed Ambulance sent for duty with 3rd D. Gds. Lieut. McCALLUM. proceeded for tempy duty with 1. R.D.C. GStH.	
"	28 5/16		1 O.R. reinforcement received. No of sick admitted to D.RS = 101. GStH.	
"	29 5/16		No 10711 S. M. SHARPE F. W. promoted Tempy. Quarter Master. proceeded to ENGLAND to take up appointment. GStH	
"	31 5/16		Capt. GRANT proceeded to take up tempy duty with "C" Battery R.H.A No of Sick admitted to D.R.S. during month = 418. GStH	

G Stew. S Hamilton Major
OC 6 C.F.A.

1577 Wt. W10791/1773 500,000 1/15 D. D. & L. A.D.S.S./Forms/C. 2118.

3rd Cav. Div

No. 6 Cavalry Field Ambulance

June 1916

Instructions regarding War Diaries and Intelligence Summaries are contained in F. S. Regs., Part II. and the Staff Manual respectively. Title pages will be prepared in manuscript.

WAR DIARY
or
~~INTELLIGENCE SUMMARY.~~
(Erase heading not required.)

Army Form C. 2118.

3 C

6 Cav F^a Amb

Vol 18

Place	Date	Hour	Summary of Events and Information	Remarks and references to Appendices
FRUGES	2 6/16		General Routine, No 57792 Pte DAVEY E.G. RAMC appointed to Acting Rank of Corporal. GHN	
"	4 6/16		Lieut. McCullum returned from Tempy. duty with 1st Royal Dgs. received orders from Hd.qrs 6th Cav. Bde. to move on the 6th inst to new billets at OFFIN. (ref. Map. ABBEVILLE 100.000) GHN.	
"	6 6/16		FLD AMB. moved into new billeting area at OFFIN. arrived there at 4 p.m. 1 Light Ambulance with 2 O.R. arrived from Tempy. duty with 3rd D.Gs. GHN.	
OFFIN	11 6/16		Capt. I.M. Grant sent to Rl. Life Gds for Tempy duty as M.O. i/c GHN.	
"	12 6/16		Capt. A Wiley ~~[illegible] IRELAND~~ sent to 1st R.Ds. as Tempy M.O. i/c. equipped a party consisting of 2 Medical Officers, 6 Other Ranks R.A.M.C, 3 Other Ranks A.S.C., (Despatch Riders and Horse holders. 11 Riding and 1 Pack horse with a sufficiency of Medical & Surgical Equipment. put these into training in jumping hedges and Trenches. so that they could be sent forward with fighting Troops to give Surgical aid until arrival of FLD. AMB. GHN	
"	16 6/16		Capt. E.R. LOVELL RAMC. attached to this unit for duty. GHN.	
"	18 6/16		Capt. A Wiley RAMC granted special leave to IRELAND from 19 6/16 to 27 6/16. GHN	
"	19 6/16		1. O.R transferred to 64 Field Amb. for duty GHN	

Instructions regarding War Diaries and Intelligence Summaries are contained in F. S. Regs., Part II. and the Staff Manual respectively. Title pages will be prepared in manuscript.

WAR DIARY
or
~~INTELLIGENCE SUMMARY.~~
(Erase heading not required.)

Army Form C. 2118.

Place	Date	Hour	Summary of Events and Information	Remarks and references to Appendices
OFFIN	20/6/16		Received under SECRET. Memo. the Order of Battle of 3rd CAVALRY DIVISION. also instructions for the Sub-division of Cavalry Field Ambulances. which are as follows:— Up to point of Concentration Field Ambulances less Motor Ambulances to remain under orders of Brigadiers. Motor Ambulances to be divisionalized and move under orders of ADMS. "B" Echelons to move forward under orders of ADMS. to be used by him to form a Divisional Dressing Station. "A" Echelon or Mobile Section of the Field Ambulance will remain under orders of Brigadiers "A" Echelon to be divided into two parts:— A¹ consisting of 2 M.Os. 6 O. Ranks RAMC., 3. O. Ranks ASC. 11 Riding horses and 1 Pack horse A² remainder of A Echelon. GHB.	
"	21/6/16		Capt. I.M. Grant RAMC returned from duty with 1st L.Gs. received SECRET MAPS of area of operations [illegible] received SECRET. orders from Bde Hdqrs. that BRIGADE would be concentrated in a new billeting area by 6 A.M. on 26/6/16 and would move to a new intermediate area on the night of 24th/25th inst. GHB.	

1577 Wt. W10791/1773 500,000 1/15 D. D. & L. A.D.S.S./Forms/C. 2118.

Instructions regarding War Diaries and Intelligence Summaries are contained in F. S. Regs., Part II. and the Staff Manual respectively. Title pages will be prepared in manuscript.

WAR DIARY
or
~~INTELLIGENCE SUMMARY.~~
(Erase heading not required.)

Army Form C. 2118.

Place	Date	Hour	Summary of Events and Information	Remarks and references to Appendices
OFFIN.	22/6/16		Capt Marshall RAMC appointed M.O. i/c N.S. Yeomanry vice Capt Lovell, RAMC. G.S.B.H.	
"	23/6/16		Received orders that Brigade would rendezvous tomorrow at 8-15 p.m. at P in PT ST. VAAST (ref. map. ABBEVILLE 100.000.) G.S.B.H.	
"	24/6/16		FIELD AMBULANCE paraded at 7 p.m. "B" Echelon having had orders to accompany Brigade "B" Echelon. left for the rendez-vous at B of BOUIN on HESDEN-MARESQUEL ROAD (ref. map ABBEVILLE 100000). I kept the two Motor Ambulances and evacuated my sick to General Hospital at ETAPLES and afterwards used them to convey the RAMC personnel of "B" Echelon and sent them on ahead to ~~[illegible]~~ MARCHEVILLE (ref. map LENS). "A" Echelon moved off at 7-30 pm to Brigade place of assembly and formed up in rear of "C" Battery R.H.A. route of March HESDEN-REGNAUVILLE-LABROYE. Sent forward 1 officer and 3 O R as billeting party to meet Staff Captain at MARCHVILLE CHURCH. Unit arrived at BRAILLY-CORNHOTTE at 1-30 AM on the 25th inst (ref map ABBEVILLE) and billeted. G.S.B.H.	
CORNHOTTE	25/6/16		Received orders that Brigade would assemble at X Roads 700 yards N of X in YVRENCHEUX (ref map ABBEVILLE) at 9.P.M. 6th CFA in rear of "C" Battery RHA. Unit paraded at 7-3 pm moved off at 8 p.m. Route of march. YVRENCH-DOMQUER-X Roads at B of CHAUSSEE-	

Army Form C. 2118.

Instructions regarding War Diaries and Intelligence Summaries are contained in F. S. Regs., Part II. and the Staff Manual respectively. Title pages will be prepared in manuscript.

WAR DIARY
or
~~INTELLIGENCE SUMMARY.~~
(Erase heading not required.)

Place	Date	Hour	Summary of Events and Information	Remarks and references to Appendices
			BRUNEHAUT – DOMART-EN-PONTHIEU. – ST. LEGER-LES-DOMART. Sent off Billeting party also "B" Echelon RAMC as before. Unit arrived at ST LEGER-LES-DOMART (ref map LENS) at 2-p.m. on the 26th inst. and billeted. GSHD.	
ST. LEGER-LES-DOMART.	26/6/16		Received orders that Brigade would assemble at N.W. entrance to VIGNACOURT at I Roads at 3 of PT. 134 at 9-30 P.M. order of march 6th C.F.A. in rear of 'C' Battery RHA. Unit paraded at 7-45 p.m. and marched off to rendez-vous at 8-15 P.M. Sent off Billeting party and RAMC personnel of "B" Echelon in Motor Ambulances to BONNEY CHURCH (ref. map AMIENS). Route of March. FLESSELLES – BERTANGLES – ALLONVILLE – QUERRIEUX. Unit arrived at BONNEY at 5-30 AM on the 27th inst. and encamped under cover of trees. RAMC personnel billeted in old barns. "B" Echelon arrived at 7-30 A.M. GSHD.	
BONNEY.	27/6/16		Received 3rd Cavalry Division Operation Order No 1. which states that 3rd Cavalry Division will be in a position to move on "Z" day at Zero hour and will move from its present billeting area South of BONNEY to a position of readiness east of ALBERT ref map AMIENS. The ADMS to be prepared to form a Divisional Dressing Station at BELLEVUE FARM in E. 5 C 1-20.000 after arrival of Division east of ALBERT. 6 C.F.A. to move in rear of IV Brigade R.H.A. GSHD.	

1577 Wt. W10791/1773 500,000 1/15 D. D. & L. A.D.S.S./Forms/C. 2118.

Army Form C. 2118.

Instructions regarding War Diaries and Intelligence Summaries are contained in F. S. Regs., Part II. and the Staff Manual respectively. Title pages will be prepared in manuscript.

WAR DIARY
or
~~INTELLIGENCE SUMMARY.~~

(Erase heading not required.)

Place	Date	Hour	Summary of Events and Information	Remarks and references to Appendices
BONNEY.	28/6/16		Capt. A Willey returned from leave. received Operation order No 1 from Brigade which states that Brigade less 'C' Battery RHA would be formed up in Brigade Bivouac ready to move at 7-30 AM tomorrow 29th inst. notified that C.F.A.s would receive their orders from A.D.M.S. Good	
"	"		Received continuation of 3rd Cav. Div. Operation order No 1 which states the Mobile Sections of all Cav. Fld Ambulances would move in order of 8th 6th 7th in rear of IV Brigade RHA. 'B' Echelon in same order will move at head of Divisional 'A' Echelon Transport. Good.	
"	28/6/16	6-40 pm.	Received orders from Brigade that for 7-30 AM tomorrow the 29th inst. read 7-3 AM. July 1st. Good.	
"	29/6/16		Received orders from Brigade that O.C. C.F.A. as Senior Medical Officer will, when on the march in the presence of the enemy or when Brigade is in action, march with Echelon II of Brigade Staff. [redacted] went forward to reconnoitre BELLEVUE FARM. Good.	
"	29/6/16	9-45 pm.	Received Medical Operation Order No 1 from A.D.M.S which states that 'A' Echelons less the Advanced Party will move in the order of march and at the time stated in Divisional Operation order, and will assemble at T Roads on the west side in E 3 D 77 1/50000	

1577 Wt. W10791/1773 500,000 1/15 D. D. & L. A.D.S.S./Forms/C. 2118.

Instructions regarding War Diaries and Intelligence Summaries are contained in F. S. Regs., Part II. and the Staff Manual respectively. Title pages will be prepared in manuscript.

WAR DIARY

or

~~INTELLIGENCE SUMMARY.~~

(Erase heading not required.)

Army Form C. 2118.

Place	Date	Hour	Summary of Events and Information	Remarks and references to Appendices
BONNEY	29th	9.45 pm	Advance party of C.F.As to move with fighting Troops. 'B' Echelons divisional under Captain R. GALLOWAY to proceed to BELLEVUE FARM in E.5.c 30.00 and be prepared to open a Dressing Station if necessary. A.D.M.S. will be at BELLEVUE FARM.	G.H.S.
BONNEY	30th		Captain I.M. GRANT attached to 1st R.D.s as M.O. vice Captain J. LANGTON BUTLER sent to 'B' Echelon 6th C.F.A. Took Regimental Medical officers up to show them position of Dressing Station and Field Ambulance. G.H.S.	

[illegible] Major
OC 6th C.F.A

1577 Wt. W10791/1773 500,000 1/15 D. D. & L. A.D.S.S./Forms/C. 2118.

3rd Cav Div

No 6 Cav F. Amb

Vol 19

July 1916

War diary of
6th Cav Fd ambulance
for July 1916

[illegible]
Lieut. Col. R.A.M.C.
A.D.M.S. 3rd Cav. Div.

3

Instructions regarding War Diaries and Intelligence Summaries are contained in F. S. Regs., Part II. and the Staff Manual respectively. Title pages will be prepared in manuscript.

WAR DIARY
or
INTELLIGENCE SUMMARY.
(Erase heading not required.)

Army Form C. 2118.

Place	Date	Hour	Summary of Events and Information	Remarks and references to Appendices
BONNEY	1/7/16	7-30 AM	Field Ambulance on parade and ready to move at 7-30 A.M. was inspected by G.O.C. 6th Cav. Bde. ordered to stand to at ½ hours notice. [illegible]	
"	1/7/16	6 pm	½ hours notice increased to 4 hours. [illegible]	
"	"	8-15 pm	Received continuation of 3rd Cav. Div. Medical Operation Order No 1. Cancelling Para. 3 of order and substituting the following 3a Heavy Sections of Cav. Fld Ambces. in the order already given, will move at the head of Echelons A1 Transport along the main road to ALBERT to the X road S.W. of second V of LAVIEVILLE where they will park with the Light section Transport of the Division, under the command of Capt. GALLOWAY No 7 C.F.A. 3b Officer Commanding combined Heavy Sections will be prepared to send forward one Officer and 21 Other Ranks with sufficient medical and surgical equipment to assist at the Main Dressing Station to be established at the Civil Hospital ALBERT by the 1st Cavalry Division and 2nd Indian Cavalry Division. 7. Medical Officer concerned will be told to instruct all walking cases when possible to proceed to No 104 Field Ambulance at the centre of ALBERT near the CHURCH. [illegible]	
BONNEY	2/7/16		Standing to at 4 hours notice. [illegible]	
"	"	5 pm	Received orders from A.D.M.S. to proceed with Light Section of Field Ambulance immediately to MORLANCOURT	

1577 Wt. W10791/1773 500,000 1/15 D. D. & L. A.D.S.S./Forms/C. 2118.

Instructions regarding War Diaries and Intelligence Summaries are contained in F. S. Regs., Part II. and the Staff Manual respectively. Title pages will be prepared in manuscript.

WAR DIARY
or
~~INTELLIGENCE SUMMARY.~~
(*Erase heading not required.*)

Army Form C. 2118.

Place	Date	Hour	Summary of Events and Information	Remarks and references to Appendices
BONNEY	2/7/16	5pm	(ref. map AMIENS 1/100000) to give assistance to Field Amb. there in dealing with German wounded, departed at 6.15 p.m. GSHH.	
MORLANCOURT	2/7/16	8 p.m	arrived at MORLANCOURT. detailed 2 Medical Officers and Tent subdivision to dress the 57 wounded already there. pitched 5 Marquees (Hospital) and prepared to deal with further cases. all ranks worked all night until 10 AM next morning GSHH	
"	3/7/16	1 p.m	ordered to hand over Hospital to 52nd Field Ambulance. Total number of German wounded admitted since 8 pm 2/7/16 = 2 Officers and 128 other ranks. the injuries were mostly due to Shell wounds and about 50% of them were serious several cases had Gas gangrene and one died GSHH	
"	3/7/16	4 pm	Handed over Hospital, having evacuated all the wounded Germans, at 4 pm and returned to BONNEY. GSHH	
BONNEY	3/7/16	6 pm	arrived at BONNEY, received orders that Brigade would probably move at 5 AM the next morning to a new billeting area. GSHH.	
BONNEY	4/7/16	2-15 AM	Received orders to be ready to move at 5-15 A.M. today to the HALLENCOURT area S of ABBEVILLE. 'B' Echelons to move at 7 A.M. GSHH	
BONNEY	4/7/16	5 15 AM	Field Ambulance moved off in rear of 6th Machine Gun Squadron. sent off billeting party to meet Staff Captain at AIRAINES CHURCH. Route of March DAOURS – YECQUEMONT – AMIENS –	

1577 Wt. W10791/1773 500,000 1/15 D. D. & L. A.D.S.S./Forms/C. 2118.

Instructions regarding War Diaries and Intelligence Summaries are contained in F. S. Regs., Part II. and the Staff Manual respectively. Title pages will be prepared in manuscript.

WAR DIARY
or
~~INTELLIGENCE SUMMARY.~~

(Erase heading not required.)

Army Form C. 2118.

Place	Date	Hour	Summary of Events and Information	Remarks and references to Appendices
BONNEY	4/7/16	5-15 AM	-AILLY-SUR-SOMME-PICQUIGNY-AIRAINES. Sent 'B' Echelon RAMC personnel in Motor Ambulances as before. billets allotted at DREUIL-LE-HAMEL. [initials]	
DREUIL-LE-HAMEL	4/7/16		arrived at 5-30 pm. after a dreary march. [initials]	
"	5/7/16 - 6		Checked equipment and replenished stores. handed [illegible] of Brigade. [initials]	
	7/7/16		Received orders from ADMS that in future 'A' Echelon of CFAs would be called Light Sections and 'B' Echelon Heavy Sections. [initials]	
"	7/7/16		Received orders from Brigade to be ready to move at short notice. [initials]	
"	8/7/16		Received orders that Brigade would assemble at Eastern edge of AIRAINES at 2-15 pm	
"		2-15 pm	Field Amb. moved off in rear of 'C' Battery RHA. 'B' Echelon in rear of Brigade. Sent a Billeting party together with RAMC personnel of Heavy Section to CORBIE CHURCH. [initials]	
CORBIE	9/7/16	3-30 AM	arrived and Bivouaced in the ETAMPS. Brigade took 13 hours and a quarter over the march both men and animals dead beat. [initials]	
CORBIE	9/7/16	4 pm	Received orders that Brigade would move to Bivouacs at VAUX-SUR-SOMME (ref map AMIENS) units moving independently. [initials]	
"	9/7/16	6-15 pm	Field Ambulance left CORBIE at 6-15 pm and arrived at VAUX at 7-15 pm. [initials]	
VAUX-SUR-SOMME	9/7/16	10 pm	Received notice that Brigade would not be required to move tomorrow 10th inst. [initials]	

1577 Wt. W10791/1773 500,000 1/15 D. D. & L. A.D.S.S./Forms/C. 2118.

Instructions regarding War Diaries and Intelligence Summaries are contained in F. S. Regs., Part II. and the Staff Manual respectively. Title pages will be prepared in manuscript.

WAR DIARY
or
~~INTELLIGENCE SUMMARY.~~
(Erase heading not required.)

Army Form C. 2118.

Place	Date	Hour	Summary of Events and Information	Remarks and references to Appendices
VAUX-SUR-SOMME	10/7/16		CAPT. T.J. BUTLER sent to take over medical charge of 3rd CAV. DIV. Supply Column. Received notice that Brigade might possibly have to move to fresh bivouacs at short notice GSHH	
"	11/7/16	10AM	ordered to stand to at 1 hours notice GSHH.	
"	11/7/16	2 pm	1 hours notice increased to 4 hours. LIEUT. V. H L. MAC SWINEY RAMC. arrived from 13th Field Ambulance for duty. GSHH.	
"	12/7/16		Received orders to attend conference at Bde. Hdqrs. at 12-30 p.m. possible forthcoming operation was explained by the G.O.C. GSHH.	
"	"	6 p.m	Received 3rd Cavalry Division Medical Operation Order No 2. as follows Ref. Map 1/100,000 Showed the Division move Eastwards from present bivouacs GSHH 1. Heavy Sections of Cavalry Field Ambulances will assemble at Zero hour in the field on the South side of the track leading from main road to the railway, immediately South of T roads about 1 Kil. S.E. of BONNEY GSHH 2. at this point the combined Heavy Sections of Cavalry Fld. Amb'ces will come under the command of Capt. R. GALLOWAY RAMC. No 7 Cavalry Field Ambulance GSHH 3. The combined Heavy Sections will leave this starting point at Zero hour and 20 minutes and move by the main CORBIE — MEAULTE road to the LE CARCAILLOT X Roads	

Instructions regarding War Diaries and Intelligence Summaries are contained in F. S. Regs., Part II. and the Staff Manual respectively. Title pages will be prepared in manuscript.

WAR DIARY
or
~~INTELLIGENCE SUMMARY.~~
(Erase heading not required.)

Army Form C. 2118.

Place	Date	Hour	Summary of Events and Information	Remarks and references to Appendices
VAUX-SUR-SOMME	12/7/16	6 p.m.	N.E. of MEAULTE, where they will park off the road. GSM MOTOR Ambulances of Cavalry Field Amb'ces. will proceed independently to the LE-CARCAILLOT X roads leaving their units at Zero hour, on arrival at X roads they will park off the road. Capt. MORAN RAMC No 8 CFA will assume Command of the Combined motor Ambulances. Issued at 4-30 p.m. 12-7-16. GSM Issued the necessary instructions to the Officer i/c. of Heavy Section and Sergeant in charge of Motor Ambulances GSM.	
"	13/7/16		on 4 hours notice. Received Brigade orders as follows. The 3rd Cav. Div. may be required to move East, tomorrow. The Brigade will stand to in bivouacs, with saddles and wagons packed, ready to move at half hours notice from 4. a.m. tomorrow. In event of Bde being ordered to move, the Bde. place of assembly will be X Roads at CHURCH, VAUX-SUR-SOMME. 6th CAV. FLD. AMB. in rear of 'C' Battery R.H.A. Route of march :- SAILLY-LE-SEC. - by track running N. of BRAY - CORBIE Road N. of contour 100. to MEAULTE (Ref. Map. 1/100 000) GSM	
"	"	12 noon.	Received continuation of 3rd CAV. DIV. Medical Operation Orders as follows :- In first Sentence of PARA I Cancel. will assemble at Zero hour, and substitute will leave their bivouacs	

1577 Wt. W10791/1773 500,000 1/15 D. D. & L. A.D.S.S./Forms/C. 2118.

Army Form C. 2118.

Instructions regarding War Diaries and Intelligence Summaries are contained in F. S. Regs., Part II. and the Staff Manual respectively. Title pages will be prepared in manuscript.

WAR DIARY
or
INTELLIGENCE SUMMARY.
(Erase heading not required.)

Place	Date	Hour	Summary of Events and Information	Remarks and references to Appendices
VAUX-SUR-SOMME	13 7/16	12 noon	In para 3. cancel "will leave this starting point at Zero hour and 20 minutes" and substitute "will leave this starting point as soon after assault as possible." Add, "Zero day will be 14 inst. Zero hour for Division will be 4 A.M." Heavy Sections of Cavalry Field Ambulances will then [be] prepared to be ready to move ½ hour after receipt of orders any time after 4 A.M. on the 14th inst. Communicate this order to all concerned. G.S.B.I.	
"	14 7/16	4 A.M.	Field Ambulance on parade and ready to move. Inspected by O.C. G.S.B.I.	
"	"	4-30 A.M.	Off saddled and standing to at ½ hours notice. G.S.B.I.	
"	"	8-45 p.m.	Received Bde. order that present degree of readiness cancelled for night. Bde to be ready at ½ hours notice from 5 A.M. G.S.B.I.	
"	15 7/16	5 A.M.	Field Ambulance on parade and ready to move. Inspected by O.C. Afterwards off saddled and standing to at ½ hour notice. G.S.B.I.	
"	16 7/16	12.38 A.M.	Received orders that Bde would be ready to move at one and a half hours notice from 6 A.M. G.S.B.I.	
"	"	12-15 p.m.	The state of readiness of Bde is changed to 4 hours after receipt of orders. G.S.B.I.	
"	17 7/16		Standing to at 4 hours notice. G.S.B.I.	
"	18 7/16		Received orders that Bde would move into a new billeting area tomorrow ~~G.S.B.I.~~ State of readiness 4 hours after receipt of orders. G.S.B.I.	

1577 Wt. W10791/1773 500,000 1/15 D. D. & L. A.D.S.S./Forms/C. 2118.

Instructions regarding War Diaries and Intelligence Summaries are contained in F. S. Regs., Part II. and the Staff Manual respectively. Title pages will be prepared in manuscript.

WAR DIARY
or
~~INTELLIGENCE SUMMARY.~~
(Erase heading not required.)

Army Form C. 2118.

Place	Date	Hour	Summary of Events and Information	Remarks and references to Appendices
VAUX-SUR-SOMME	18 7/16	10.45pm	Received orders that Bde would move into bivouac at LA NEUVILLE tomorrow (ref map AMIENS 1/100000.) 6. Cav FLD AMB to leave at 3-30pm. GSrdH.	
"	19 7/16	3-30pm	Unit moved off to new billeting area. Sent billeting party and guide to meet Staff Captain at LA NEUVILLE CHURCH at 11 A.M. GSrdH.	
LA NEUVILLE	19 7/16	5pm	Arrived at LA.NEUVILLE men bivouaced in field. pitched tents and opened small Rest Station for Sick GSrdH.	
"				
"	21 7/16		under orders from ADMS. 3rd Cav. Div. sent 1 NCO and 6 men to No 5. CCS for Temp. duty. G.O.C 6th Cav. Bde ordered an inspection by S.M.O. of the whole of the Bde for Scabies. GSrdH	
"	22 7/16		Inspected 1st R.Dr found 29 cases of Scabies. Sent 2 Med. Offs and 6 O.R. to 21 C.C.S. for Temp. duty. GSrdH	
"	23 7/16		Inspected 3rd D.Gs found no case of scabies. GSrdH	
"	24 7/16		Inspected N.S.Y. found 24 cases of scabies also that over 50 % of the men did not wear under pants. recommended that every man be compelled to wear them GSrdH	
"	25 7/16		Inspected the remainder of the Bde. 1 Case of Scabies found in C Batt. R.H.A. no other cases found GSrdH.	
"	26 7/16		Sent 1 Motor Ambulance with 2 Drivers to report for duty to OC Digging party No 8 C.F.A. GSrdH	

1577 Wt. W10791/1773 500,000 1/15 D. D. & L. A.D.S.S./Forms/C. 2118.

Instructions regarding War Diaries and Intelligence Summaries are contained in F. S. Regs., Part II. and the Staff Manual respectively. Title pages will be prepared in manuscript.

WAR DIARY
or
~~INTELLIGENCE SUMMARY.~~

(*Erase heading not required.*)

Army Form C. 2118.

Place	Date	Hour	Summary of Events and Information	Remarks and references to Appendices
LA NEUVILLE	27/7/16		Under orders from A.D.M.S. 3rd CAV DIV sent 1 M.O. for tempy duty to O.C. Digging Party No. 8 C.F.A at BECOURT (ref map AMIENS 1/100000) [illegible]	
"	29/7/16		Arranged to take over Medical Charge of Divisional Digging Party at BECOURT on Aug 1st 16 from No 8 C.F.A. [illegible]	
"	31/7/16		Received orders that Bde would move to a new billeting area tomorrow. Recalled all the Officers and men on Tempy duty. [illegible]	
"	"	6 p.m.	Received orders that Bde would assemble at [illegible] of LA NEUVILLE at 6 A.M. tomorrow and march to SOUES (ref map AMIENS 1/100000) 6 C.F.A. in rear of "C" Bty R.H.A. [illegible]	

[illegible] for Major
O.C. 6 C.F.A

1577 Wt. W10791/1773 500,000 1/15 D. D. & L. A.D.S.S./Forms/C. 2118.

38

August/16

DIARY of

Vol 20

6th Cavalry Field Ambulance

Month of August 1916.

Instructions regarding War Diaries and Intelligence Summaries are contained in F. S. Regs., Part II. and the Staff Manual respectively. Title pages will be prepared in manuscript.

WAR DIARY
or
~~INTELLIGENCE SUMMARY~~.
(Erase heading not required.)

Army Form C. 2118.

Place	Date	Hour	Summary of Events and Information	Remarks and references to Appendices
SOUES. S.A.H. ~~LANEUVILLE~~	1-8-16	9.15 PM.	Recd orders that Bgde will march tomorrow to St RIQUIER area. Place of assembly Western Exit of SOUES 1000 yards S. of M in 7m at 5 AM. 6th C.F.A. in rear of C Battery R.F.A. (Ref map 1/100000 AMIENS.). S.A.H.	
"	2-8-16	5 AM	Bgde moved off as above. Sent Billeting party & guide to meet Staff Capt at CAOURS Church at 8 A.M. MILLENCOURT was the place given as Billeting area to 6th CFA, which arrived there at 2.30 P.M. Unit went into Bivouacs - & opened temporary Bgde Hosp. S.A.H. B Echelons marched separately from A Echelons, & were Divisionalised. B Echelon 6th CFA joined A Echelon at MILLENCOURT at 5 PM. S.A.H	
MILLENCOURT.	3-8-16		General Routine S.A.H	
		11.30 PM.	Recd orders that Bgde will march tomorrow to Bivouacs at 4.30 AM, on the AUTHIE River between SAUCHOY and DOMPIERRE (Ref map ABBEVILLE Sheet 14 1/100000). S.A.H	

1577 Wt. W10791/1773 500,000 1/15 D. D. & L. A.D.S.S./Forms/C. 2118.

Instructions regarding War Diaries and Intelligence Summaries are contained in F. S. Regs., Part II. and the Staff Manual respectively. Title pages will be prepared in manuscript.

WAR DIARY
or
INTELLIGENCE SUMMARY.
(Erase heading not required.)

Army Form C. 2118.

Place	Date	Hour	Summary of Events and Information	Remarks and references to Appendices
MILLENCOURT	3/8/16	11.55 PM	Recd further orders that Bgde would move to FRUGES Area on Aug 4th & 5th billeting night of 4th/5th at ROUSSENT - MAINTENAY Gd & Pt PREAUX - St REMY AU BOIS. (Ref. map. ABBEVILLE Sheet 14 1/100000). Place of assembly X Roads just N. of M in MILLENCOURT EN PONTHIEU at 5 A.M. 6th Cav. F. Amb. in Rear of 6th M/Gun Squadron.	GAA
"	4/8/16		Billeting party & Guide were sent to meet Staff Capt. at MAINTENAY CHURCH at 8 A.M.	
			In accordance with above orders Unit marched at 5 AM & arrived at MAINTENAY at 10 A.M. Billeting area given to 6th C.F.A. was MAINTENAY.	
			B Echelon marched separately - & was Divisionalised, arriving at MAINTENAY at 12.30 PM, when it joined A Echelon. Unit went into Bivouacs. Temporary Bgde Hosp. was opened. GAA	

1577 Wt. W10791/1773 500,000 1/15 D. D. & L. A.D.S.S./Forms/C. 2118.

Army Form C. 2118.

Instructions regarding War Diaries and Intelligence Summaries are contained in F. S. Regs., Part II. and the Staff Manual respectively. Title pages will be prepared in manuscript.

WAR DIARY
or
INTELLIGENCE SUMMARY.
(Erase heading not required.)

Place	Date	Hour	Summary of Events and Information	Remarks and references to Appendices
MAINTENAY	4/8/16	7.15 PM	Orders recd that Bgde will march to permanent billets tomorrow. Place of Assembly at Y Roads N of M of MAINTENAY at 8.30 A.M. B. Echelon 6th C.F.A. will march with A Echelon 6th C.F.A. 6th C.F.A. in rear of 3rd D.G. Wire recd from Bgde that in permanent Billets – allotment of areas will be as before. S.A.H.	
OFFIN	5/8/16		In accordance with orders Unit marched as above & arrived at OFFIN at 10.30 A.M. S.A.H.	
"	6/8/16		General Routine. Brigade H. of ? opened. Arrangements are being made to take in & treat all cases of Scabies in the Brigade, also for all blankets & clothing to be disinfected by "Thresh" S.A.H.	
"	7/8/16		General Routine. S.A.H.	
	8/8/16		Arrangements are now completed for treating Scabies & disinfecting Clothes. Capt WILEY was today granted Special leave to ENGLAND leave dating from 8/8/16 to 17/8/16. S.A.H.	

1577 Wt. W10791/1773 500,000 1/15 D. D. & L. A.D.S.S./Forms/C. 2118.

Instructions regarding War Diaries and Intelligence Summaries are contained in F. S. Regs., Part II. and the Staff Manual respectively. Title pages will be prepared in manuscript.

WAR DIARY
or
INTELLIGENCE SUMMARY.
(Erase heading not required.)

Army Form C. 2118.

Place	Date	Hour	Summary of Events and Information	Remarks and references to Appendices
OFFIN.	9/8/16		General Routine. Disinfection of clothes & blankets being completed, & treatment of cases of Scabies being carried on. The Bgde Hosp opened by 6th CFA, is taking all Brigade Sick. Necessary cases for evacuation are being sent to No 26 Gen. Hosp. ETAPLES. SAH	
"			No. of Cases admitted to Brigade Hosp from 1/8/16 to 7/8/16 is 72. This number includes 35 verminous & scabies cases which are being treated by 6th CFA. SAH.	
"			1 Corp A.S.C. H.T. arrived for duty. 1 Driver A.S.C. H.T. Evac. Sick. 1 G.S. Wagon 2 Drs & 4 mules attached for purpose of drawing rations from Rail Head (BOURAINVILLE.) for Bde H.Qs & 13th M.V.S. G.R.O. 1295 (Precautions against fire) republished in Regl Orders. SAH	
"			R.O. from ADMS Recd (21709/1) - Sick to be evacuated to No 20 Field Amb. HESDIN. Scabies cases are to be treated in No 6 CFA. Infectious case Evac to Isolation Hosp. ETAPLES. SAH.	

Instructions regarding War Diaries and Intelligence Summaries are contained in F. S. Regs., Part II. and the Staff Manual respectively. Title pages will be prepared in manuscript.

WAR DIARY
or
INTELLIGENCE SUMMARY.
(Erase heading not required.)

Army Form C. 2118.

Place	Date	Hour	Summary of Events and Information	Remarks and references to Appendices
OFFIN.	10/8/16		R.O. recd from ADVS No. 208. RO's No 196 of May 8th & 205 of June 5th 1916 are cancelled & the following substituted: Dental & Eye cases are sent to ETAPLES - Dental cases to No 6. Convalesc. Depot. Eye cases to No 24 Gen. Hospital. GAH.	
	11/8/16		Major E HAMMERTON granted Special leave to U.K. from 14th to 22nd inst. During absence of Major HAMMERTON Capt HOAR is appointed O.C. GAH	
	13/8/16		Sanction granted by ADVS to purchase green vegetables at the rate of ½ lb. per head for all cases of Scabies when undergoing treatment in 6th CVA. GAH	
	14/8/16		Capt (Bvt) LOWRY CORRY 1 Batman & 1 horse proceeded to Div. HQs	
			1 Pte Sergt RAVC. granted leave from 15/8/16 to 15/9/16 on completion of service (Authy G.O.C. 6th Cav. Bgde) GAH.	
	15/8/16		6 Pte RAVC. arrived for duty. GAH	

Instructions regarding War Diaries and Intelligence Summaries are contained in F. S. Regs., Part II. and the Staff Manual respectively. Title pages will be prepared in manuscript.

WAR DIARY

or

~~INTELLIGENCE SUMMARY.~~

(Erase heading not required.)

Army Form C. 2118.

Place	Date	Hour	Summary of Events and Information	Remarks and references to Appendices
OFFIN.	15 8/16		Recd D.9/280/7. d. 14-4-16 & D.M.S. Reserve Army 9/19. re Protection of Reg. Aid Posts & advanced dressing Station against gas attacks. S.A.H.	
"	17 8/16		1 O.R. R.A.M.C. (Cook) arrived for duty from No 7. C.F.A.	
			No. of cases admitted to Bgde Hosp. from 8 8/16 to 14 8/16 40. S.A.H.	
"	18 8/16		Capt A. Wiley rejoined unit from leave. S.A.H.	
"	19 8/16		1 O.R. R.A.M.C. transferred to No 7 C.F.A. S.A.H.	
"	22 8/16		Major S.H.L. HAMMERTON rejoined from leave S.A.H.	
			The A.D.M.S. inspected the medical & sanitary arrangements of 3rd Dragoon Guards. S.A.H.	
"	24 8/16		Lieut P.A. MACCULLUM proceeded to 1st Royal Dragoons for temp. duty	
	26.		A.D.M.S. inspected the medical & sanitary arrangements of 1st Royal Dragoons – C Battery R.H.A. & 6th M.G. Squadron S.A.H.	

1577 Wt. W10791/1773 500,000 1/15 D. D. & L. A.D.S.S./Forms/C. 2118.

Instructions regarding War Diaries and Intelligence Summaries are contained in F. S. Regs., Part II. and the Staff Manual respectively. Title pages will be prepared in manuscript.

WAR DIARY
~~or~~
~~INTELLIGENCE SUMMARY.~~
(Erase heading not required.)

Army Form C. 2118.

Place	Date	Hour	Summary of Events and Information	Remarks and references to Appendices
OFFIN.	25/8/16		A.D.M.S. inspected the Medical & Sanitary arrangements of N.S.Y. (Yeomanry) No of Cases admitted to Brigade HP. from 15/8/16 to 21/8/16 — 39. [illegible]	
HESMOND	26/8/16		Unit under Brigade instructions moved to-day from its Billeting area in OFFIN to a new Billeting area at The CHATEAU HESMOND (Ref Map No 11. ABBEVILLE 1/100000)	[illegible]
"			Lieut McCullum rejoined 6 C.F.A from 1st R.Ds. Capt C.R. Lovell proceeds to 1st R.D.s for Temp. duty. Lieut McCullum & 12 O.R.s RAMC under instructions from A.D.M.S. proceeds to No 44 C.C.S. for Temp. duty. 1 O.R. RAMC (TF) H.T. reverts to RAMC G.D. & from 7th rate A.S.C. Corps pay to 5th rate RAMC Corps pay	
"			Recd Memo from D.G.M.S. No D.G.D/2288/74 calling attention to the considerable amount of gastro-intestinal trouble amongst troops - & specially officers.	

1577 Wt. W10791/1773 500,000 1/15 D. D. & L. A.D.S.S./Forms/C. 2118.

Instructions regarding War Diaries and Intelligence Summaries are contained in F. S. Regs., Part II. and the Staff Manual respectively. Title pages will be prepared in manuscript.

WAR DIARY
or
~~INTELLIGENCE SUMMARY.~~
(Erase heading not required.)

Army Form C. 2118.

Place	Date	Hour	Summary of Events and Information	Remarks and references to Appendices
HESDIGNEUL	26/8/16		Special attention should be given to the Conditions of Officers Messes & Kitchens of Headquarters of formations. S.A.H.	
"	28/8/16		Memo from D.M.S. Reserve Army No. 232d/24/8/16 Calling attention to cases of patients who arrive at C.C.S. deeply under the influence of Morphia. The greatest care should be taken to ascertain that the drug has not been taken by the patient from a private store before administering another dose. S.A.H.	
"	29/8/16		Lieut. V.H.L. McSwiney R.A.M.C. proceeded to 49th Div for duty - & has been struck off the strength. S.A.H.	
"	30		Order recd from A.D.M.S. 21810 "All cases of diarrhoea in 6th Cav. Bgde to be reported to this Office."	
"			No of cases admitted to Bgd H.P. 22/8/16 to 28/8/16 — 31.	
			" " " " 29/8/16 - 31/8/16 — 18.	
			S.A.H.	

Instructions regarding War Diaries and Intelligence Summaries are contained in F. S. Regs., Part II. and the Staff Manual respectively. Title pages will be prepared in manuscript.

WAR DIARY

or

~~INTELLIGENCE SUMMARY.~~

(*Erase heading not required.*)

Army Form C. 2118.

Place	Date	Hour	Summary of Events and Information	Remarks and references to Appendices
HESDIN	31/8/16.		Total Cases admitted to Bg. H.P. during August 1916	
			220.	
			S Cabins 56. (44 from 6th Cav. Bgde.)	
			10 " 7 " "	
			8 " 8 " "	
			S.A.H.	
			G. Stewart Hamilton Major	
			O.C. 6. C.F.A	

T.134. Wt. W708-776. 500000. 4/15. Sir J. C. & S.

140/1788

6th Cav. Field Amb.

Sept 1916

Vol 21

Diary of
6th Cavalry Field Amb:
September
1916.

Instructions regarding War Diaries and Intelligence Summaries are contained in F. S. Regs., Part II. and the Staff Manual respectively. Title pages will be prepared in manuscript.

WAR DIARY

or

~~INTELLIGENCE SUMMARY.~~

(Erase heading not required.)

Army Form C. 2118.

Place	Date	Hour	Summary of Events and Information	Remarks and references to Appendices
			Ref. Map. No 14 1/100000 ABBEVILLE.	
HESMOND	1/9/16		One O.R. Evacuated to H. Order of Battle received from Div. H.Q. SHA	
"	2/9/16		G.O.C. inspected unit. Capt LOVELL rejoined from 1st R.D.s SHA	
"	3/9/16		Capt LOVELL proceeded to No 44 C.C.S. in relief of Lieut McCULLUM for temp. duty. Lieut McCULLUM rejoined Unit - & was granted leave from 4th to 12th inst. inclusive. SHA	
"	5/9/16		2nd Whlr. CHAPMAN H.T. No T4/108122 ASC promoted to rank of Whlr. Corp. to date from Aug 28 1916 (Auth. ASC Sect No 13942 d/4. 9/16.	
			Inspection of Transport by O.C. A.S.C. 3rd Cav. Div. SHA	
"	6/9/16		Memo from Bg. H.Q. recd that Div. will be moving from present Billets on any day after 9th inst. SHA	
"	8/9/16		Sick admitted to Bg. HP. from Sept 1st to Sept 7th 38 - of which Diarrhoea 12 cases & Scabies 5 cases. SHA	
"	9/9/16		No. 30668 S.M. RICHARDSON, F RAMC joined unit from No 77 F.A.	

T.2134. Wt. W708–776. 500000. 4/15. Sir J. C. & S.

Instructions regarding War Diaries and Intelligence Summaries are contained in F. S. Regs., Part II. and the Staff Manual respectively. Title pages will be prepared in manuscript.

WAR DIARY
~~or~~
~~INTELLIGENCE SUMMARY.~~

(*Erase heading not required.*)

Army Form C. 2118.

Place	Date	Hour	Summary of Events and Information	Remarks and references to Appendices
HESMOND	9/9/16		Wire recd from Bgd. H.Q. that Division will march from present Billeting area on Sept 10th 1916.	
			Memo from A.D.M.S. that office of A.D.M.S. will remain open at FRUGES on Sept 10th. All sick on 10/9/16 to be Evac. to No 20 F.A.	
			Orders recd from Bgd. H.Q. that Bgds will march tomorrow Sept 10th to a Bivouac on the AUTHIE RIVER. The march will be continued on 11th 12th & 13th. On the 10th point of Assembly at level crossing 800 yds S.E. of BEURANVILLE STATION at 10.20 AM. 6th C.F.A. in rear of N.S.Y. Billeting officer proceeded to meet Staff Capt. at Church at SAULCHOY at 10.30 AM.	
			Ref. Map. ABBEVILLE No 14. 1/100000. [signature]	
ARGOULES.	10/9/16		In accordance with above orders, No 6 C.F.A. went into Bivouacs at ARGOULES, arriving at 1 P.M.	
			1 G.S. Waggon 2 Drivers & 4 Mules ex from 3rd Cav. Div. Res. Park	

T.134. Wt. W708–776. 500000. 4/15. Sir J. C. & S.

Instructions regarding War Diaries and Intelligence Summaries are contained in F. S. Regs., Part II. and the Staff Manual respectively. Title pages will be prepared in manuscript.

WAR DIARY
~~or~~
~~INTELLIGENCE~~ SUMMARY.
(*Erase heading not required.*)

Army Form C. 2118.

Place	Date	Hour	Summary of Events and Information	Remarks and references to Appendices
ARGOULES	10/9/16		No 1/45925 Pte EYRES J. ASC. M.T. arrived for duty with Sunbeam Motor Amb. No. A 17007 in accordance with instructions recd from ADMS.	
			Memo recd from ADMS that his Office will close at FRUGES at 12.30 P.M. 11/9/16 & open at GUESCHART at 3.30 P.M. 11/9/16: Ref. Map. LENS 11. 1/100000.	
			Sick on 11/9/16 will be evac. to No 20 F.A.	
			Wire recd from Bde H.Q. that Bgde will move to new area about noon tomorrow. Billeting Officer will meet Staff Capt at X Roads just East of final L in NEUILLY-L-HOPITAL at 12 Noon. S.F.H.	
			Ref. Map. ABBEVILLE 14. 1/100000.	
ARGOULES	11/9/16		Orders recd from Bgd H.Q. that Bgde will march today to Billeting area - CANCHY - MILLENCOURT.	
			Place of assembly at 6 X Roads just (S.W.) LE PETIT CHEMIN at 2 P.M. 6 CFA in rear of 6th N.I. Glen. Sq.	

T.2134. Wt. W708-776. 500000. 4/15. Sir J. C. & S.

Instructions regarding War Diaries and Intelligence Summaries are contained in F. S. Regs., Part II. and the Staff Manual respectively. Title pages will be prepared in manuscript.

WAR DIARY
or
INTELLIGENCE SUMMARY.
(Erase heading not required.)

Army Form C. 2118.

Place	Date	Hour	Summary of Events and Information	Remarks and references to Appendices
CANCHY	11/9/16		Bgd. marched as above. 6th CFA went into Bivouacs at CANCHY arriving there at 6 P.M.	
"	"		Orders recd from Bg. H.Q. at 9.30 P.M. that Bgde will march tomorrow 12th inst. to LA CHAUSSEE (ref Map. AMIENS 17. 1/100000) & will halt there until 14th inst. Continuing the march on that day to Y. area S.W. of VECQUEMONT. (ref Map AMIENS 17. 1/100000) Assembly point for 12th inst. will be X Roads 650 yards W of B of BOIS de L'ABBEY. at 10 A.M. 6th CFA in rear of 6th D/Am. Sg. Billeting officer to meet Staff Capt at LA CHAUSSEE Church at 12 noon 12th inst. SAA	
TIRANCOURT (LA CHAUSSEE)	12/9/16		Bgd marched as above, & 6th CFA went into Bivouac at TIRANCOURT (LA CHAUSSEE) arriving there at 6 P.M.	
"	13/9/16		Bgd Remained here to day. CAPT LOVELL & 12 O.R. rejoined unit from No 44 C.C.S. SAA	

T.134. Wt. W708–776. 500000. 4/15. Sir J. C. & S.

Instructions regarding War Diaries and Intelligence Summaries are contained in F. S. Regs., Part II. and the Staff Manual respectively. Title pages will be prepared in manuscript.

WAR DIARY

or

~~INTELLIGENCE~~ SUMMARY.

(*Erase heading not required.*)

Army Form C. 2118.

Place	Date	Hour	Summary of Events and Information	Remarks and references to Appendices
TIRANCOURT.	13/9/16	.	Orders recd from Bgd. H.Q. that Bgd will march tomorrow 14th inst to X area & Bivouac N. of BUSSY (Ref map. AMIENS. 17. 1/100000) Assembly point W. end of St SAVEUR at 8 A.M. 6th CFA in rear of C Battery RHA.	
			Orders from A.D.M.S. that sick will be evac. to New Zealand S.H AMIENS. Infectious cases & self inflicted wounds to No 39 C.C.S. ALLONVILLE. [illegible]	
BUSSY-LES-DAOURS	14/9/16		Bgde marched as above. No 6 CFA. went into Bivouacs in X Area N of BUSSY.	
			M/148925 Pte Gyers of A.S.C. M.T. was transferred to No 8 CFA.	
"	"		Order recd from Bgd. H.Q. that Bgde will move tomorrow to a position of readiness S & W. of BONNAY. Starting point T Roads 200 yards N of T in VECQUEMONT Time 8 A.M. 6th CFA. in rear of 6th M Gun. Sq. After 11 AM. Bgd will be prepared to move S. of the River	

Instructions regarding War Diaries and Intelligence Summaries are contained in F. S. Regs., Part II. and the Staff Manual respectively. Title pages will be prepared in manuscript.

WAR DIARY

~~or~~

~~INTELLIGENCE~~ ~~SUMMARY~~.

(Erase heading not required.)

Army Form C. 2118

Place	Date	Hour	Summary of Events and Information	Remarks and references to Appendices
BUSSY LES DAOURS	14/9/16		at 1/2 an hours notice	
			Secret orders recd from ADMS.	
			1. 3rd Cav. Div. comes under orders of Cav. Corps midnight 13/14th Sept 1916.	
			2. Sick will be evac. in Div. Cars to No 1 NEW ZEALAND S.H. AMIENS.	
			3. List of possible C.C.S. given to which cases may be evacuated - according to circumstances.	
			4. Position of Advanced Depots Med Stores - & Mobile Laboratories given.	
			5. Cav Corps Hd Qrs. at DAOURS.	
			Memo (Secret) from ADMS recd.	
			1. During operations all references will be to 1/40000 Map 57.C.	
			2. West of Map 57C all references will be to the 1/100000 Sheet	
			Secret orders recd from ADMS as follows —	

WAR DIARY

or

INTELLIGENCE SUMMARY.

(*Erase heading not required.*)

Army Form C. 2118.

Instructions regarding War Diaries and Intelligence Summaries are contained in F. S. Regs., Part II. and the Staff Manual respectively. Title pages will be prepared in manuscript.

Place	Date	Hour	Summary of Events and Information	Remarks and references to Appendices
BUSSY LES DAOURS	14/9/16		1 Heavy Sect. of CFA will be divisionalised. 2. Each heavy Section i/c of an Officer RAMC will assemble with Tail of Column at + Roads 200 yards N of T in VECQUEMONT not before 10.5 AM. They will move under Command of Capt GALLOWAY, in rear of Ammunition Column to assembly area W.N.W. of LA NEUVILLE, where they will park & await further orders. 3 Motor Ambulances of Each CFA will assemble at Church at VECQUEMONT at 10.45 AM under Command of the Senior MT NCO, & await further orders from ADMS. SAH.	
W of BONNAY	15/9/16		Bgde moved as above to W. of BONNAY. Motor Ambulance with 1 Sergt & 5 O.R. MT ASC proceeded to be Divisionalised under A.D.M.S. B Echelons of 6th 7th & 8th CFA proceeded to be Divisionalised	

Instructions regarding War Diaries and Intelligence Summaries are contained in F. S. Regs., Part II. and the Staff Manual respectively. Title pages will be prepared in manuscript.

WAR DIARY
or
INTELLIGENCE SUMMARY.
(*Erase heading not required.*)

Army Form C. 2118.

Place	Date	Hour	Summary of Events and Information	Remarks and references to Appendices
N of BONNAY	15/9/16		under A.D.M.S. - i/c of Capt GALLOWAY	
			Wire recd from Bgde H.Q. that Bgde will bivouac tonight in its present position, & be prepared to move at 1/2 an hours notice from 8 A.M. 16/9/16.	
			One Motor Cyclist attached to A.D.M.S. for [illegible]	
			Lieut McCULLY rejoined unit from Camp [illegible]	
	16/9/16		12 O.R's under instructions from A.D.M.S. proceeded for Camp duty with Divisional working party	
			Sanitary instructions were issued to all units of Bgde by Major HAMMERTON S.M.O. of Bgde - whilst Bgde was in Camp.	
			1. Latrines dug at 3% strength of unit, away from Cook house, & screened. Sanitary orderlies to be constantly on duty.	
			2. Horse manure to be placed well away from Camp - & burnt, all refuse & tins to be burnt.	

T2134. Wt. W708-776. 500000. 4/15. Sir J. C. & S.

Army Form C. 2118.

Instructions regarding War Diaries and Intelligence Summaries are contained in F. S. Regs., Part II. and the Staff Manual respectively. Title pages will be prepared in manuscript.

WAR DIARY
~~or~~
~~INTELLIGENCE~~ SUMMARY.
(*Erase heading not required.*)

Place	Date	Hour	Summary of Events and Information	Remarks and references to Appendices
N. of BONNAY	16/9/16		3. All drinking water must be Chlorinated.	[initials]
"	17/9/16		Orders recd from Bgd H.Q. at 1 A.M. today that Bgd will move to fresh Bivouac area at S of PONT NOYELLE at 8 A.M.	[initials]
S. of PONT NOYELLE	17/9/16		Wire recd from Bgd. H.Q. that State of readiness is relaxed altogether.	
			Bgde as above ordered moved at 8 A.M. to area S of PONT NOYELLE & went into Bivouac there	[initials]
"	18/9/16		Sick will be evac. whilst in present area to NEW ZEALAND S.A. by Motor Amb. (Instruction from ADMS)	[initials]
"	18/9/16 to 21/9/16		General Routine. Weather has been constantly wet. Bivouac area bad - deep mud - & men constantly wet. Something has been done to relieve things by Bell Tents supplied by Brigade, but only a very small % can find cover from the wet except in Temp. Bivouacs made by themselves. No 6 Ct A were supplied with 2 Bell Tents.	

T.134. Wt. W708-776. 500000. 4/15. Sir J. C. & S.

Instructions regarding War Diaries and Intelligence Summaries are contained in F. S. Regs., Part II. and the Staff Manual respectively. Title pages will be prepared in manuscript.

WAR DIARY ~~or~~ ~~INTELLIGENCE SUMMARY.~~

(Erase heading not required.)

Army Form C. 2118

Place	Date	Hour	Summary of Events and Information	Remarks and references to Appendices
St Pont Noyelles	18/9/16 to	21/9/16	On 20/9/16 Capt WILLEY proceeded on temp duty as M.O. i/c Detail with Div. Working Party.	
			On 21/9/16 Capt LOVELL proceeded on temp duty with details of Div. Working Party, under instruction from A.D.M.S.	
			Cases admitted into Bg Hosp from 8th to 14th 9/16 36 of which were 5 Diarrhoea & 1 Scabies	
			Cases admitted into Bg Hp from 14 to 21st 9/16 31, of which were 9 Diarrhoea & 2 Scabies. SAH	
		21/9/16	Orders recd from Bgde. at 9pm. that Bgd. will march tomorrow Sept 22nd to Bivouac at SOUES - LONGPRE. (Ref. AMIENS. 1/100000). Place of assembly present Bivouac area. 6th CFA in rear of 6th M.G. Sqn. B. Echelons will be Divisionalised & billet night 22nd/23rd at St PIERRE a GOUY. Orders from ADMS, all sick to be evacuated to AMIENS. SAH	

T.134. Wt. W708-776. 500000. 4/15. Sir J. C. & S.

Instructions regarding War Diaries and Intelligence Summaries are contained in F. S. Regs., Part II. and the Staff Manual respectively. Title pages will be prepared in manuscript.

WAR DIARY

~~or~~

~~INTELLIGENCE SUMMARY.~~

(Erase heading not required.)

Army Form C. 2118.

Place	Date	Hour	Summary of Events and Information	Remarks and references to Appendices
SOUES	22/9/16		March carried out as in previous instructions. Brigade orders recd 9 P.M. that Bgde will march tomorrow 23/9/16 to Billeting area St ACHEUL - BACHIMONT. Place & time of assembly - Farm 1000 yds S of O in HANGEST SUR SOMME - 9.45 AM. 6th CFA in rear of C Batt. RHA (Ref. Map. LENS. 1/100000)	SAH
DRUCAS (WAVAN)	23/9/16		March carried out as above, 6th CFA. went into Billets at DRUCAT. (WAVANS). Orders recd from ADMS. Sick will be evac. to HESDIN. No 20 F.A. (LENS 1/100000). Orders recd from Bgd - that Bgde will move to new billeting area North of AUTHIE RIVER from RAYE SUR AUTHIE to LA HOUSSOYE. Starting point Y roads 600 yds East of Y in LANNOY. Time 7 AM. 6 CFA in rear of 6th D. G. Squad. B Echelons will march in rear of Bgde. SAH	

T. 134. Wt. W708-776. 500000. 4/15. Sir J. C. & S.

Instructions regarding War Diaries and Intelligence Summaries are contained in F. S. Regs., Part II. and the Staff Manual respectively. Title pages will be prepared in manuscript.

WAR DIARY
~~or~~
~~INTELLIGENCE SUMMARY.~~
(Erase heading not required.)

Army Form C. 2118.

Place	Date	Hour	Summary of Events and Information	Remarks and references to Appendices
DOURIEZ	24/9/16		Brigade marched as above, & went into Billets at DOURIEZ (ABBEVILLE 14 / 1/100000). G.H.	
"	25/9/16		Capt WILEY & Capt LOVELL returned to No 6 C.F.A. from temp. duty with Divisional Working Party. G.H.	
"	27/9/16		Major G.H.L. HAMMERTON - O.C. of 6th C.F.A. left this unit to take over Command of 69th F.A.	
			Lieut. P.A. McCULLUM proceeded to 3rd D.G.s for temp. duty during absence of CAPT ROWN - on leave. G.H.	
"	28/9/16 - 29/9/16		General Routine G.H.	
"	29/9/16		Orders recd from Bgde that 6 C.F.A. will move tomorrow to new Billeting area at RANG DE FLIERS. (ABBEVILLE 14/100000) The march to be made independently. G.H.	
RANG DE FLIERS	30/9/16		6th C.F.A marched as above, & went into Billets at RANG DE FLIERS.	
			Orders from AD.M.S. to Evac. Sick to ETAPLES.	

T.2134. Wt. W708-776. 500000. 4/15. Sir J. C. & S.

Instructions regarding War Diaries and Intelligence Summaries are contained in F. S. Regs., Part II. and the Staff Manual respectively. Title pages will be prepared in manuscript.

WAR DIARY

or

~~INTELLIGENCE SUMMARY.~~

(*Erase heading not required.*)

Army Form C. 2118.

Place	Date	Hour	Summary of Events and Information	Remarks and references to Appendices
RANGE DE FLIERS	30/9/16		CAPT. C F G T HEAP appointed to Command of 6th C F A - vice Major E H L HAMMERTON - to 6th F.A. (Auth. A.D.M.S. Z 1902/2/d 30/9/16) to date from 28th/9/16	
			Bgd. Hosp. opened. Arrangements for treatment of Cases of Scabies - & Diarrhoea in the Bgd made	
			Arrangements for treatment of Dental Cases made	
			Cases admitted into Bgde Hosp from 23rd to 30th incl. 48 - of which 9 were Scabies & 14 Diarrhoea.	
			Cases admitted into Bgde H.P. during Sept 1916 153 - of which 17 were Scabies & 40 were diarrhoea	G.H.
			G H Heap Capt O.C. 6th C F A.	

T.134. Wt. W708-776. 500000. 4/15. Sir J. C. & S.

6th Cav. Field Ambulance

Oct 1916.

Vol 22

WAR DIARY

of

No. 6 Cavalry Field Ambulance

October 1916

Instructions regarding War Diaries and Intelligence Summaries are contained in F. S. Regs., Part II. and the Staff Manual respectively. Title pages will be prepared in manuscript.

WAR DIARY
or
INTELLIGENCE SUMMARY.
(Erase heading not required.)

Army Form C. 2118.

Place	Date	Hour	Summary of Events and Information	Remarks and references to Appendices
RANG du FLIERS	2/10/16	10.15 PM	Clock put back at 1 AM to midnight	
			No 1143 Pte CARNES. J R.A.M.C transferred to No 7 C.F.A A.W.	
"	3/10/16	3 [illegible]	Lieut CLARKE, A.H R.A.M.C T.C. arrived for duty with unit A.W.	
"	4/10/16		Foden disinfector placed at disposal of 6th C.F.A. All blankets belonging to the unit and hospital disinfected, also all blankets and kit of scabies patients A.W.	
"	5/10/16		No M/07831 CLAYTON. A Pte A.S.C. M.T. returned from temporary duty with A.D.M.S 3rd Cav Div. A.W.	
"	7/10/16		Capt R. MARSHALL. R.A.M.C m.o i/c N.S.Y evacuated to the Duchess of Westminster's hospital	
	"		Capt E.R. LOVELL proceeded for temporary duty with N.S.Y vice Capt MARSHALL	
	"		Patients admitted into 6th C.F.A hospital from Oct 1st to Oct 7th were 33 of which 3 were suffering from diarrhoea and 3 were scabies A.W.	

T.134. Wt. W708–776. 500000. 4/15. Sir J. C. & S.

Instructions regarding War Diaries and Intelligence Summaries are contained in F. S. Regs., Part II. and the Staff Manual respectively. Title pages will be prepared in manuscript.

WAR DIARY
or
INTELLIGENCE SUMMARY.
(Erase heading not required.)

Army Form C. 2118.

Place	Date	Hour	Summary of Events and Information	Remarks and references to Appendices
RANG du FLIERS	9/10/16	10.15 AM	2 L.D. horses reinforcements received	
			18 dental cases collected from Brigade taken to No 6 Con. Depot ETAPLES for treatment	
	9/10/16		Motor ambulance No A1542 Sunbeam sent to workshops 3rd Cav Div for repairs	
〃	〃		Lieut A. NEILSON RAMC T.C arrived for duty with the unit	
	10/10/16		12 dental cases collected from Brigade taken to No 6 Con Depot ETAPLES for treatment AW.	
〃	14/10/16	10.45	Lieut P.A. McCALLUM returned from temporary duty as M O i/c 3rd D.G.	
	〃	〃	Number of patients admitted to C.F.A. hospital from Oct 8th to Oct 14 was 25 including Scabies 3; Diarrhoea 2 AW.	
	16/10/16		12 Dental cases collected from Brigade and taken to No 6 Convalescent Depot ETAPLES for treatment AW	

Instructions regarding War Diaries and Intelligence Summaries are contained in F. S. Regs., Part II. and the Staff Manual respectively. Title pages will be prepared in manuscript.

WAR DIARY
or
INTELLIGENCE SUMMARY.
(Erase heading not required.)

Army Form C. 2118.

Place	Date	Hour	Summary of Events and Information	Remarks and references to Appendices
RANG du FLIERS	17/10/16	11 AM	No 1372 Sgt E. MEIGH, R.A.M.C. T.F. proceeded to ENGLAND, for training in Cadet Unit. A.N.	
"	19/10/16		No 57792 L/Cpl DAVEY, E.C R.A.M.C appointed to the rank of acting sergeant with pay from the 17th inst vice Sgt MEIGH. authy D.G.M.S Cir memo No 14 para 2(a) d/4/10/15 + A.D.M.S 21971 d/18/10/16 A.N.	
MERLIMONT PLAGE	21/10/16		Under instructions from Headquarters 6th C.B (L140 d/20/10/16) the unit moved to new billeting area at MERLIMONT PLAGE departing from RANG du FLIERS at 10 AM, and marched independently. Arrived at MERLIMONT. PLAGE at 11.30	
			Patients admitted to 6th C.F.A Hospital from Oct 15th to Oct 21st – 33 which included 2 cases of Scabies and 6 of Diarrhoea A.N.	
"	26/10/16	10.45 am	Lieut A. H. CLARKE R.A.M.C proceeded for temporary duty as M.O. i/c charge of 3rd Cavalry Division Supply column A.N.	
"	27/10/16	-	Lieut A. NEILSON. R.A.M.C granted leave to SCOTLAND from 28/10/16 to 1/11/16 A.N.	

T2134. Wt. W708–776. 500000. 4/15. Sir J. C. & S.

Instructions regarding War Diaries and Intelligence Summaries are contained in F. S. Regs., Part II. and the Staff Manual respectively. Title pages will be prepared in manuscript.

WAR DIARY
or
INTELLIGENCE SUMMARY.
(Erase heading not required.)

Army Form C. 2118.

Place	Date	Hour	Summary of Events and Information	Remarks and references to Appendices
MERLIMONT PLAGE	28/10/16	11 AM	Pte (a/cpl) R. MOORE. R.A.M.C T.F. proceeds for duty with the ARTIST'S RIFLES subsequently to take a course at the Cadet School ETAPLES on the 27/11/16 (Authy AG No A/18393; A.D.M.S 21917 26/10/16) A.H.	
"	30/10/16		Capt E. R. LOVELL R.A.M.C S.R. returned from temporary duty as M.O. i/c NORTH SOMERSET, YEOMANRY on the return of Capt MARSHALL from leave	
			Admissions to 6th C.F.A hospital from Oct 22nd to Oct 31st inclusive - General 25, Scabies 10, Diarrhoea 4 } total 39	
			Total admissions for the month of October were 130 A.H.	

P. A. Heap Capt.

OFFICER COMMANDING
Nº 6 CAVALRY FIELD AMBULANCE.

T2134. Wt. W708-776. 500000. 4/15. Sir J. C. & S.

Nov. 1916

3rd Cav. Div

140/1849

Vol 23

WAR DIARY

of

No 6 Cavalry Field Ambulance

for the month of

November 1916

Instructions regarding War Diaries and Intelligence Summaries are contained in F. S. Regs., Part II. and the Staff Manual respectively. Title pages will be prepared in manuscript.

WAR DIARY
or
INTELLIGENCE SUMMARY.
(Erase heading not required.)

Army Form C. 2118.

Place	Date	Hour	Summary of Events and Information	Remarks and references to Appendices
MERLIMONT PLAGE	1/11/16	11.AM.	General routine AW	
"	4/11/16		No M2/021959 Pte LYNNE H.L. proceeded to No 8 C.F.A. with motor ambulance No 9393 "NAPIER" for temporary duty AW.	
	5/11/16		General routine AW.	
	6/11/16		General routine AW.	
	7/11/16		No 1485 Cpl EDWARDS. E.G. R.A.M.C T.F. evacuated to No 26 General Hospital	
	"		No 44225 Pte CLACY G.A. RAMC proceeded to R.E. 3rd Field Squadron for duty and is taken off the strength accordingly.	
	"		Admissions to hospital for week ending Nov 7th — 19 AW.	
	9/11/16		No 1569 L/cpl GOODMAN S.F. R.A.M.C T.F. arrived for duty from No 34 C.C.S AW.	
	11/11/16		No 1254 Pte BROMILOW, T. R.A.M.C T.F. evacuated to No 26 General Hospital	
	"		One L.D. horse reinforcement arrived	
	"		Inspection of Divisional Rest Station by MAJOR-General J. VAUGHAN, C.B. D.S.O	
	"		Stabling for the horses is in the process of erection, in the mean time, most of the horses are picketted in the open AW.	

T.134. Wt. W708-776. 500000. 4/15. Sir J. C. & S.

Instructions regarding War Diaries and Intelligence Summaries are contained in F. S. Regs., Part II. and the Staff Manual respectively. Title pages will be prepared in manuscript.

WAR DIARY
or
INTELLIGENCE SUMMARY.
(Erase heading not required.)

Army Form C. 2118.

Place	Date	Hour	Summary of Events and Information	Remarks and references to Appendices
MERLIMONT PLAGE	12th/11/16	11.30AM	General routine AN.	
	13th/11/16	"	General routine	
"	14th/11/16		Capt S.R. LOVELL, R.A.M.C granted leave to ENGLAND from Nov 14th to Nov 21st AN	
	"		Lieut A NEILSON R.A.M.C. T.C promoted to the rank of Captain (London Gazette 18/10/16)	
	"		No T/20690 C/Sgt HALLAM. R A.S.C H.T. was awarded the military medal for bravery in the field (London Gazette 9/11/16)	
	"		Admissions to hospital for week ending November 14th were 44 of which cases 1 was diarrhoea and nine (9) were scabies AN.	
			Patients admitted to the Divisional Rest Station for week ending Nov 14th 57 of which 14 were scabies and 3 were diarrhoea AN.	
	15/11/16		No 1539 L/Cpl GOODMAN S.F R.A.M.C. T.F. proceeded to 98th Field Ambulance for duty (authy C.R. 3379/MC. d/14/11/16) AN.	
	16/11/16		General routine AN.	

T.134. Wt. W708-776. 500000. 4/15. Sir J. C. & S.

Instructions regarding War Diaries and Intelligence Summaries are contained in F. S. Regs., Part II. and the Staff Manual respectively. Title pages will be prepared in manuscript.

WAR DIARY
or
INTELLIGENCE SUMMARY.
(Erase heading not required.)

Army Form C. 2118.

Place	Date	Hour	Summary of Events and Information	Remarks and references to Appendices
MERLIMONT PLAGE				
	17/11/16	1 P.M.	The following men arrived for duty and are taken on the strength accordingly	
			No 65253 Pte JACOBS. J. R.A.M.C.	
			No 88504 " JOYNT. E. R.A.M.C	
			No 88623 " JEBBETT, A.C. R.A.M.C AM.	
	18/11/16		General routine AM.	
	19/11/16		General routine AM.	
	20/11/16		CAPT. E. F. HEAP R.A.M.C proceeded on leave to England for a fortnight	AM.
	"		The field ambulance and Divisional Rest Station were inspected by D.D.M.S Cavalry Corps AM	
	21/11/16		Under instructions from A.D.M.S 3rd Cav Div a party of twelve (12) other ranks proceeded for temporary duty with the 7th Pioneer Battalion	AM
			Patients admitted to Divisional Rest Station for week ending Nov 21st were 64, of which 14 were scabies and 2 diarrhoea	
			Of these 64 cases 36 were from the 6th Cavalry Brigade of which 11 were scabies and 2 diarrhoea AM.	
	22/11/16		General routine AM.	

T.134. Wt. W708-776. 500000. 4/15. Sir J. C. & S.

Instructions regarding War Diaries and Intelligence Summaries are contained in F. S. Regs., Part II. and the Staff Manual respectively. Title pages will be prepared in manuscript.

WAR DIARY
or
INTELLIGENCE SUMMARY.
(Erase heading not required.)

Army Form C. [illegible]118.

Place	Date	Hour	Summary of Events and Information	Remarks and references to Appendices
MERLIMONT PLAGE	23/11/16	10.30am	General routine AH	
	24/11/16		General routine AH	
	25/11/16		No M1/09371 Pte W. KERSHAW, A.S.C. M.T. proceeded with motor ambulance No 1111 for temporary duty with A.D.M.S 3rd Cav Div AH.	
	26/11/16		No 1462 Pte T.H. OLIVER RAMC T.F. whilst on leave to England was admitted to the 1st WESTERN GENERAL H. LIVERPOOL AH.	
	27/11/16		General routine AH	
	29/11/16		General routine AH	
	30/11/16		The number of cases admitted to the Divisional Rest Station from Nov 22nd to 30th was 71 of which 12 were scabies + 2 diarrhoea, of this 71 39 were from the 6th Cav Brigade of which 4 were scabies and 1 diarrhoea. Total number of cases admitted to hospital from 6th Cav Brigade were 138 of which 4 were diarrhoea + 24 were scabies. Total admission to the Divisional Rest Station from Nov 10th to Nov 30th were 186 of which 40 were scabies & 7 were diarrhoea AH	

G A Heap Capt.
OFFICER COMMANDING
No 6 CAVALRY FIELD AMBULANCE

T.134. Wt. W708–776. 500000. 4/15. Sir J. C. & S.

Dec 1916

3rd Cav Div

140/1900

Vol 24

WAR DIARY

of

6th Cav: Field Ambulance

December 1916

Instructions regarding War Diaries and Intelligence Summaries are contained in F. S. Regs., Part II. and the Staff Manual respectively. Title pages will be prepared in manuscript.

WAR DIARY
or
INTELLIGENCE SUMMARY.
(*Erase heading not required.*)

Army Form C. 2118.

Place	Date	Hour	Summary of Events and Information	Remarks and references to Appendices.
MERLIMONT PLAGE	Dec 1st 1916	10 AM	No 88395 Pte HUTTON, J R.A.M.C arrived for duty and was taken on the strength accordingly [illegible]	
"	Dec 2-7		General routine. [illegible]	
"	Dec 8th		Number of cases from 6th Cav Brigade admitted to the D.R.S for week ending Dec 7th 1916 was 31 of which 2 were diarrhoea cases	
"			Total admissions to Divisional Rest Station for week ending Dec 8th were 69 of which 8 were scabies and 6 diarrhoea	
"	"		No 79894 Pte TAYLOR, J R.A.M.C arrived for duty from No 7 C.F.A and was taken on the strength accordingly [illegible]	
"	Dec 9th		General routine [illegible]	
	10/12/16		General routine [illegible]	
"	11/12/16		Capt A. WILEY R.A.M.C granted leave of absence to Ireland from Dec 1st to Dec 21st [illegible]	
"	12/12/16		General routine	
	14/12/16		Under instructions from A.D.M.S 3rd Cav Div, one officer (Capt E.R. LOVELL) and 12 O.Rs proceeded for temporary duty with the 7th PIONEER BATTALION in relief of one officer (7th C.F.A) and 12 O.Rs (6th C.F.A) [illegible]	

Instructions regarding War Diaries and Intelligence Summaries are contained in F. S. Regs., Part II. and the Staff Manual respectively. Title pages will be prepared in manuscript.

Army Form C. 2118.

WAR DIARY
or
INTELLIGENCE SUMMARY.
(Erase heading not required.)

Place	Date	Hour	Summary of Events and Information	Remarks and references to Appendices
MERLIMONT PLAGE	15/12/16	4.30pm	12 O.R returned from temporary duty with the 7th Pioneer Battalion	
〃	〃		No 1539 Dr L R ADAMS, RAMC H.T was evacuated to No 23 General H and is taken off the strength	
	〃		Number of cases from 6th Cav Brigade admitted to D.R.S for week ending Dec 14th was 18 of which one (1) was scabies	
			Total admissions to D.R.S for week ending Dec 14th was 31 of which two (2) were scabies AM.	
〃	16/12/16		No M2/031959 Pte H.L. LYNNE A.S.C M.T. with motor ambulance No 9393 returned from temporary duty with 8th C.F.A AM	
	18/12/16		General routine AM	
〃	19/12/16		No M1/09371 Pte KERSHAW A.S.C M.T. with motor ambulance No 1111 returned from temporary duty with A.D.M.S 3rd Cav Div AM.	
〃	20/12/16		No 1545 S/Sgt BURROWS A.E. RAMC T.F. proceeded to England preparatory to taking a temporary commission in the infantry under instruction from 6th Cav Brigade L388/2d/18/12/16 AM.	

Instructions regarding War Diaries and Intelligence Summaries are contained in F. S. Regs., Part II. and the Staff Manual respectively. Title pages will be prepared in manuscript.

WAR DIARY
or
INTELLIGENCE SUMMARY.
(Erase heading not required.)

Army Form C. 2118.

Place	Date	Hour	Summary of Events and Information	Remarks and references to Appendices
MERLIMONT PLAGE	20/12/16		Capt. A. NEILSON RAMC and No 958 Sgt G.L. McARTHUR RAMC proceeded for temporary duty with the 6th Pioneer Battalion AN.	
"	21/12/16		General routine AN	
HESMOND	22/12/16		Under instructions from H.Q. 6th Cav Brigade the unit moved into the new billeting area at HESMOND, having handed over the D.R.S and billets to No 8 C.F.A	
	"		Number of cases from 6th Cav Brigade for week ending Dec 21st was 27 of which 3 were scabies AN	
"	24/12/16		General routine AN.	
	26/12/16		One light ambulance, 2 horses, 1 driver and 1 orderly were attached to the 1st Royal Dragoons and 3rd Dragoon Guards for the collection of sick.	
			No 53076 Pte W. NEWTON RAMC and No M1/07831 Pte D.R. CLAYTON A.S.C M.T. proceeded for temporary duty with the A.D.M.S 3rd Cav Div AN.	

Instructions regarding War Diaries and Intelligence Summaries are contained in F. S. Regs., Part II. and the Staff Manual respectively. Title pages will be prepared in manuscript.

WAR DIARY
or
INTELLIGENCE SUMMARY.
(Erase heading not required.)

Army Form C. 2118.

Place	Date	Hour	Summary of Events and Information	Remarks and references to Appendices
HESMOND				
	26/12/16		No 8809 Pte SCHOFIELD, H. R.A.M.C. proceeded to England preparatory to taking a temporary commission in the infantry under instructions from 6th Cav. Brigade L/388/4 d/26/12/16 AH	
"	28/12/16		Lieut P. A. McCALLUM, R.A.M.C. granted leave to Scotland from 29/12/16 to 8/1/17 AH	
"	30/12/16		General routine AH.	
"	31/12/16		Number of cases admitted to Hospital from the 6th Cav Brigade from Dec 22nd to Dec 31st was sixteen (16) of which two (2) were scabies and two (2) were diarrhoea	
"			Total number of cases admitted to hospital from 6th Cav Brigade for the month of December was ninety two (92) of which four (4) were diarrhoea and six (6) were scabies AH.	

E. A. Heap Capt.

OFFICER COMMANDING
No 6 CAVALRY FIELD AMBULANCE.

Jan. 1917

3rd Cav Div

140/947

Vol 25

Diary of

6th Cav. Field Ambulance

January 1917

Instructions regarding War Diaries and Intelligence Summaries are contained in F. S. Regs., Part II. and the Staff Manual respectively. Title pages will be prepared in manuscript.

WAR DIARY
or
INTELLIGENCE SUMMARY.
(Erase heading not required.)

Army Form C. 2118.

Place	Date	Hour	Summary of Events and Information	Remarks and references to Appendices
HESMOND				
	1/1/17	10.30am	No 43838 Pte J. CORE R.A.M.C was evacuated to No 4 Casualty Clearing Station on the 26/12/16 whilst on temporary duty with the 7th Pioneer Battalion	AW.
"	2/1/17		Lieut A H. CLARKE returned from temporary duty with 4th Brigade Royal Horse Artillery Ammunition Column AW.	
"	3/1/17		Pte CLAYTON D.R. (No M/07231 A.S.C. M.T.) returned from temporary duty with A.D.M.S 3rd Cav Div AW.	
"	5/1/17		General routine AW.	
"	6/1/17		No 47952 Pte W. J. GRIGGLESTON, R.A.M.C proceeded to 4th Brigade R.H.A Ammunition Column in relief of No 1409 Pte S. PIMBLETT who rejoined this unit.	
	"		No 55016 Pte ROBERTSON D M R.A.M.C proceeded to 13th Course School of Cookery St POL for three (3) weeks training AW.	
"	7/1/17		No 1006 Sgt A. SANDHAM proceeded to 3rd Cav Div ANTI-GAS School for five (5) days instruction	
	"		Patients admitted into hospital for week ending Jan 7th were ten (10) of which one was scabies AW.	

T.134. Wt. W708-776. 500000. 4/15. Sir J. C. & S.

Instructions regarding War Diaries and Intelligence Summaries are contained in F. S. Regs., Part II. and the Staff Manual respectively. Title pages will be prepared in manuscript.

WAR DIARY
or
INTELLIGENCE SUMMARY.
(Erase heading not required.)

Army Form C. 2118.

Place	Date	Hour	Summary of Events and Information	Remarks and references to Appendices
HESMOND	8/1/17		No 1462 Pte T.H. OLIVER R.A.M.C arrived for duty with this unit	
			No 20289 Pte F. GRIFFITHS R.A.M.C was evacuated to No 51 Gen H. A.M.	
"	9/1/17		Lieut P.A. McCALLUM R.A.M.C returned from leave of absence to Scotland A.M.	
"	10/1/17		General routine A.M.	
	11/1/17		Lieut P.A. McCALLUM R.A.M.C proceed to 1st R Dr for temporary duty during the absence on leave of CAPT. I.M. GRANT R.A.M.C	
"	–		No 394 Pte EXELBY T. R.A.M.C and No 70390 Pte EVANS W.W. arrived for duty A.M.	
	–		No 10000 Pte ANDERSON, C R.A.M.C whilst on temporary duty with the 7th Pioneer Battalion was evacuated to No 4 C.C.S on the 20/12/16 and this day rejoined the unit as a reinforcement A.M.	
"	12/1/17		General routine	
			Patients admitted into hospital for week ending Jan 14th were 14 of which five (5) were scabies A.M.	
	14/1/17		General routine A.M.	

T.134. Wt. W708–776. 500000. 4/15. Sir J. C. & S.

Instructions regarding War Diaries and Intelligence Summaries are contained in F. S. Regs., Part II. and the Staff Manual respectively. Title pages will be prepared in manuscript.

WAR DIARY
or
INTELLIGENCE SUMMARY.
(Erase heading not required.)

Army Form C. 2118.

Place	Date	Hour	Summary of Events and Information	Remarks and references to Appendices
HESMOND	17/1/17		The O.C. A.S.C inspected the transport of the unit at BEAURAINVILLE and later wrote expressing his thorough satisfaction with the same in every way	
"	"		Lieut A.H. CLARKE proceeded for duty with the 6th Pioneer Battalion in relief of Capt A. NEILSON A.N.	
"	18/1/17		Capt H. DUNKERLEY R.A.M.C arrived for duty and was taken on the strength accordingly A.N.	
"	19/1/17		No 1485 Cpl EDWARDS P.G R.A.M.C arrived for duty A.N.	
	20/1/17		Capt A. NEILSON returned from temporary duty with the 6th Pioneer Battalion A.N.	
	21/1/17		The number of patients admitted to hospital for weekending Jan 21st was nine (9) of which three (3) were scabies A.N.	
	22/1/17		Cpl J. QUINN R.A.M.C proceeded to 3rd Cav Div anti-gas school for five (5) days course of instructions	
	"		Capt A. NEILSON R.A.M.C proceeded to the Corps gas school for instruction A.N.	

Instructions regarding War Diaries and Intelligence Summaries are contained in F. S. Regs., Part II. and the Staff Manual respectively. Title pages will be prepared in manuscript.

WAR DIARY
or
INTELLIGENCE SUMMARY.
(Erase heading not required.)

Army Form C. 2118.

Place	Date	Hour	Summary of Events and Information	Remarks and references to Appendices
HESMOND	23/1/17		No 53076 Pte NEWTON. W. RAMC was transferred to the A.D.M.S. Office A.W.	
"	24/1/17		A.D.M.S. 3rd Cav Div inspected the ambulance	
"			No. M1/5246 Cpl FLEET, G A.S.C. M.T. was awarded the military medal (London Gazette 23/1/17) A.W.	
	25/1/17		Capt F.P. HEAP RAMC proceed on leave to England from Jan 26th to Feb 5th.	
			During the absence of Capt HEAP on leave, Capt A. WILEY assumed command of the ambulance A.W.	
	"		No 43838 Pte J. CORE RAMC & No 90215 Pte R. STRAITON, RAMC arrived for duty A.W.	
	27/1/17		Lieut P.A. McCALLUM returned from duty as MO i/c 1st R Ds	
	28/1/17		General routine A.W.	
	31/1/17		Patients admitted into hospital from Jan 22nd to 31st numbered 18 of which 3 were scabies	
			Total number of patients admitted during the month was 51 of which 12 were scabies A.W.	

F.A. Heap Capt.
OFFICER COMMANDING
No 6 CAVALRY FIELD AMBULANCE.

2353 Wt. W2544/1454 700,000 5/15 D. D. & L. A.D.S.S./Forms/C. 2118.

Mar. 1917

240/2086

Vol 27

WAR DIARY

of

6th Cav. Field Ambulance

MARCH 1917

Army Form C. 2118.

Instructions regarding War Diaries and Intelligence Summaries are contained in F. S. Regs., Part II. and the Staff Manual respectively. Title pages will be prepared in manuscript.

WAR DIARY
or
INTELLIGENCE SUMMARY.

(Erase heading not required.)

Place	Date	Hour	Summary of Events and Information	Remarks and references to Appendices
HESMOND	1.3.14		Lieut P.A. McCALLUM RAMC. TC. was granted leave of absence to SCOTLAND from March 1st to 14th upon completion + renewal of contract SRL.	
"	3.3.14		General Routine SRL.	
	5.3.14		Capt E.R. LOVELL R.AMC. SR. was granted special leave of absence to England from March 5th to 15th SRL.	
	6.3.14		Capt A. WILEY RAMC. TC. proceeded to LONDON. ENGLAND to report to the War Office upon completion of his contract and was taken off the strength accordingly SRL	
	7.3.14		Patients admitted to hospital for week ending March 7th 19 (nineteen) of which 9 (nine) were scabies SRL	
	9.3.14		General routine SRL.	
	11.3.14		Capt H.V. FITZGERALD RAMC TC. arrived for duty and was taken on the strength accordingly.	
			Capt H. DUNKERLEY RAMC. TC. returned from temporary duty with D.D.M.S. CAV CORPS. SRL	
	12.3.14		General routine SRL.	

2353 Wt. W2544/1454 700,000 5/15 D. D. & L. A.D.S.S./Forms/C. 2118.

Army Form C. 2118.

WAR DIARY
or
INTELLIGENCE SUMMARY.
(*Erase heading not required.*)

Instructions regarding War Diaries and Intelligence Summaries are contained in F. S. Regs., Part II. and the Staff Manual respectively. Title pages will be prepared in manuscript.

Place	Date	Hour	Summary of Events and Information	Remarks and references to Appendices
HESMOND	14.3.17		Patients admitted to hospital for week ending March 14th 20 (twenty) of which 10 (ten) were Scabies	
			Capt H DUNKERLEY RAMC. TC. proceeded to Divisional Gas School for a course of instruction ERL.	
	15.3.17		Lieut A. CLARKE. RAMC TC and 6 (six) O.R's returned from temporary duty with the 6th PIANEER BATTALION	
			CAPT. E. R. LOVELL, RAMC. SR. returned from leave of absence to ENGLAND ERL.	
	16.3.17		No T4/35439 Dr. ASHADOWN E ASC with one (1) light ambulance proceeded to 4th C.F.A. for temporary duty in relief of No T1/S.R/405 Dr GAMBLE. H. ASC who rejoined the unit today	
			~~CAPT~~ ERL LIEUT. P. A. McCALLUM returned from leave of absence to SCOTLAND ERL.	
	19.3.17		CAPT. H. DUNKERLEY. RAMC TC. returned from a course of instruction at the Divisional Gas School. ERL.	
	ERL ~~[illegible]~~		CAPT H DUNKERLEY RAMC. TC. proceeded to the NORTH SOMERSET YEOMANRY	

2353 Wt. W2544/1454 700,000 5/15 D. D. & L. A.D.S.S./Forms/C. 2118.

Instructions regarding War Diaries and Intelligence Summaries are contained in F. S. Regs., Part II. and the Staff Manual respectively. Title pages will be prepared in manuscript.

WAR DIARY
or
INTELLIGENCE SUMMARY.
(Erase heading not required.)

Army Form C. 2118.

Place	Date	Hour	Summary of Events and Information	Remarks and references to Appendices
HESMOND	17.3.17 (cont)		as Medical Officer in charge and was taken off the strength accordingly ERL.	
	19.3.17		CAPT. A NEILSON RAMC.TC. proceeded to 3rd DRAGOON GUARDS as temporary M.O. i/c during the absence of CAPT. H.A. RONN RAMC.TC through sickness	
			No 958 Sgt G.L. McARTHUR RAMC.TF proceeded to 'C' Battery RHA to give a three days course of instruction in stretcher bearing and first aid to the stretcher bearers of this unit ERL	
	20.3.17		General routine ERL	
	21.3.17		Patients admitted to H week ending 21.3.17. 17 (Seventeen) of which 5 (five) were Scabies ERL	
	22.3.17		T/35439 Dr ASHDOWN F. A.S.C. H.T. + 2 (two) horses with a light ambulance returned from temporary duty with the 7th CFA ERL	
	23.3.17		General routine ERL	
	24.3.17		At 11.0 p.m. the time was advanced 1 (one) hour ERL	
	25.3.17		General routine ERL.	

Army Form C. 2118.

Instructions regarding War Diaries and Intelligence Summaries are contained in F. S. Regs., Part II. and the Staff Manual respectively. Title pages will be prepared in manuscript.

WAR DIARY
or
INTELLIGENCE SUMMARY.
(Erase heading not required.)

Place	Date	Hour	Summary of Events and Information	Remarks and references to Appendices
HESMOND	24.3.14		No M2/103145 Pte MOSES G. ASC. MT. with motor ambulance No 9393 proceeded to 8th CFA for temporary duty	
			LIEUT. P.A. McCALLUM, RAMC. TC. promoted to the rank of temporary Captain. London Gazette March 24th 1914 (as from March 4th 1914)	ERL
			CAPT. A. NEILSON, RAMC. TC. returned from temporary duty with 3rd DGs.	ERL
	28.3.14		CAPT A NEILSON. RAMC. TC and No 45210 PTE. BELL. J. RAMC (batman) proceeded to join the 3rd CAV. DIV. DISMOUNTED BATTALION for duty	ERL
	29.3.14		General routine	ERL
	31.3.14		No 20591 PTE. S. PIMBLETT. RAMC. TF proceeded to 3rd Cav. Div. Supply Column for duty in relief of No 1040 PTE J DAVIES RAMC. TF. two taken off the strength, PTE DAVIES being taken on the strength	ERL
			Patients admitted to HP from March 22nd – 31st 35 (thirty five) of which 12 (twelve) were scabies	
			Total admissions to the HP during the month 91 (ninety one) of which 36 (thirty six) were Scabies. 5 (five) scabies were from	

Instructions regarding War Diaries and Intelligence Summaries are contained in F. S. Regs., Part II. and the Staff Manual respectively. Title pages will be prepared in manuscript.

WAR DIARY
or
INTELLIGENCE SUMMARY.
(Erase heading not required.)

Army Form C. 2118.

Place	Date	Hour	Summary of Events and Information	Remarks and references to Appendices
HESMOND	31.3.17 (Cont)		G Battery RHA + 2 (two) from Aux Horse Transport During the month the personnel have been equipped + fitted with the small box respirator and frequent lectures + drills in the use of these have been given GRL.	
			C A Heap Capt OFFICER COMMANDING No 6 CAVALRY FIELD AMBULANCE.	

T2134. Wt. W708–776. 500000. 4/15. Sir J. C. & S.

Feb. 1917

3rd Cav. Div.

140/2042. Vol 2 ~~1~~ 6

WAR DIARY

of

No 6 Cavalry Field Ambulance

February 1917

Instructions regarding War Diaries and Intelligence Summaries are contained in F. S. Regs., Part II. and the Staff Manual respectively. Title pages will be prepared in manuscript.

WAR DIARY
or
INTELLIGENCE SUMMARY.
(Erase heading not required.)

Army Form C. 2118.

Place	Date	Hour	Summary of Events and Information	Remarks and references to Appendices
HESMOND	1/2/17	10 AM	Capt A. NEILSON, RAMC proceeded for temporary duty with the 3rd D.G. during the absence of Capt H. RONN on leave AM	
"	3/2/17		General routine AM.	
"	5/2/17		General routine AM.	
"	6/2/17		Capt E.F. HEAP RAMC returned from leave of absence to England AM	
	7/2/17		One NCO and 5 privates RAMC proceeded to the 6th Pioneer Battalion for duty.	
"			No T4/108122 Wlr CHAPMAN, H.P. A.S.C proceeded to the 3rd Cav Div Wheelwrights Workshop for duty AM.	
"	8/2/17		General routine AM.	
	9/2/17		Capt E.R. LOVELL RAMC and two other ranks returned from temporary duty with the 7th Pioneer Battalion	
	"		No 958 Sgt G. McARTHUR, RAMC returned from temporary duty with the 6th Pioneer Battalion AM.	
	10/2/17		No T/21189 Dr GRIFFITHS, W A.S.C H.T. was evacuated to No 26 Gen H AM	
	11/2/17		General routine AM.	

2353 Wt. W2514/1454 700,000 5/15 D. D. & L. A.D.S.S./Forms/C. 2118.

Army Form C. 2118.

WAR DIARY
or
INTELLIGENCE SUMMARY.
(Erase heading not required.)

Instructions regarding War Diaries and Intelligence Summaries are contained in F. S. Regs., Part II. and the Staff Manual respectively. Title pages will be prepared in manuscript.

Place	Date	Hour	Summary of Events and Information	Remarks and references to Appendices
HESMOND	13/2/17		Capt A. NEILSON RAMC returned from temporary duty with the 3rd D.G.	AN
"	14/2/17		General routine Patients admitted into Hospital for week ending Feb 14th were (10) of which two (2) were scabies AN.	
"	15/2/17		General routine AN.	
"	17/2/17		No T/SR/705 Driver GAMBLE H. ASC with light ambulance & two (2) horses proceeded to No 7 Cav Field Ambulance for temporary duty AN.	
"	19/2/17		General routine AN.	
	20/2/17		Capt H. DUNKERLEY RAMC and No 1495 Pte HUGHES, W RAMC proceeded to the D.D.M.S Cav Corps for temporary duty AN.	
	21/2/17		Patients admitted to hospital for week ending February 21st were twelve (12) of which 1 was Scabies AN.	
	24/2/17		General routine AN	
	28/2/17		Lieut P.A. McCALLUM RAMC proceeded to Scotland on special leave	
	"		Patients admitted to hospital for week ending Feb 28th were 9 of which two were scabies Total admissions to hospital for the month were 41, of which 7 were scabies and 1 was diarrhoea AN	

G H Heap Capt

OFFICER COMMANDING
No 6 CAVALRY FIELD AMBULANCE.

2353 Wt. W2544/1454 700,000 5/15 D. D. & L. A.D.S.S./Forms/C. 2118.

April 1917

S

140/2086

Vol 2 8

WAR DIARY

of

No. 6 Cavalry Field Ambulance

for

APRIL 1917

B.E.F.

2

Summary of Medical War Diaries of

6th CAVALRY FIELD AMBULANCE

3rd Cav.Div., Cav.Corps,
3rd Army (from 8/4/17 till 13/5/17.

WESTERN FRONT 1917.

O.C. Captain E.F.G.T. Heap.

Summarised under the following heagings :

PHASE "B": BATTLE OF ARRAS, APRIL - MAY 1917.

1st Period - Attack on Vimy Ridge, April.

2nd Period - Capture of Siegfried Line, May.

6th CAV. F.A.,

WESTERN FRONT 1917.
April.

3rd Cav.Div., Cav.Corps, 3rd Army.
from 8/4/17.

O.C. Capt. E.F.G.T. Heap.

Phase "B": Battle of Arras, April - May 1917.

1st Period - Attack on Vimy Ridge, April.

H.Q. at VACQUERIE-LE-BOUCQ.

April

8th **Moves** To FOSSEUX.

9th **Evacuations** Wlkg. W. to Bastion Coll.Post, Arras.

L.D.W. & Stg. to Cave A.D.S., Arras, or nearest A.D.S.

Operations "Zero" 5.30 a.m.

Moves To ARRAS.

10th To Cross Roads by T. in HALTE, Arras-St.Pol Road, 4½ Kilos. from Arras.

To H.32.d.(51 B & C).

11th **Evacuation** 3 light Amb. Wagons proceeded along main Cambrai-Arras Road to 200 yds. West of Cross Roads, Feuchy Chapel by 5 p.m. After dusk W. cleared from line Monchy-le-Preux to Les Fosses Farm, and evacuated to Inf. D.Ss. All evacuated by 9 p.m.

12th **Moves** To ARRAS RACE-COURSE.

Moves Detachment Light Section to Bde. Fosseux.

15th **Moves** Heavy Section rejoined H.Q. Fosseux.

16th To LE BOISLE.

Casualties Admitted for week ended April 7th 34.

" " " " " 14th 78.

Casualties R.A.M.C. 0 & 1 Shell-shock, 0 & 1 W.

19th **Moves** To MAINTENAY.

Casualties Admitted for week ended April 21st 35.

20th/30th **Operations R.A.M.C.** Routine.

6th CAV. F.A.,

WESTERN FRONT 1917.
April.

3rd Cav.Div., Cav.Corps, 3rd Army.
from 8/4/17.

O.C. Capt. E.F.G.T. Heap.

Phase "B": Battle of Arras, April - May 1917.

1st Period - Attack on Vimy Ridge, April.

H.Q. at VACQUERIE-LE-BOUCQ.

April

8th Moves To FOSSEUX.

9th Evacuations Wlkg. W. to Bastion Coll.Post, Arras.

L.D.W. & Stg. to Cave A.D.S., Arras, or nearest A.D.S.

Operations "Zero" 5.30 a.m.

Moves To ARRAS.

10th To Cross Roads by T. in HALTE, Arras-St.Pol Road, 4½ Kilos. from Arras.

To H.32.d.(51 B & C).

11th Evacuation 3 light Amb. Wagons proceeded along main Cambrai-Arras Road to 200 yds. West of Cross Roads, Feuchy Chapel by 5 p.m. After dusk W. cleared from line Monchy-le-Preux to Les Fosses Farm, and evacuated to Inf. D.Ss. All evacuated by 9 p.m.

12th Moves To ARRAS RACE-COURSE.

Moves Detachment Light Section to Bde. Fosseux.

15th Moves Heavy Section rejoined H.Q. Fosseux.

16th To LE BOISLE.

Casualties Admitted for week ended April 7th 34.

" " " " " 14th 78.

Casualties R.A.M.C. 0 & 1 Shell-shock, 0 & 1 W.

19th Moves To MAINTENAY.

Casualties Admitted for week ended April 21st 35.

20th/30th Operations R.A.M.C. Routine.

Army Form C. 2118

Instructions regarding War Diaries and Intelligence Summaries are contained in F. S. Regs., Part II. and the Staff Manual respectively. Title Pages will be prepared in manuscript.

WAR DIARY
or
INTELLIGENCE SUMMARY
(Erase heading not required.)

Place	Date	Hour	Summary of Events and Information	Remarks and references to Appendices
HESMOND	1.4.17		General Routine ERL	
	2.4.17		Wire from 6th Cav Bde B.M.103 stated Bde will move into area PLUMOISON, BOUIN, AUBIN ST VAAST, ECQUEMICOURT, CONTES on Thursday April 5th further details follow tomorrow ERL	
	3.4.17		No M2/103175 Pte G MOSES ASC MT with M.A. 9393 returned from temporary duty with 8th CFA Wire from Bde SC/480 that billeting party would meet Staff Capt at BOUIN Church 10.30 am 4th April ERL	
	4.4.17		T4/108122 a/Cpl Whlr CHAPMAN ASC AT returned from temp'y duty with 3rd Cav Div Wheelers Workshop. Orders from Bde L488 that Brigade would concentrate by 12 noon on April 5th in area ECQUEMICOURT-CONTES-AUBIN ST. VAAST-Pt St. VAAST-BOUIN, PLUMOISON ~~Dismounted~~ ERL Heavy section of 6th CFA will accompany their unit 6th CFA will leave HESMOND at 9.45 am ROUTE - Level crossing 660 yards E of BEAURAINVILLE Stn - ECQUEMICOURT to billets at BOUIN to be east of MARESQUEL by 12 noon	

1875 Wt. W593/826 1,000,000 4/15 J.B.C. & A. A.D.S.S./Forms/C. 2118.

Instructions regarding War Diaries and Intelligence Summaries are contained in F. S. Regs., Part II. and the Staff Manual respectively. Title Pages will be prepared in manuscript.

WAR DIARY
or
INTELLIGENCE SUMMARY
(Erase heading not required.)

Army Form C. 2118

Place	Date	Hour	Summary of Events and Information	Remarks and references to Appendices
HESMOND	4.4.17 cont.	pm 4.30	Under instructions from ADMS dated 3/4/17 ~~the~~ dismounted men, strength 32 O R's (thirty two), under senior NCO reported to O.C. 3rd Cav. Div. Supply Colm. to proceed by lorries to concentration point on 5/4/17.	
			Wire from Bde L 488/1 that 6 CFA will be billeted in CONTES and not at BOUIN. 6th CFA will therefore march by HESMOND via Road junction at B in BEAURAINVILLE direct to CONTES starting at 9.45 am. (Ref. Map LENS 1/100,000)	
			No T/291091 Dr AUSTWICK F. ASC. HT + No T/293490 Dr TEMPLE H. ASC HT. arrived for duty and were taken on the strength. ERL	
	5.4.17	9.0am	CAPT H.V. FITZGERALD RAMC TC proceeded to BEAURAINVILLE to report to OC Div Batt to proceed with this unit by lorry to take over MO i/c of Forward Working Party at ARRAS in relief of CAPT NEILSON RAMC TC who had gone on special leave to U.K. He took two F.M Panniers with him	
CONTES			~~Wire~~ Orders from Bde L 493 Ref Map LENS 1/100.000 that brigade will march on 6th. Starting point road junction on MONTREUIL-HESDIN road 880 yds North of C of MARCONELLE 9.15 am. Billeting area VACQUERIE-LE-BOUCQ - Pt. FORTEL - FORTEL. Orders follow.	
			Wire from Bde Billeting parties to meet Staff Capt at Road junction west	

1875 Wt. W593/826 1,000,000 4/15 J.B.C. & A. A.D.S.S./Forms/C. 2118.

Instructions regarding War Diaries and Intelligence Summaries are contained in F. S. Regs., Part II. and the Staff Manual respectively. Title Pages will be prepared in manuscript.

WAR DIARY
or
INTELLIGENCE SUMMARY
(Erase heading not required.)

Army Form C. 2118

Place	Date	Hour	Summary of Events and Information	Remarks and references to Appendices
CONTES	5.4.14		of V in VACQUERIE-LE-BOUCQ at 9.30 am 6th inst	
		6.15 pm	Orders from Bde L 493/1 cancelling L 493 of even date Move postponed for 24 hrs. March to take place on 7th	
			Orders from Bde Heavy sections of CFA to assemble with B echelons of units & to march under B.T.O. They will assemble in order of march of units at X Roads at Church of PLUMOISON at 9.30 am clear of the main MONTREUIL - HESDIN road. All cyclists to be at starting point at 9.10 am & march under senior NCO	ERL
	6.4.14		Unit remained at CONTES	ERL
VACQUERIE-LE-BOUCQ	7.4.14		Orders from Bde (ref. Map 1/100,000 LENS Sheet) that Bde will march tomorrow 8th inst to billets in FOSSEUX. Starting point X Roads just West of M of MON LEBLOND on main FREVENT - DOULLENS road Head of Bde to pass starting point at 2.30 pm. Order of march Bde HQ, 6th Sig Troop, NSY, 3rd D.G's, Royals, 'C' Battery, 6th M.G.S, Light section CFA, A1 Echelon A2 Echelon, Heavy section 6th CFA. Route X Roads ABRE - Southern outskirts REBREUVIETTE - IVERGNY - SUS-St-LEGER - SOMBRIN. All cyclists to be at head of Bde at starting point at 2.25 pm to march under senior NCO. Heavy Section 6 CFA will march in rear of 6th Cav. Bde column under an officer	

1875 Wt. W593/826 1,000,000 4/15 J.B.C. & A. A.D.S.S./Forms/C. 2118.

Instructions regarding War Diaries and Intelligence Summaries are contained in F. S. Regs., Part II. and the Staff Manual respectively. Title Pages will be prepared in manuscript.

WAR DIARY
or
INTELLIGENCE SUMMARY
(Erase heading not required.)

Army Form C. 2118

Place	Date	Hour	Summary of Events and Information	Remarks and references to Appendices
VACQUERIE-LE-BOUCQ	7.4.17		detailed by OC 6th CFA. Heavy sections 6th, 7th + 8th CFA's will be divisionalized on arrival in GOUY-EN-ARTOIS area + will bivouac under orders of ADMS	
			Horse rugs will be carried rolled round horses necks to FOSSEUX	
			Message from ADMS to evacuate ordinary sick whilst in concentration area to St POL, FREVENT or DOULLENS as forward CCS's are reserved for reception of wounded.	
			Message from ADMS Please arrange to carry your 3 (three) wheeled stretchers during forthcoming operations with your light section SRR	
FOSSEUX	7.4.17		On arrival in FOSSEUX the heavy section proceeded to GOUY-EN-ARTOIS area where it came under the command of CAPT SLANEY RAMC.	
	8.4.17		Concentration order No 1 ADMS	
			after Zero hour on Z day the division will be at 1 hours notice	
			When the division moves one light ambulance + a corporal RAMC as wagon orderly will be detailed by each CFA to accompany the Regts of the Bde on their march to the eastern outskirts of ARRAS. This ambulance will follow closely after the rear regiment of the Bde, collect all casualties + evacuate them to Dressing station in the GRANDE PLACE at the railway crossing at the East outskirts of ARRAS the wagon will return + park just off the main road ½ mile on the N side of ARRAS	

Instructions regarding War Diaries and Intelligence Summaries are contained in F. S. Regs., Part II. and the Staff Manual respectively. Title pages will be prepared in manuscript.

WAR DIARY
or
INTELLIGENCE SUMMARY.
(Erase heading not required.)

Army Form C. 2118.

Place	Date	Hour	Summary of Events and Information	Remarks and references to Appendices
FOSSEUX.	8.4.14		On the order to move being received light sections in the order 8 CFA, 6 CFA, 7 CFA will follow the 7th Brigade and park just off the road at the X roads ½ Kil N.NE. of the X in FOSSEUX (LENS 11. 1/100,000) & await further orders from ADMS. Horses harnessed in, but poles down. Wheeled stretcher carriers ready for early use	
			Combined heavy sections to remain in billets at GOUY ready to move at ½ hrs notice	
			Motor ambulances to move independently from GOUY not sooner than 1 hour after the light sections have moved & concentrate with light sections	
			Orders from ADMS that pack mounted sections will each carry 6 petrol tins full of water on specially arranged pack saddle. All ambulance wagons & cars will carry water in tanks & petrol tins. Water carts of light & heavy sections will carry as many petrol tins full of water as can be arranged. Should stretcher bearers be sent out, each squad of 4 bearers will carry one tin of water if sufficient tins can be found	
			Operation order No 2. ADMS. Ref. Map 51 B+C 1/40,000 & LENS 11 1/100,000	

T2134. Wt. W708-776. 500000. 4/15. Sir J. C. & S.

Instructions regarding War Diaries and Intelligence Summaries are contained in F. S. Regs., Part II. and the Staff Manual respectively. Title pages will be prepared in manuscript.

WAR DIARY
or
INTELLIGENCE SUMMARY.
(Erase heading not required.)

Army Form C. 2118.

Place	Date	Hour	Summary of Events and Information	Remarks and references to Appendices
FOSSEUX	8.4.17		Pack mounted sections will accompany their respective Bn HQ's. The OC. CFA or OC. section will get in touch with R.M.O's as soon as possible & deal with casualties, collecting them in groups under any available shelter & near roads or tracks. A series of relay posts is to be established along the main ARRAS-CAMBRAI road and casualties will be brought along that road & handed over to the nearest relay party. Light sections of CFA: will be concentrated as per Concentration Order No1. & be prepared to move off on ¼ hours notice to form an advanced dressing station under orders from ADMS. This dressing station will probably be in LES FOSSES Fm. N.11 b 9.4 on the main ARRAS-CAMBRAI road. Light wagons will be sent out to get in touch with Pack mounted sections as soon as possible Motor ambulances will move independently to the same concentration point as light sections where they will be divisionalised under Senior MT. NCO	

T2134. Wt. W708-776. 500000. 4/15. Sir J. C. & S.

Instructions regarding War Diaries and Intelligence Summaries are contained in F. S. Regs., Part II. and the Staff Manual respectively. Title pages will be prepared in manuscript.

WAR DIARY
or
INTELLIGENCE SUMMARY.
(Erase heading not required.)

Army Form C. 2118.

Place	Date	Hour	Summary of Events and Information	Remarks and references to Appendices
FOSSEUX	8.4.17		& await further orders from ADMS The combined heavy sections under command of Capt SLANEY RAMC will remain at GOUY ready to move at ½ hours notice. The O.C. combined heavy sections will be prepared to send forward on ¼ hrs notice 2 (two) Sgts, 4 (four) Corpls + 32 (thirty two) privates RAMC to act as stretcher bearers. 7 (seven) motor ambulance cars will be sent to convey this party. It will be formed into 8 (eight) squads & each squad will carry 1 long stretcher, 1 blanket & if possible one large water bottle or petrol tin of water ADMS will be at H. 32 central (51 B) All walking wounded from the division will be directed to the 'BASTION' collecting post ARRAS. Lying & sitting cases will be taken to the nearest infantry advanced dressing station or the 'CAVE' A.D.S. ARRAS No 08765 Pte J. H. EVANS ASC MT transferred to base with Motor ambulance. 17004 JRR	

T2134. Wt. W708-776. 500000. 4/15. Sir J. C. & S.

Instructions regarding War Diaries and Intelligence Summaries are contained in F. S. Regs., Part II. and the Staff Manual respectively. Title pages will be prepared in manuscript.

WAR DIARY
or
INTELLIGENCE SUMMARY.
(Erase heading not required.)

Army Form C. 2118.

Place	Date	Hour	Summary of Events and Information	Remarks and references to Appendices
FOSSEUX	8.4.17		3rd Cav. Div. Concentration order No 2.	
			(a) 8th Cav Bde will move to just short of the western exit of ARRAS in G.21.a.4.4 thence due East to the road point in G.21 b. 5.4 where it will join the cavalry track "A" which it will follow to eastern end of H. 31 b (1/20,000)	
			(b) 6th Cav. Bde will move into area vacated by the 8th Bde	
			Div. Report Centre will move up to the head of the 8th Brigade at the Eastern end of H. 31. b.	
			6th Cav Bde Concentration order No 2. Ref Map 51 B. N.W & S.W (1/20,000) & 51 B & C 1/40,000	
			6th Cav Bde will move via DUISANS - Fork roads L 8. c - L 9 a & c on the main St POL - ARRAS road to G 13. d. 9. 4 & will close up so that its tail is East of railway in L.9	
			Bde report centre at head of Bde.	
			Subsequent to this Concentration the Bde will move into area vacated by 8th Bde & thence in accordance with 6th Cav. Bde Operation order No 1.	
			6th Cav Bde Operation order No 1.	
			After Zero + 2 hours on Z day the Bde will remain standing to at 1 hrs	

T2134. Wt. W708 -776. 500000. 4/15. Sir J. C. & S.

Instructions regarding War Diaries and Intelligence Summaries are contained in F. S. Regs., Part II. and the Staff Manual respectively. Title pages will be prepared in manuscript.

WAR DIARY
or
INTELLIGENCE SUMMARY.
(*Erase heading not required.*)

Army Form C. 2118.

Place	Date	Hour	Summary of Events and Information	Remarks and references to Appendices
FOSSEUX	8.4.17		notice. as soon as the order to move is received the 6th Cav. Bde will follow 8th Bde & halt with its head West of DUISANS & its tail East of GOUVES	
			order of March Bde H.Q., 6th Sig. Troop, 3rd D.G's, 1 Sect 'C' Battery, Royals, 'C' Battery less 1 sect, Field Troop R.E., 6th M.G.S less 3 sections, N.S.Y., Pack-mounted sect C.F.A.	
			Pack mounted section of C.F.A will move with the Bde under all circumstances. Light sections C.F.A's will be collected so soon as Divn has carried out its first concentration park just off the road P.12.a 3.8 & await orders of A.D.M.S.	
			6th Cav Bde Operation order No 1 Ref Map 51 B. N.W & S.W. 1/20,000 & 51 B & C 1/40,000	
			6th Cav Bde will move south of MONCHY-LE-PREUX & seize VIS-EN-ARTOIS gaining touch with the left of the 2nd CAV. DIV.	
			3rd D.G's plus 1 section C Battery will act as advanced Guard & will seize Southern edge of Spur in O.15.a.9.4 - BOIS-DU-VERT - Road in O.3.d.9.0 exclusive. When this objective is gained main body 6th C.F.A pack mounted section in rear will move from CROSSING over WANCOURT -	

Army Form C. 2118.

Instructions regarding War Diaries and Intelligence Summaries are contained in F. S. Regs., Part II. and the Staff Manual respectively. Title pages will be prepared in manuscript.

WAR DIARY
or
INTELLIGENCE SUMMARY.
(Erase heading not required.)

Place	Date	Hour	Summary of Events and Information	Remarks and references to Appendices
FOSSEUX	8.4.17		FEUCHY line about N 4 a 9 8 - SOUTH of MONCHY to a position about O 7 c 5 5	
			Advanced divisional HQ will be in O 7 b 9 6 as soon as 6th & 8th Bdes have completed first bound	
			Bde report centres will be established	
			(a) at H 33 d 8 4 when 3rd DGs are just East of WANCOURT - FEUCHY line	
			(b) at N 12 b 3 6 when 3rd DGs are moving forward to first objective	
			(c) at O 7 b 9 6 when 3rd DGs have gained their objective. SRK	
FOSSEUX	9.4.17	12.35 am	Message from Bde P.804 Bde will stand to from 7.30 am today at 1 hrs notice	
		2.0 am	L 804/1 Zero hour is fixed at 5 30 am today 9th	
		9.40 am	BM 123 from Bde. The Bde will turn out at once + will move in accordance with 6 CB concentration order No1. Report by orderly when ready to move	
		10.0 am	N 48 from ADMS During first concentration ADMS will be at Div report centre at N exit of DUISANS	
ARRAS.		4.0 pm	Bde having moved, pack mounted section 6th CFA in rear of Bde orders received to remain for the night in present position	

WAR DIARY
or
INTELLIGENCE SUMMARY.
(Erase heading not required.)

Army Form C. 2118.

Instructions regarding War Diaries and Intelligence Summaries are contained in F. S. Regs., Part II. and the Staff Manual respectively. Title pages will be prepared in manuscript.

Place	Date	Hour	Summary of Events and Information	Remarks and references to Appendices
ARRAS	9.4.17	8.45pm	BM 130 from BDE. Units will be saddled up & on the cavalry track alongside their present bivouacs at 5 am tomorrow morning. Order of march the same as today. Unit commanders will come to Bde H.Q at 5 am tomorrow	
		10.30pm	Units will saddle up on the cavalry track at 11.30 pm tonight, facing west. Further orders follow.	
		11.30pm	Bde marched back to bivouacs at X roads by T in HALTE on the main ARRAS – St POL road 4½ Kil from ARRAS (LENS 1/100,000) [illegible]	
X roads by T in HALTE on the ARRAS – St POL road 4½ Kil from ARRAS (Ref Map LENS 1/100,000)	10.4.17	8.15am	~~When Bde~~ BM 134 from Bde stating that when Bde is standing to at one hours notice no officer or man is to leave the lines except under special leave from CO. Message from Bde to consume 1 iron ration for todays consumption & refill from Echelon A 11	
		8.30am	BM. 138 from Bde. Units will be saddled up at 11 am today in bivouac	
		10.0am	BM. 139 from Bde 2nd & 3rd Cav Divs will be ready to move from present bivouacs after 11 am. 3rd Cav Div will move in same order of march as yesterday morning. In consequence the Bde less 1 squad 3rd DGs will	

Instructions regarding War Diaries and Intelligence Summaries are contained in F. S. Regs., Part II. and the Staff Manual respectively. Title pages will be prepared in manuscript.

WAR DIARY
or
INTELLIGENCE SUMMARY.
(*Erase heading not required.*)

Army Form C. 2118.

Place	Date	Hour	Summary of Events and Information	Remarks and references to Appendices
Xroads by T in HALTE on the ARRAS–ST POL Road 4½ kilos from ARRAS (ref Map LENS 1/100,000)	10.4.14		Stand to saddled up in bivouac from 11 am onwards 6th Cav Bde Concentration order No 2 of 9.4.14 + 6 CB Operation order No 1 of 8.4.14 will hold good when Bde moves Divisional report centre S.E. Corner GRAND PLACE ARRAS	
H 32 d (51 B/C 1/40,000)		9.10 pm	Message from Bde that Units ~~will~~ off saddle, put horses sacks and saddle up again, ⅓ of the unit at a time. Units will be prepared to move at 5 am tomorrow No M2/150186 Pte BRIDGEWATER B.S. A.&C.M.T. with motor ambulance 14643 arrived for duty	
H.32 d (ref Map 51 B/C 1/40,000)	11.4.14	4.45 am.	Division will be prepared to advance at 6 am in consequence 6th Cav BDE less 3rd DG's will be disposed in H 32 d ready to move at 6 am according to 6th Cav. Bde Operation order No 1. (Brigade message BM 148) During the fighting on 11th the pack mounted section dealt with + evacuated all casualties, as far forward as Bde HQ's, to infantry dressing stations. Three light ambulance wagons managed to	

Army Form C. 2118.

Instructions regarding War Diaries and Intelligence Summaries are contained in F. S. Regs., Part II. and the Staff Manual respectively. Title pages will be prepared in manuscript.

WAR DIARY
or
INTELLIGENCE SUMMARY.
(Erase heading not required.)

Place	Date	Hour	Summary of Events and Information	Remarks and references to Appendices
H32d (Ref Map 51 B+C 1/40,000)	11.4.17		proceed along main CAMBRAI – ARRAS road to about 200 yds west of X roads at FEUCHY CHAPEL by 5 pm. After dusk stretcher bearers from the light section collected wounded from line running from MONCHY-LE-PREUX to LES-FOSSES Fm + evacuated them by means of these light ambulance wagons to infantry dressing stations + by 9.0 pm before the last regiment of the Bde was relieved all casualties in the Bde had been evacuated	
		9.0pm	The Bde moved back into bivouacs on the racecourse ARRAS. ERL	
ARRAS. racecourse	12.4.17	9.30 am	The Bde moved back into billets in FOSSEUX area.	
FOSSEUX			Light section C+A under orders from ADMS rejoined the Bde at FOSSEUX + ~~later in the evening the heavy section of C+A + all dismounted men.~~ ERL ERL	
	15.4.17		Heavy section C+A rejoined this evening together with all dismounted men.	
			Orders from Bde Ref Map 1/100,000 LENS ~~+~~ ABBEVILLE sheets.	
			Bde will march tomorrow 16th inst to billeting area LABROYE – LE BOISLE –	

T2134. Wt. W708–776. 500000. 4/15. Sir J. C. & S.

Instructions regarding War Diaries and Intelligence Summaries are contained in F. S. Regs., Part II. and the Staff Manual respectively. Title pages will be prepared in manuscript.

WAR DIARY
or
INTELLIGENCE SUMMARY.
(Erase heading not required.)

Army Form C. 2118.

Place	Date	Hour	Summary of Events and Information	Remarks and references to Appendices
FOSSEUX	15.4.17		GENNE IVERGNY - VITZ VILLEROY - WILLENCOURT - LANNOY - VAULX - LE PONCHEL Starting point road junction SW exit of FOSSEUX. Head of Bde will pass starting point at 8 am. Order of March. All cyclists of Bde, Bde HQs & Sig. Troop, 3rd DGs, N.S.Y, ROYALS, 6th MGS, C Battery RHA, 6th CFA. A Echelon of all units, 13th MVS Route. SOMBRIN - SUS St LEGER - IVERGNY - Southern outskirts of REBREUVIETTE - Southern outskirts BONNIERES - VILLERS L'HOPITAL - WAVANS - AUXI LE CHATEAU B Echelon in order of march of units will pass starting point at 9 am brigaded under Bde T.O (Heavy section of CFA accompanied B Echelons) All dismounted men of the Bde under an Officer to be detailed by OC Royals, will assemble in front of CINEMA HUT, FOSSEUX in GOUY-EN-ARTOIS road at 8.30 am & will march to Mairie GOUY-EN-ARTOIS from whence they will be conveyed by motor lorries at 9.30 am to billets Billeting parties will meet Staff Capt at road junction N.E of AUXI LE CHATEAU station on AUXI - DOULLENS road at 12 noon Units will leave behind a party under an Officer to clear up	

T2134. Wt. W708-776. 500000. 4/15. Sir J. C. & S.

Instructions regarding War Diaries and Intelligence Summaries are contained in F. S. Regs., Part II. and the Staff Manual respectively. Title pages will be prepared in manuscript.

WAR DIARY
or
INTELLIGENCE SUMMARY.
(Erase heading not required.)

Army Form C. 2118.

Place	Date	Hour	Summary of Events and Information	Remarks and references to Appendices
FOSSEUX	15.4.17		billets	
			No 50398 Pte C. WIGGINS RAMC N.A. was evacuated on the 13th inst suffering from shell shock.	
			No 1183 Pte GREGNALL RAMC TF was evacuated on the 11th inst suffering from wound in face	
LE BOISLE (ref map ABBEVILLE 1/100,000)		5 pm	Unit arrived in billets followed later by heavy section less one G.S. wagon broken down on the road. This was towed in on the 16th	
			Patients admitted to H' week ending April 7th 34 (thirty four) of which 1 (one) was diarrhoea + 6 (six) Scabies	
			Patients admitted to H' week ending April 14th 78 (seventy eight) of which 1 (one) was scabies	
	14.4.17		No M2/103145 Pte G. MOSES ASC MT proceeded to ADMS 3rd Cav D. with M.A. No 1542 for temporary duty	
			CAPT A NEILSON, RAMC TC returned from special leave of absence in U.K.	
	18.4.17		No 88502 Pte JOYNT E. RAMC proceeded to N.S.Y. for water cart duty in relief of	

T2134. Wt. W708–776. 500000. 4/15. Sir J. C. & S.

Instructions regarding War Diaries and Intelligence Summaries are contained in F. S. Regs., Part II. and the Staff Manual respectively. Title pages will be prepared in manuscript.

WAR DIARY
or
INTELLIGENCE SUMMARY.
(Erase heading not required.)

Army Form C. 2118.

Place	Date	Hour	Summary of Events and Information	Remarks and references to Appendices
LE BOISLE	18.4.17		No 339051 Pte STANBRIDGE JR who rejoined this unit the same day	
			Orders from Bde that Brigade will march westwards tomorrow 19th inst	
			B Echelon of Bde HQ. Royals, C Battery 13th MVS + Heavy section 1 CFA will	
			assemble at church at LE BOISLE at 9.25 am + march under Bde T.O.	
			route as for Bde H.Q.	
			6th CFA. Starting point Road junction at Church LE BOISLE, time 9.35 am.	
			Route DOMPIERRE, billeting area MAINTENAY	
			Billeting Officer will meet the Staff Capt at MAINTENAY church at 8.30 am	
			Message from Bde cancelling previous ~~...~~ message of 13th inst putting	
			the Bde at 4 hours notice	
			SRL	
MAINTENAY	19.4.17	12.45 pm	Unit arrived in the new billeting area.	
	20.4.17		Patients admitted to H week ending April 21st 35 (thirty five) of which 3 (five)	
			were scabies + 1 (one) diarrhoea.	
			No T/291091 Dr AUSTWICK F.B. ASC MT was evacuated to H + taken off the strength	
			CAPT. H.V. FITZGERALD RAMC TC + No 45'40 Pte BELL J RAMC arrived from temp	

T2134. Wt. W708–776. 500000. 4/15. Sir J. C. & S.

Instructions regarding War Diaries and Intelligence Summaries are contained in F. S. Regs., Part II. and the Staff Manual respectively. Title pages will be prepared in manuscript.

WAR DIARY
or
INTELLIGENCE SUMMARY.
(Erase heading not required.)

Army Form C. 2118.

Place	Date	Hour	Summary of Events and Information	Remarks and references to Appendices
MAINTENAY	24.4.14		duty with the 3rd CAV. DIV Dismounted Battn. GRL	
	23.4.14		No M2/103145 Pte MOSES G. ASC MT with M.A 1542 returned from temp. duty with ADMS	
	25.4.14		CAPT A NEILSON RAMC TC + No 45210 Pte BELL, J RAMC proceeded for temp duty with DDMS. Cav. Corps. GRL	
	26.4.14		No M2/031959 Pte LYNNE H.L. ASC MT proceeded with M.A 9393 for temp duty with N.Y.C.F.A. GRL	
	28.4.14		Transport of both Light + Heavy Sections was inspected by the OC ASC. GRL	
	30.4.14		CAPT. H.V. FITZGERALD RAMC TC proceeded to 3rd D. G's for temp duty during the absence on leave of MO i/c CAPT HARDMAN RAMC TC.	
			CAPT. E.F. HEAP proceeded to BOULOGNE on 5 days leave of absence.	
			LIEUT A. CLARKE RAMC TC proceeded for temp duty to 1st R.D's as MO i/c during absence of CAPT. I.M. GRANT, granted 14 days special leave of absence in the UK	
			Patients admitted to H from 22nd to 30th 39 (thirty nine) of which 12 (twelve) were Scabies	
			Total admissions to H for April 186 (one hundred + eighty six) of which 24 (twenty four) were Scabies + 2 (two) diarrhoea GRL	

E.F. Heap Capt
OFFICER COMMANDING
No 6 CAVALRY FIELD AMBULANCE.

May. 1917

S

140/2161

Vol 29

WAR DIARY

of

No 6 Cav. Field Ambulance

for month of

May 1917

B.E.F.

Summary of Medical War Diaries of

6th CAVALRY FIELD AMBULANCE

3rd Cav.Div., Cav.Corps,
3rd Army (from 8/4/17. (till 13/5/17.

WESTERN FRONT 1917.

O.C. Captain E.F.G.T. Heap.

Summarised under the following heagings :

PHASE "B": BATTLE OF ARRAS, APRIL - MAY 1917.

1st Period - Attack on Vimy Ridge, April.

2nd Period - Capture of Siegfried Line, May.

6th CAV. F.A., WESTERN FRONT 1917.
May.

3rd Cav.Div., Cav.Corps, 3rd Army till 13/5/17.

O.C. Capt. E.F.G.T. Heap.

Phase "B": Battle of Arras, April - May 1917.

2nd Period - Capture of Siegfried Line, May.

H.Q. at MAINTENAY.

May

1st /12th	Operations R.A.M.C.	Routine.
13th	Moves & Transfer	To TORTE-FONTAINE en route for 4th Army Area.

6th CAV. F.A.,

WESTERN FRONT 1917.
May.

3rd Cav.Div., Cav.Corps, 3rd Army till 13/5/17.

O.C. Capt. E.F.G.T. Heap.

Phase "B": Battle of Arras, April - May 1917.

2nd Period - Capture of Siegfried Line, May.

H.Q. at MAINTENAY.

May

1st /12th	Operations R.A.M.C.	Routine.
13th	Moves & Transfer	To TORTE-FONTAINE en route for 4th Army Area.

Instructions regarding War Diaries and Intelligence Summaries are contained in F. S. Regs., Part II. and the Staff Manual respectively. Title pages will be prepared in manuscript.

WAR DIARY
or
INTELLIGENCE SUMMARY.
(Erase heading not required.)

Army Form C. 2118.

Place	Date	Hour	Summary of Events and Information	Remarks and references to Appendices
MAINTENAY	1/5/17 to 7/5/17		General Routine	
(ref map 1/100,000 ABBEVILLE)			No 1974 Sgt. C.D. FERGUSON RAMC was awarded the military medal on April 30th 1917 (Auth Hq Qts 3 Cav. Div 6239 d/30/4/17)	
			Patients admitted to H.P. week ending May 4th 14 (seventeen) of which two were Scabies	ERL
	8/5/17 to 10/5/17		General Routine	ERL
	11/5/17		Capt A. NEILSON RAMC(TC) + 1 (one) O.R. returned from temp. duty with DDMS Cav Corps	
			No 10000 Pte ANDERSON RAMC evacuated to 26 G.H.	ERL
	12/5/17		Under instructions from 6th C Bde L/9 b5/1 CAPT HV FITZGERALD RAMC + 33 OR's (representing dismounted personnel) proceeded to BEAURAINVILLE for entrainment. He took with him 1 medical companion and a surgical Haversack. Remainder of ambulance left MAINTENAY at 11.am + reached TORTEFONTAINE at 1.0am. Billets were provided. 1 officer + 6 OR's remained behind to clean up billets + settle	

T2134. Wt. W708-776. 500000. 4/15. Sir J. C. & S.

Instructions regarding War Diaries and Intelligence Summaries are contained in F. S. Regs., Part II. and the Staff Manual respectively. Title pages will be prepared in manuscript.

WAR DIARY
or
INTELLIGENCE SUMMARY.
(Erase heading not required.)

Army Form C. 2118.

Place	Date	Hour	Summary of Events and Information	Remarks and references to Appendices
MAINTENAY			claims SRL	
TORTEFONTAINE (ABBEVILLE 1/100,000)	13/5/17	10am	Ambulance moved under C Bde L969 d/12/5/17 to billets at FROHEN-LE-GRAND (ref map LENS 1/100,000) Arrived at 2.30pm Horses were watered & fed en route. SRL	
FROHEN-LE-GRAND (LENS 1/100,000)	14/5/17	9.0am	Under instructions from 6 C Bde L/995 proceeded to billeting area of HAVERNAS (LENS 1/100,000) arrived ~~there~~ at 2.30pm No T/325?28 Dr EDGAR J ASC HT evacuated to H? Patients admitted to H? week ending May 14th 31 (thirty one) of which 1 (one) was diarrhoea SRL	
HAVERNAS (LENS 1/100,000)	15/5/17	9am	Unit proceeded (auth. 6 C Bde L999 d/14/5/17) to BUSSY-LES-DAOURS (ref map AMIENS 1/100,000) where ~~they~~ it remained for 16th SRL	
BUSSY-LES-DAOURS (AMIENS 1/100,000)	17/5/17	8.30am	Unit proceeded (auth. 6 C Bde) to BAYONVILLERS (ref map AMIENS 1/100000) where they rested for one day. Men were in huts & half of the horses under shelters SRL	
BAYONVILLERS (AMIENS 1/100,000)	18/5/17		CAPT HEAP & 1 other officer proceeded to BUIRE (ref map St QUENTIN 1/100,000) with brigade party to see the site of the future camp.	

T2134. Wt. W708–776. 500000. 4/15. Sir J. C. & S.

Instructions regarding War Diaries and Intelligence Summaries are contained in F. S. Regs., Part II. and the Staff Manual respectively. Title pages will be prepared in manuscript.

WAR DIARY
or
INTELLIGENCE SUMMARY.
(Erase heading not required.)

Army Form C. 2118.

Place	Date	Hour	Summary of Events and Information	Remarks and references to Appendices
			any suitable place in the village was allotted to the 6 CHA. The village is one mass of ruins + no houses are left standing. Three gardens were chosen for where tents and bivouacs could be erected and sites for horses lines were found near. SRL	
	19/5/17	7.0am	Under instruction from 6 CBde. Unit marched with Bde to BUIRE (St QUENTIN 1/100,000). Horses were watered + fed just EAST of BRIE (ref map AMIENS 1/100,000) Arrived at BUIRE 2.30 pm. There were no tents issued for patients so no hospital was opened, all cases being evacuated to D.RS opened at DOIGNT (AMIENS 1/100,000) SRL	
BUIRE (St QUENTIN 1/100,000)	20/5/17		CAPT H.V. FITZGERALD RAMC T(C) + 31 OR's rejoined the unit SRL.	
	21/5/17		Under instructions from A.D.MS. 3.CD. H/402/3 d/20/5/17 the heavy section proceeded to DOINGT (ref map 1/100,000 AMIENS) for duty at Corps Scabies Station + D.R.S. CAPT. A NEILSON was in charge of Heavy Section	
			Patients passed through the ambulance for week ending 21st	

Instructions regarding War Diaries and Intelligence Summaries are contained in F. S. Regs., Part II. and the Staff Manual respectively. Title pages will be prepared in manuscript.

WAR DIARY
or
INTELLIGENCE SUMMARY.
(Erase heading not required.)

Army Form C. 2118.

Place	Date	Hour	Summary of Events and Information	Remarks and references to Appendices
			22 (twenty two) of which 1 (one) was diarrhoea + 2 (two) scabies SRL	
	24.5.17		CAPT HEAP + LIEUT CLARKE with 20 O.R's proceeded ~~work~~ for duty with the Bde dismounted party (ADMS 3CD A402/6 d 22/5/17) this party ~~opened~~ took over from 2nd Cav Div Fd Amb a collecting post at EPEHY (ref map 1/40,000 Sheet 62C) at F1C central. The accomodation for wounded was unsatisfactory. There was room for five lying cases at most + protection was merely shrapnel proof. The only place available being a cellar. Two good dug outs are at present in process of construction + are nearly completed. I am strongly of opinion that adequate protection for wounded should be provided as early as possible when any new line is taken over + should not be left until apparently every other matter has been seen into + provided for. This criticism applies even more strongly to Regtl Aid Posts where accomodation +	

Instructions regarding War Diaries and Intelligence Summaries are contained in F. S. Regs., Part II. and the Staff Manual respectively. Title pages will be prepared in manuscript.

WAR DIARY
or
INTELLIGENCE SUMMARY.
(Erase heading not required.)

Army Form C. 2118.

Place	Date	Hour	Summary of Events and Information	Remarks and references to Appendices
			protection where practically nil. Fortunately no marked groups of casualties occurred but had such been the case it would have necessitated the wounded lying out in the open at Regl. Aid Posts possibly under fire & certainly under adverse conditions. In trench construction & making of Regimental or Battn. HQrs I am of opinion that sufficient interest is not taken & facilities given to RAMC to carry out their duties efficiently.	
			This collecting post was responsible for collection of all sick & wounded over a sector held by one cavalry division i.e. III Cav. DIV. This was divided into two sub sectors each of which had a Regt Aid Post. These were situated at F 4 a 2.9. (sheet 62c) & X 26 a 6 4 (sheet 57c 1/40,000).	
			Wounded could be evacuated by day & night from Regt aid posts either walking or by stretchers. Wheeled transport i.e. light ambulances or motor ambulances could be taken	

Instructions regarding War Diaries and Intelligence Summaries are contained in F. S. Regs., Part II. and the Staff Manual respectively. Title pages will be prepared in manuscript.

WAR DIARY
or
INTELLIGENCE SUMMARY.
(Erase heading not required.)

Army Form C. 2118.

Place	Date	Hour	Summary of Events and Information	Remarks and references to Appendices
			up to Regt Aid Posts at night only, but two wheeled stretchers were always kept, together with 2 RAMC bearers from collecting post, at Aid Posts to facilitate any urgent evacuations during the day.	
			Collecting post evacuated to a main dressing station at VILLERS FAUCON (E 22 d 1/40,000 sheet 62c) + for this purpose one motor ambulance was kept at the collecting post + when it ~~pro~~ proceeded to the MDS, another car ~~from~~ was [SRL] sent out at once on its arrival at MDS to replace. This could be done both day + night.	
			~~1~~ 1 OR ASC MT (motor cyclist) detailed by orders of ADMS to proceed to CORPS REST STATION DOINGT (ref map 1/100,000 AMIENS sheet) SRL.	SRL
	24.5.17		One (1) OR RAMC arrived for duty SRL.	
	28.5.17		Three light ambulances detailed to proceed to transport lines of 6th CAV. BDE at VILLERS FAUCON to be ready to be used by	

T2134. Wt. W708-776. 500000. 4/15. Sir J. C. & S.

Instructions regarding War Diaries and Intelligence Summaries are contained in F. S. Regs., Part II. and the Staff Manual respectively. Title pages will be prepared in manuscript.

WAR DIARY
or
INTELLIGENCE SUMMARY.
(Erase heading not required.)

Army Form C. 2118.

Place	Date	Hour	Summary of Events and Information	Remarks and references to Appendices
			collecting post if required	ERL
	30.5.17		1. OR. RAMC proceeded to England prior to taking a commission in infantry	
			CAPT HV FITZGERALD with 3 OR's (2 RAMC + 1 ASC Batman) proceeded to HARBONNIERE for temp duty at MO ½ details AMIENS 1/100,000	ERL
	31.5.17		Patients admitted ~~passing through~~ light section for period May 22nd – 31st 4 of which 2 were Diarrhoea + 1 Scabies all other cases being sent on direct to CORPS REST STATION.	ERL
			The Collecting POST at EPEHY evacuated up to 31st May 26 sick + 12 wounded	ERL.

G A Heap Capt.
OFFICER COMMANDING
Nº 6 CAVALRY FIELD AMBULANCE.

24

Vol 30

June. 1917

140/2230

WAR DIARY

6th C. F. A

Month of June 1917

Army Form C. 2118.

WAR DIARY
or
INTELLIGENCE SUMMARY.
(Erase heading not required.)

Instructions regarding War Diaries and Intelligence Summaries are contained in F. S. Regs., Part II. and the Staff Manual respectively. Title pages will be prepared in manuscript.

Place	Date	Hour	Summary of Events and Information	Remarks and references to Appendices
BUIRE. (St QUENTIN. 1/100,000)	3/6/17		CAPT E F HEAP + LIEUT CLARKE + 9 OR's returned from duty at collecting post with dismounted party of 6th Bde	SRL
	4/6/17		LIEUT A CLARKE + 1 OR + 1 riding horse SRL proceeded to ADMS 3rd CAV. DIV for temporary duty	SRL
	5/6/17		CAPT P.A. McCALLUM + 1 OR proceeded to 36 CCS for temporary duty	SRL
	10/6/17		Six OR's returned from duty at collecting post EPEHY	SRL
	11/6/17		one (1) OR RAMC reinforcement received	SRL
			Transport + ASC personnel of heavy section less water cart + 1 GS Wagon (in workshop) + 2 OR's returned from Corps Rest Station	SRL
	13/6/17		2 OR's ASC H.T. reinforcements received	SRL
	19/6/17		LIEUT CLARKE + 1 OR + 1 riding horse SRL returned from temp duty with ADMS.	SRL
	22/6/17		CAPT E R LOVELL + LIEUT A H CLARKE + 20 OR's, with three light ambulance wagons + 2 motor ambulances proceeded for duty at the A.D.S EPEHY (1/40,000 62c.)	
			CAPT P.A. McCALLUM + 1 OR returned from temp duty at 36 CCS	SRL
	24/6/17		1. OR RAMC evacuated to 39 CCS	SRL

T2134. Wt. W708–776. 500000. 4/15. Sir J. C. & S.

Instructions regarding War Diaries and Intelligence Summaries are contained in F. S. Regs., Part II. and the Staff Manual respectively. Title pages will be prepared in manuscript.

WAR DIARY
or
INTELLIGENCE SUMMARY.
(Erase heading not required.)

Army Form C. 2118.

Place	Date	Hour	Summary of Events and Information	Remarks and references to Appendices
	24/6/17		No T4/8?17 L/Cpl WINDRED ASC-AT proceeded to A.D.S for temporary duty	SRL
	24/6/17		1. OR ASC MT exchanged with 1 OR ASC M.T from 3rd CAV DIV SUPPLY Co'n. The personnel at the A.D.S were reinforced by 1 officer + 12 O.R. for one night from No 4 C.S.A. SRL as a raid had been arranged. LIEUT CLARKE + 4 OR's RAMC proceeded to X 22 d. 4 4 (1/40,000 57.C) + formed an advanced regimental aid post. No provision had been made for the reception of wounded but a rough shelter was soon erected with sand bags etc. This post was between the outposts + the front line trenches. Two wheeled stretchers + three long stretchers + nine O.R. (under a Sgt) were sent up along the road as far as the barrier at X 22 C 3. 4. The former party were in position by 12 midnight + the latter by 12 30 am (25th). Arrangements were made for the three light ambulances to be at the A.D.S by dusk in case they should be needed.	SRL
	25/6/17	1.10am	Raid commenced at 1.10 am	

T2134. Wt. W708-776. 500000. 4/15. Sir J. C. & S.

Army Form C. 2118.

Instructions regarding War Diaries and Intelligence Summaries are contained in F. S. Regs., Part II. and the Staff Manual respectively. Title pages will be prepared in manuscript.

WAR DIARY
or
INTELLIGENCE SUMMARY.
(Erase heading not required.)

Place	Date	Hour	Summary of Events and Information	Remarks and references to Appendices
	25.6.17	1.45am	When the barrage had died down & word had been received from HQrs (Sector) that there were a number of casualties the three light ambulance wagons & 1 motor ambulance were sent to FALLEN TREE. X 24 b 3.6. These were just sufficient to remove all casualties (5 lying & 6 sitting)	SRL
	28.6.17		CAPT LOVELL & LIEUT CLARKE with 24 O.R. returned from duty at ADS	
			1 OR (Clerk) returned from duty at the M.D. Station	SRL
	29.6.17		CAPT A NEILSON & 26 O.R. returned from duty at the Corps Rest Station	SRL

July 1/1917

R. Heap Capt
OFFICER COMMANDING
No 6 CAVALRY FIELD AMBULANCE

T2134. Wt. W708–776. 500000. 4/15. Sir J. C. & S.

July 1917

Vol 31

140/2298

WAR DIARY

of

6th C. F. Ambulance

for month of

JULY 1917

Instructions regarding War Diaries and Intelligence Summaries are contained in F. S. Regs., Part II. and the Staff Manual respectively. Title pages will be prepared in manuscript.

WAR DIARY
or
INTELLIGENCE SUMMARY.
(Erase heading not required.)

Army Form C. 2118.

Place	Date	Hour	Summary of Events and Information	Remarks and references to Appendices
BUIRE (St QUENTIN 1/100,000)	1.7.17		4 ORs proceeded to the 4th Army School of Sanitation for a four days course. SRL	
	2.7.17		CAPT A NEILSON RAMC.TC + 3 ORs proceeded to 3rd Cav Div Dismounted Batt for duty.	
			24 OR proceeded to join dismounted personnel of Bde for transport to new area. SRL	
	3.7.17	7.0am	Unit proceeded to Bde starting point - road junction I 30 c 0 1 (1/40,000 Sheet 62c). Thence to billets at SUZANNE (R/Map 1/100,000 AMIENS) arriving at 1.0 pm. SRL	
SUZANNE (AMIENS 1/100,000)	4.7.17	8.15 am	Unit proceeded to Bde starting point, X roads just S.W. of S of BRAY-SUR-SOMME thence to billets at HEILLY arriving at 1.0 pm. SRL	
HEILLY (AMIENS 1/100,000)	5.7.17	9.0am	Unit less Heavy Section proceeded to Bde starting point Road junction 440 yds NE of CONTAY church (LENS 1/100,000). HEAVY Section proceeded at 7.45 am to join B Echelons of Bde at X Roads 450 yds NNE of T of RIBEMONT. Unit arrived in ORVILLE (LENS 1/100,000) by 2.30 pm. SRL	
ORVILLE (LENS 1/100,000)	6.7.17	9.30am	Unit proceeded to Bde starting point T Roads 300 Yds S.W. of Church	

Instructions regarding War Diaries and Intelligence Summaries are contained in F. S. Regs., Part II. and the Staff Manual respectively. Title pages will be prepared in manuscript.

WAR DIARY
or
INTELLIGENCE SUMMARY.
(*Erase heading not required.*)

Army Form C. 2118.

Place	Date	Hour	Summary of Events and Information	Remarks and references to Appendices
ORVILLE (LENS 1/100,000)			LUCHEUX thence to billets at REBREUVIETTE	ERR
REBREUVIETTE (1/100,000 LENS)	7.7.17	10am	Light Section proceeded via FREVENT to Bde starting point X Rds 1000 yds North of the H in HERLIN-LE-SEC (on main FREVENT-ST POL Road) Thence to billets in AUCHEL (HAZEBROUCK 5a 1/100,000) Heavy Section marched from starting point & turning on the ETREE-WAMIN-FREVENT Rd 1 Kilometre SOUTH of F in FREVENT	
AUCHEL (HAZEBROUCK 1/100,000)	7.7.17		Unit was billeted in a french school part of which was prepared for reception of Sick. Rooms were furnished with canvass stretched on wooden frames for beds & these proved extremely useful.	
			CAPT HV FITZGERALD + 3 ORs returned from temporary duty at HARBONNIER (AMIENS 1/100,000) on the 5th July	ERR
			Patients admitted to H. 1-7th incl 32 of which 1 was Scabies & 6 Diarrhoea	
	9.7.17		1 OR ASC MT proceeded with motor cyclist for temp duty with ADMS	

Instructions regarding War Diaries and Intelligence Summaries are contained in F. S. Regs., Part II. and the Staff Manual respectively. Title pages will be prepared in manuscript.

WAR DIARY
or
INTELLIGENCE SUMMARY.
(Erase heading not required.)

Army Form C. 2118.

Place	Date	Hour	Summary of Events and Information	Remarks and references to Appendices
AUCHEL (HAZEBROUCK 1/100,000)	10.4.17		CAPT NEILSON + 3 OR's returned from temp duty with dismounted Batt	
			28 OR's rejoined unit having proceeded with dismounted personnel. This included 4 OR's who had proceeded to the 1st Army School of Instruction	SRL
	13.4.17		3 OR's RAMC arrived for duty	SRL
	14.4.17		Patients admitted to H 8th – 14th (incl) 40 of which 2 were Scabies + 7 Diarrhoea.	SRL
	16.4.17	8.15	Unit proceeded independently according to march table to billets at LES LAURIERS arriving there at 9.0 am	SRL
LES LAURIERS (HAZEBROUCK 1/100000)	18.4.17		There is no accomodation for a hospital. RAMC men are in barns + bivouacs, ASC in bivouacs. No stabling, horses are in a field.	SRL
	19.4.17		CAPT E F HEAD proceeded on leave of absence to England from 20th – 30th inst	SRL
	20.4.17		G.O.C. 6th Cav. Bde inspected the unit.	

T2134. Wt. W708–776. 500000. 4/15. Sir J. C. & S.

Instructions regarding War Diaries and Intelligence Summaries are contained in F. S. Regs., Part II. and the Staff Manual respectively. Title pages will be prepared in manuscript.

WAR DIARY
or
INTELLIGENCE SUMMARY.
(Erase heading not required.)

Army Form C. 2118.

Place	Date	Hour	Summary of Events and Information	Remarks and references to Appendices
LES LAURIERS (HAZEBROUCK 1/100,000)			Patients admitted to H 15th – 21st 36 of which 4 were Scabies + 6 Diarrhoea	ERL
	24.7.17		1 OR ASC HT + 1 OR RAMC evacuated + struck off the strength	ERL
	26.7.17		CAPT HV FITZGERALD granted leave to SCOTLAND from 24th – 10th Aug on completion + renewal of contract	ERL
	27.7.17		1 OR RAMC transferred to 7th CFA	ERL
	31.7.17		CAPT E F HEAP returned from leave of absence in ENGLAND	
	31.7.17	3.30 pm	ADMS 3rd Cav Div inspected the pack mounted section	ERL
			Patients admitted to H 22 – 31 42 of which 2 were Scabies + 5 Diarrhoea. On 26th we obtained from Bde 3 bell tents + together with operating tent + 2 bell tents of this unit a small hospital was erected in a field	
			Total admission to H during month of July 150 of which 9 were Scabies + 24 Diarrhoea.	ERL

EF Heap Capt
OFFICER COMMANDING
No 6 CAVALRY FIELD AMBULANCE.

T2134. Wt. W708 – 776. 500000. 4/15. Sir J. C. & S.

Aug. 1917.

17

Vol 32

140/2304

WAR DIARY

of

No 6 Cavalry Field Ambulance

for Month of

AUGUST. 1917

Army Form C. 2118.

Instructions regarding War Diaries and Intelligence Summaries are contained in F. S. Regs., Part II. and the Staff Manual respectively. Title pages will be prepared in manuscript.

WAR DIARY
or
INTELLIGENCE SUMMARY.
(Erase heading not required.)

Place	Date	Hour	Summary of Events and Information	Remarks and references to Appendices
LES LAURIERS (HAZEBROUCK 1/100,000)	2.8.17		No 341183 Cpl KEDWARDS RAMC. TF proceeded to base to be released for munition work	SRL
	4.8.17		1 driver ASC HT arrived for duty	SRL
	6.8.17		No 54792 Pte (A/Sgt) DAVEY EC RAMC promoted to substantive rank of Cpl as from June 28th 1917 (RAMC orders 28/6/17	
			Corps Pay of No 58070 Pte (A/Cpl) FAIRWEATHER W RAMC raised from 5th - 4th rate (as from 28/6/17).	SRL
			1 OR RAMC rejoined unit from hospital	SRL
	7.8.17		LIEUT A.H. CLARKE proceeded to NSH for temp. duty	
			Patients admitted to Hosp week ending Aug 7th 22 of which five (5) were ~~Scabies~~ Diarrhoea SRL + two (2) Scabies	SRL
	10.8.17		No 75607 Pte V.W ROCHE RAMC appointed acting Corporal with pay from Aug 2/17 (Auth DGMS B 1450/1281 d. 8.8.17)	SRL
	12.8.17		Capt ER LOVELL granted leave to England from 13 - 23rd inst.	SRL
	14.8.17		Capt A. NEILSON proceeded to 3rd D.G's for temp duty	SRL
			Patients admitted to H week ending Aug 14th seventeen (17) of	

T2134. Wt. W708-776. 500000. 4/15. Sir J. C. & S.

Instructions regarding War Diaries and Intelligence Summaries are contained in F. S. Regs., Part II. and the Staff Manual respectively. Title pages will be prepared in manuscript.

WAR DIARY
or
INTELLIGENCE SUMMARY.
(Erase heading not required.)

Army Form C. 2118.

Place	Date	Hour	Summary of Events and Information	Remarks and references to Appendices
LES LAURIERS	14.8.14		which two (2) were Diarrhoea and four (4) Scabies	SRL
(HAZEBROUCK. 1/100.000)	19.8.14		CAPT RA McCALLUM granted leave to Scotland from 20th – 30th inst	SRL
			LIEUT AH CLARKE returned from temp. duty with NSY	SRL
	1		CAPT HV. FITZGERALD granted extension of leave from 10th – 18th inst.	
			(Auth. War Office telegram 9/8/14)	SRL
	20.8.14		No 58010 a/Cpl FAIRWEATHER RAMC was admitted to Military H GREAT	
			YARMOUTH on Aug 25th whilst on leave.	SRL
	21.8.14		OC. ASC 3 Cav Div inspected the transport of the unit	
			Patients admitted to H week ending Aug 21st eighteen (18) of which	
			one (1) was Scabies	SRL
	26.8.14		1 Sgt + 1 Cpl RAMC arrived for duty	SRL
	30.8.14		No 58010 a/Cpl FAIRWEATHER RAMC rejoined from H	
			Lieut CLARKE granted leave to England from Aug 31st – Sept 10th	SRL
	31.8.14		Patients admitted to H from Aug 22nd – 31st twenty five (25) of which one	
			(1) was Diarrhoea + three (3) Scabies	
			Total patients admitted to H during month eighty two (82) of which	

T2134. Wt. W708 –776. 500000. 4/15. Sir J. C. & S.

Instructions regarding War Diaries and Intelligence Summaries are contained in F. S. Regs., Part II. and the Staff Manual respectively. Title pages will be prepared in manuscript.

WAR DIARY
or
INTELLIGENCE SUMMARY.
(Erase heading not required.)

Army Form C. 2118.

Place	Date	Hour	Summary of Events and Information	Remarks and references to Appendices
LES LAURIERS (HAZEBROUCK) 1/100,000			eight (8) were Diarrhoea and ten (10) Scabies ERL.	
			C. A. Heap Capt. OFFICER COMMANDING № 6 CAVALRY FIELD AMBULANCE.	

T2134. Wt. W708-776. 500000. 4/15. Sir J. C. & S.

17 140/2433 Vol 3

WAR DIARY

of

No 6 Cav Field Ambulance

for month of

September 1917

Instructions regarding War Diaries and Intelligence Summaries are contained in F. S. Regs., Part II. and the Staff Manual respectively. Title pages will be prepared in manuscript.

WAR DIARY
or
~~INTELLIGENCE SUMMARY~~
(Erase heading not required.)

Army Form C. 2118.

No 6 CAVALRY FIELD AMBULANCE
No. ....
Date Sept 1917
III CAVALRY DIV

Place	Date	Hour	Summary of Events and Information	Remarks and references to Appendices
LES LAURIERS (HAZEBROUCK 1/100,000)	1.9.17		Light ambulance wagon and pair of horses driven by T/32501 Dr WEST H.G. ASC HT won 1st prize at Cav. Corps Horse Show for best two horsed ambulance (light) class	SRL
	3.9.17		CAPT A NEILSON returned from temp duty with 3rd D.G.s	SRL
	7.9.17		Patients admitted to H. week ending Sept 7th sixteen (16) of which 2 (two) were Scabies and 1 (one) Diarrhoea	SRL
	8.9.17		ADMS 3 CAV. DIV. inspected personnel & transport of Unit Hospital & billets	SRL
	10.9.17		No 45604 a/Cpl ROCHE V.W. RAMC reverted to a/Cpl without pay from Aug 26/17 Auth DGMS Cav Memo No 20 d/21/8/17	SRL
	14.9.17		Patients admitted to H. week ending 14th 13 (thirteen) of which 2 (two) were Scabies & 1 (one) Diarrhoea	SRL
	16.9.17		LIEUT A CLARKE proceeded to 1st R.D.s for temp duty.	
	17.9.17		CAPT C.M. WILLMOTT RAMC TC + 2 OR's attached to 3rd CAV DIV Supply Column were taken on the strength from 15/9/17	SRL

SRL

T2134. Wt. W708-776. 500000. 4/15. Sir J. C. & S.

2

Instructions regarding War Diaries and Intelligence Summaries are contained in F. S. Regs., Part II. and the Staff Manual respectively. Title pages will be prepared in manuscript.

WAR DIARY
or
~~INTELLIGENCE SUMMARY~~.
(Erase heading not required.)

Army Form C. 2118.

Place	Date	Hour	Summary of Events and Information	Remarks and references to Appendices
LES LAURIERS (HAZEBROUCK 1/100,000)	19.9.17		CAPT A NEILSON granted leave to ENGLAND from 20/9/17 to 30/9/17	
			1 OR RAMC transferred to 31st DIV.	SRL
	21.9.17		LIEUT A CLARKE RAMC TC appointed M.O. i/c N.S.Y. & struck off the strength	
			Patients admitted to H week ending 21st 12 (twelve) of which 1 (one) was Scabies + 1 (one) Diarrhoea	SRL
	24.9.17		1 OR RAMC attached to C Battery RHA taken on the strength. He remains for duty with C Battery	
			1 OR RAMC exchanged for 1 OR RAMC attached to 6th M.G.S.	SRL
	29.9.17		No 339091 Dr FORTAY J A, RAMC T.F. transferred from Transport to Bearer Section. Pay reduced from 4th rate Corps pay ASC to 5th rate Corps Pay RAMC.	SRL
	30.9.17		Patients admitted to H from Sep 22nd – 30th 14 (fourteen) of which 3 (three) were Scabies	
			Total Patients admitted to H during the month of September 55 (fifty five) of which 8 (eight) were Scabies and	SRL

Instructions regarding War Diaries and Intelligence Summaries are contained in F. S. Regs., Part II. and the Staff Manual respectively. Title pages will be prepared in manuscript.

3

WAR DIARY

or

~~INTELLIGENCE SUMMARY.~~

(Erase heading not required.)

No 6 CAVALRY FIELD AMBULANCE
No. ____ Date Sept 1914
1st CAVALRY DIVISION

Army Form C. 2118.

Place	Date	Hour	Summary of Events and Information	Remarks and references to Appendices
LES LAURIERS (HAZEBROUCK 1/100,000)	30.9.14 (cont)		3 (three) Diarrhoea — GRL	

GR Lovell Capt RAMC

GA Heap Capt RAMC

OFFICER COMMANDING
No 6 CAVALRY FIELD AMBULANCE.

T2134. Wt. W708-776. 500000. 4/15. Sir J. C. & S.

Nov. 1917

140/2578

No. 6. Cav. F. A.

Instructions regarding War Diaries and Intelligence Summaries are contained in F. S. Regs., Part II. and the Staff Manual respectively. Title pages will be prepared in manuscript.

WAR DIARY
or
~~INTELLIGENCE~~ SUMMARY.
(*Erase heading not required.*)

Army Form C. 2118.

No 6 CAVALRY FIELD AMBULANCE
No.
Date
3rd CAVALRY DIVISION

Vol 35

Place	Date	Hour	Summary of Events and Information	Remarks and references to Appendices
PONT REMY (ABBEVILLE 1/100000) K6	3.11.17		2 NCO's + 4 ptes proceeded to 3rd Cav Div Pioneer Batt in relief of similar number who returned on 5th inst. SRL	
	6.11.17		No 1974 Sgt C.D. FERGUSON RAMC appointed a/2MS with pay from Oct 25th Auth. DGMS 1450/1594 d 4/11/17. SRL	
	7.11.17		No 091429 Dr Moulds G ASC AT proceeded to ASC AT Base Depot for reclassification (Authy 6th Cav Bde 4/15/12 d 5/11/17.	
			Patients admitted to H week ending Nov 7th 8 (eight) of which 1 (one) ~~were~~ was in Scabies SRL	
	12.11.17		Capt A. NEILSON RAMC proceeded to 1st R.D's for temp duty Capt GRANT RAMC having been transferred to the home establishment	
			No 73554 Pte HARPER G.D. RAMC evacuated to S 12 Kot C.F.A SRL	
	14.11.17		No 339091 Pte FORTAY J.A. RAMC transfd to 1/10th Liverpool Regt with a view to taking a commission in the Infantry (HQ 3rd Cav Div 6434 d 13/11/17.)	
			Patients admitted to H week ending 14th 13 (thirteen) of which 1 (one) was Scabies + 1 (one) Diarrhea SRL	
			SRL	

T2134. Wt. W708–776. 500000. 4/15. Sir J. C. & S.

Instru[illegible]s regarding War Diaries and Intelligence Su[illegible]es are contained in F. S. Regs., Part II. and the Staff Manual respectively. Title pages will be prepared in manuscript.

WAR DIARY
or
~~INTELLIGENCE SUMMARY.~~ II

(*Erase heading not required.*)

Army F[illegible] C. 211[illegible]

No. .... Date 9 Nov 1917

Place	Date	Hour	Summary of Events and Information	Remarks and references to Appendices
PONT REMY (ABBEVILLE 1/100,000) K6	15.11.17		CAPT. H.V. FITZGERALD + 24 O.R. returned from temp duty with 3rd CAV DIV. PIONEER BATT.	SRL
	16.11.17		Dismounted personnel proceeded to VIGNACOURT (LENS 1/100,000 G6) proceeding the following day by lorry to CAPPY (AMIENS 1/100,000 J1)	SRL
	17.11.17	9.30am	Unit less dismounted men, proceeded with Brigade to billets at AGNICOURT (AMIENS 1/100,000 F1) arriving in billets at 5 p.m.	
			Received 6th CAV BDE L.S.15 d 16/11/17 which detailed 3rd D. Gds. + N.S.Y. to provide 1 mounted orderly each for duty with P.M.S. These orderlies to be asked for direct from Regts. by OC 6 CFA in any future operations	SRL
AGNICOURT (AMIENS 1/100,000 F1)	18.11.17	4.15pm	Unit, less dismounted men, proceeded with Brigade by a night march to forward area, arriving at CAPPY (AMIENS 1/100,000 J1) ~~[illegible]~~ SRL at 10.30 p.m. G.S. rations issued at CAPPY	SRL
CAPPY (AMIENS 1/100,000 J1)	19.11.17		1 riding horse returned to unit from 3rd CAV DIV PIONEER BATT.	
		12 noon	1 Pte 3rd D.G.s + 1 Pte N.S.Y. attached for duty with Pack Mounted Section.	
			2 Ptes RAMC proceeded to Walking Wounded Station at BUS (LENS 1/100,000 L6)	SRL

Instructions regarding War Diaries and Intelligence Summaries are contained in F. S. Regs., Part II. and the Staff Manual respectively. Title pages will be prepared in manuscript.

WAR DIARY
or III
~~INTELLIGENCE~~ SUMMARY.
(*Erase heading not required.*)

Army Form C. 2118.

Place	Date	Hour	Summary of Events and Information	Remarks and references to Appendices
CAPPY (AMIENS J1 1/100,000)	19.11.14 (cont)		to record casualties to cavalry passing through.	
			~~Operation~~ SRL ADMS' Operation orders Nos 5 & 6 & Cav Corps Medical Arrangements Operation order No 14a made known to all M.O's of unit.	
			Secret orders received from BDE re probable move of 3rd CAV DIV from BRAY (AMIENS 1/100,000 I1) to FINS (VALENCIENNES NE A6 ~~[illegible]~~ 1/100,000) area. P.M.S to follow Brigade. C.F.A's to be divisionalized. SRL	
	20.11.14	9.0am	Unit standing to at ½ hrs notice. Notice later extended to 1 hour & horses off saddled	
		*	Message from Bde (timed 3.5 pm) saying 'There is every probability of the Division moving to the FINS area tonight.'	
			Message from Bde (timed 8.5 pm) Unit will be ready to move from billets at ½ hrs notice after receipt of orders at unit HQ's after 6.30 am 21st Nov. SRL	
	21.11.14		Message from Bde (timed 3.50 pm) saying units need not be in a state of readiness to move till tomorrow morning, unless they hear to the	
			SRL	

Instructions regarding War Diaries and Intelligence Summaries are contained in F. S. Regs., Part II. and the Staff Manual respectively. Title pages will be prepared in manuscript.

WAR DIARY
or IV
~~INTELLIGENCE~~ SUMMARY.
(Erase heading not required.)

Army Form C. 2118.

No 6 CAVALRY FIELD AMBULANCE No. ___ Date Nov 19 III CAVALRY DIVISION

Place	Date	Hour	Summary of Events and Information	Remarks and references to Appendices
CAPPY (AMIENS J1 1/100,000)	21.11.17 (cont)		contrary	
			Message from BDE Units to be ready to move at 1 hrs notice from receipt of orders at units HQ after 6 30 am 22nd inst	SRL
	~~22.11.17~~		~~Message from BDE (timed 2 45 pm) cancelling state of readiness~~	SRL
			Patients admitted to FA week ending 21st 25 (twenty five) of which 1 (one) was Diarrhoea	SRL
	22.11.17		Message from BDE (timed 2 45 pm) cancelling state of readiness	
			No 339033 Sgt SANDHAM RAMC appointed to A/S Sgt with Pay (auth DDMS 1450/1687 d 19/11/17	SRL
	23.11.17	8.50 am	Unit proceeded with Brigade to CONTAY (LENS F6 1/100,000) area. Dismounted men conveyed in lorries. Unit arrived in billets at LA VICOGNE (LENS 1/100,000 D6) 5. 30 pm	
			1 PTE 3rd D Gs + 1 PTE N SY returned to their units.	SRL
LA VICOGNE (LENS 1/100,000 D6)	24.11.17		Message from BDE (timed 6 30 pm) after 6 30 am tomorrow 25th inst units to be at 2 hrs notice to move after receipt of orders at BDE HQ. Provisional starting point for move eastwards notified	SRL
				SRL

T2134. Wt. W708-776. 500000. 4/15. Sir J. C. & S.

Instructions regarding War Diaries and Intelligence Summaries are contained in F. S. Regs., Part II. and the Staff Manual respectively. Title pages will be prepared in manuscript.

WAR DIARY
or
~~INTELLIGENCE~~ SUMMARY.
(*Erase heading not required.*)

V

Army Form C. 2118

Place	Date	Hour	Summary of Events and Information	Remarks and references to Appendices
LA VICOGNE (LENS 1/100,000)	25.11.14		Message from Bde (timed 6.40pm) cancelling state of readiness until further orders	SRL
	27.11.14		CAPT CH STRINGER RAMC granted leave to IRELAND from 28th Nov ~~Nov 28~~ 31st Dec 12th	SRL
			1 Dr ASC AT arrived from 3rd CAV DIV for duty	
			INTERPRETER de COMYS arrived for duty from 3rd Cav. DIV	SRL
	29.11.14		CAPT. A NEILSON having been relieved by Capt J LYONS RAMC returned from temp duty with 7th RDs.	
			Orders received for dismounted brigade.	SRL
	30.11.14	11.40am	Message from Bde cancelling all previous orders. Units put on 1 hours notice	
			Message from Bde (timed 2.45pm) Units to be prepared to move mounted at 1 hours notice on Gap organization, ~~tatts~~ SRL to send up dismounted battn. also	
			No 88395 PTE J HUTTON RAMC evacuated to 3rd CAV STAT. HP	
			Patients admitted to HP from Nov 22nd – 30th 20 (twenty) of which 2 (two) were	SRL

T2134. Wt. W708–776. 500000. 4/15. Sir J. C. & S.

Instructions regarding War Diaries and Intelligence Summaries are contained in F. S. Regs., Part II. and the Staff Manual respectively. Title pages will be prepared in manuscript.

WAR DIARY
or
~~INTELLIGENCE SUMMARY.~~
(*Erase heading not required.*)

VI

Army Form C. 2118.

No. 6 CAVALRY FIELD AMBULANCE
No. ____
Date Nov 1914
III CAVALRY

Place	Date	Hour	Summary of Events and Information	Remarks and references to Appendices
LA VICOGNE (LENS 11 D6) (400 000)	30.11.14	6 a.m.	Scabies Total patients admitted to H.P. during the month 66 (sixty six) of which 4 (four) were Scabies + 2 (two) Diarrhoea Cases evacuated during month Officers sick 4 Wounded 0 = 4 O.R.s " 52 " 0 = 52 56 During first few days of the month the Hospital at PONT REMY was furnished with beds etc from Red Cross Stores + was very well equipped. Accomodation 10 beds with sheets etc + sufficient room for twenty more stretchers. On receiving orders to move most of the cases were evacuated the remainder returned to duty + the Hospital closed down J.R. Powell Capt RAMC	RRA RRA

T2134. Wt. W708–776. 500000. 4/15. Sir J. C. & S.

Oct. 1917 16 140/2499 Vol 34

WAR DIARY
of
No 6 Cav. Field Ambulance
for month of
OCTOBER 1917

Army Form C. 2118.

Instructions regarding War Diaries and Intelligence Summaries are contained in F. S. Regs., Part II. and the Staff Manual respectively. Title pages will be prepared in manuscript.

WAR DIARY
or
~~INTELLIGENCE SUMMARY.~~

(Erase heading not required.)

No. 6 CAVALRY FIELD AMBULANCE
No.
Date Oct 1917
III CAVALRY DIVISION

Place	Date	Hour	Summary of Events and Information	Remarks and references to Appendices
LES LAURIERS	3.10.17		CAPT H.V. FITZGERALD + 1 O.R. (batman) proceeded to Corps Gas School for a three day course of instruction	SRL
HAZEBROUCK				SRL
(100,000)	4.10.17		4 OR's RAMC transferred to 31st Div	
	5.10.17		CAPT E F HEAP proceeded to ENGLAND on completion of contract + was struck off the strength	
			1 Cpl RAMC evacuated to 51 CCS + struck off the strength	
			The Pack Mounted Section attended a Brigade Scheme with object of practicing communication between H.Q. of Regts + the R.M.S.	SRL
	7.10.17	1.am	Winter time came into force	
			Warning order received that division might be required to move at short notice on 9th	
			Patients admitted to H.P. week ending 7th fifteen, of which two were Scabies + one Diarrhoea	SRL
	8.10.17		CAPT. C.H. STRINGER arrived to take command of the unit vice CAPT E F HEAP	SRL

T2134. Wt. W708-776. 500000. 4/15. Sir J. C. & S.

Instructions regarding War Diaries and Intelligence Summaries are contained in F. S. Regs., Part II. and the Staff Manual respectively. Title pages will be prepared in manuscript.

WAR DIARY
or
~~INTELLIGENCE SUMMARY.~~ II

(*Erase heading not required.*)

Army Form C. 2118.

Place	Date	Hour	Summary of Events and Information	Remarks and references to Appendices
LES LAURIERS	11.10.17		1 OR RAMC exchanged for 1 OR RAMC att 6th MG.S	RRL
HAZEBROUCK 1/100,000	14.10.17		Patients admitted to H.P. week ending 14th 10 (ten) of which (one) was Diarrhoea	RRL
	15.10.17		Warning order received that division will move to area S.W. of DOULLENS within next few days	RRL
	19.10.17		Unit moved with brigade to billets at HUCLIER (LENS 1/100,000) Dismounted men arranged for by lorry transport	RRL
HUCLIER (LENS 1/100,000).	21.10.17		One Officer proceeded with brigade billeting party to PONT REMY (ABBEVILLE 1/100,000) to reconnoitre final area. Patients admitted to H.P. week ending 21st 13 (thirteen) of which 7 (seven) were Scabies. CAPT NEILSON took over medical charge of No 1 section 3rd Cavalry Reserve Park visiting them each morning until 30th inst	RRL
	22.10.17		Unit moved with Brigade to billets at ~~BA~~ CANETTEMONT (LENS 1/100,000) Dismounted party proceeded to final area at PONT REMY (ABBEVILLE 1/100,000) by lorry + ~~[illegible]~~	RRL

T2134. Wt. W708-776. 500000. 4/15. Sir J. C. & S.

Instructions regarding War Diaries and Intelligence Summaries are contained in F. S. Regs., Part II. and the Staff Manual respectively. Title pages will be prepared in manuscript.

WAR DIARY
or
~~INTELLIGENCE SUMMARY~~.
(Erase heading not required.)

III

No. 6 CAVALRY FIELD AMBULANCE
Date Oct 1917
3rd CAVALRY DIV

Army Form C. 2118.

Place	Date	Hour	Summary of Events and Information	Remarks and references to Appendices
CANETTEMONT (LENS 1/100,000)	23.10.17		Unit moved with Brigade billets at DOMESMONT LENS 1/100,000 Billeting party having billeted at DOMESMONT proceeded on to PONT REMY (LENS 1/100,000)	RRF
DOMESMONT (LENS 1/100,000)	24.10.17		Unit moved with Brigade to final billets at PONT REMY (LENS 1/100,000)	RRF
PONT REMY (ABBEVILLE 1/100,000)	28.10.17		1 Sergt RAMC + 20 OR's RAMC ~~[illegible]~~ joined 3rd CAV. DIV. PIONEER BATT for duty.	
			CAPT HV FITZGERALD + 4 OR's (1 ASC Batman + 3 OR's RAMC) joined 3rd CAV. DIV PIONEER BATT to take over medical charge	
			1 riding horse sent for use of CAPT FITZGERALD	
			1 Cpl RAMC + 1 driver ASC HT taken on the strength	RRF
	30.10.17		2 Ptes RAMC proceeded to Reinforcement Camp ETAPLES for transfer to Infantry	
			Patients admitted to H 22nd – 31st 13 (thirteen) of which 7 (seven) were Scabies	
			Total Patients admitted to H for October 51 (fifty one) of which	RRF

T2134. Wt. W708–776. 500000. 4/15. Sir J. C. & S.

Instructions regarding War Diaries and Intelligence Summaries are contained in F. S. Regs., Part II. and the Staff Manual respectively. Title pages will be prepared in manuscript.

WAR DIARY
or
~~INTELLIGENCE~~ ~~SUMMARY~~.
IV
(*Erase heading not required.*)

Army Form C. 2118.

Place	Date	Hour	Summary of Events and Information	Remarks and references to Appendices
PONT REMY ABBEVILLE (1/100,000)			9 (nine) were Scabies + 3 (three) Diarrhoea The unit is in good billets. Cover for all the horses has been found but stables are very scattered. There are three large billets for the men (two for ASC + 1 for RAMC). The RAMC men have a very good billet but it has a stone cement floor. Straw has been obtained for these + palliasses have been ~~made from~~ ERL improvised. Special fire orders have been posted in each billet + fire buckets provided. A large concert hall has been obtained for a hospital suitable for about 50 patients + a smaller room a few yards away for a Scabies hospital Sick are now collected by horsed ambulances, only urgent cases being sent for by ambulance car. ERL E R Lovell Capt RAMC SR	

T2134. Wt. W708-776. 500000. 4/15. Sir J. C. & S.

Dec. 1917

140/2618

No. 6. Cav. F.A.

6th Cav Fd Amb
Vol 6

Army Form C. 2118.

Instructions regarding War Diaries and Intelligence Summaries are contained in F. S. Regs., Part II. and the Staff Manual respectively. Title pages will be prepared in manuscript.

WAR DIARY
or
~~INTELLIGENCE SUMMARY.~~
(Erase heading not required.)

Place	Date	Hour	Summary of Events and Information	Remarks and references to Appendices
LA VICOGNE (LENS 1/100,000)	1.12.17		Capt. H.Y. FITZGERALD, R.A.M.C. + 8 other ranks (5 O.R. Ramc + 3 A.S.C. M.T. O.R.) with two motor ambulances left at 2 am. this morning to report to A.D.M.S. ~~Cav~~ 3rd Cav. Division. Authority A.D.M.S. operation order No 7. d/30/11/17. This party in conjunction with a similar party from Nos. 7 + 8 C.F.As, was to form a temporary medical unit to care for the Dismounted Brigade (3rd Cav. Div) until ~~No~~ 7 C.F.A. moved up to the line.	
			4 Other Ranks Ramc. (To act as battalion stretcher bearers), 1 A.S.C. H.T. driver with water cart, + 1 water cart orderly (Ramc) with push cycle, left this morning to proceed up to the line with the 6th Dismounted Battalion (3rd Cav. Div). Authority G.S. 3rd Cav. Div. G/407/5. d/4/11/17. C.T.S.	
ALLONVILLE (AMIENS 1/100,000)	2.12.17		Unit moved to ALLONVILLE today. Authority 6th Cav. Brig. L/535. d/1/12/17. This authority cancels 6th Cav. Brig. M/570/1. d/30/11/17 ordering the unit to be ready to move at one hour's notice.	
			Capt. A NEILSON, Ramc, 1 Sergt + 6 O.R. Ramc left this afternoon for temporary duty with IIIrd Corps Main Dressing Station at V.18.c. (Ref map 57C. 1/40,000). Authority A.D.M.S. H/981. d/2/12/17. C.T.S.	

2353 Wt. W2514/1454 700,000 5/15 D. D. & L. A.D.S.S./Forms/C. 2118.

Army Form C. 2118.

Instructions regarding War Diaries and Intelligence Summaries are contained in F. S. Regs., Part II. and the Staff Manual respectively. Title pages will be prepared in manuscript.

WAR DIARY
or
~~INTELLIGENCE SUMMARY.~~

(Erase heading not required.)

II

NO 6 CAVALRY FIELD AMBULANCE
No. ......
Date ......
III CAVALRY DIVISION

Place	Date	Hour	Summary of Events and Information	Remarks and references to Appendices
ALLONVILLE (Amiens 1/100,000)	3.12.17		Capt. H V FITZGERALD, RAMC + 8 O.R. RAMC with 2 motor ambulances (vide above 1/12/17) returned to this unit. Owing to No 7 C.F.A. having moved up the line with the Dismounted Brigade, 3rd Cav. Div., this unit (No 6 C.F.A.) took over medical charge of the 7th Cav. Brigade. As one Regimental Med. Off. from each Brigade was detailed in medical charge of each dismounted Battalion in the line, this also involved detailing a medical officer to see the daily sick of one regiment in each of the 6th + 7th Cav. Brigades. This was arranged for by sending out a Med. Off. from the Field Ambulance daily. In cases of urgency arrangements were made for Regiments without a permanent Med. Off. to apply to the nearest Regimental M.O, or direct to the Field Ambulance. Authority for above arrangements – A.D.M.S. H/980 d/1/12/17. C.W.J.	
	5.12.17		One motor ambulance sent to No 8 C.F.A. for temporary duty. C.W.J.	
	7.12.17		Patients admitted to Hospital for week ending Dec. 7 = 19. (Scabies, Diarrhoea, etc.) C.W.J.	
	8.12.17		Capt. NEILSON, RAMC 1 Sgt. + 6 O.R. who went to 3rd Corps M.D.S. on 3rd inst, were transferred today to No 5 C.C.S. TINCOURT for temporary duty. C.W.J.	

2353 Wt. W2544/1454 700,000 5/15 D. D. & L. A.D.S.S./Forms/C. 2118.

Instructions regarding War Diaries and Intelligence Summaries are contained in F. S. Regs., Part II. and the Staff Manual respectively. Title pages will be prepared in manuscript.

WAR DIARY

or

~~INTELLIGENCE SUMMARY.~~ III

(Erase heading not required.)

Army Form [redacted]2118.

Place	Date	Hour	Summary of Events and Information	Remarks and references to Appendices
ALLONVILLE (Amiens 1/100,000)	11.12.17		2 Corporals + 10 other ranks, R.A.M.C. proceeded today to 407 C.F.A. for temporary duty while that unit is in medical charge of the 3rd Cav. Dismounted Brigade. C.W.S.	
	13.12.17		New nomenclature for Cavalry Corps units when organised for acting dismounted is as follows:– 3rd Dismounted Division composed of 6th, 7th + 8th Dismounted Brigades. The words "Cavalry" + "Battalion" [are?] no longer used. Authority 6th Cav. Brigade L531/21, d/13/12/17 C.W.S.	
	14.12.17		Patients admitted to Hospital during week ending 14th inst = 26 (Scabies 3, Diarrhoea 1). C.W.S.	
	16.12.17		Capt. H.Y. FITZGERALD, R.A.M.C. proceeded to 408 C.F.A. for temporary duty. Authority A.D.M.S. M/223/25 d/15/12/17. C.W.S.	
	17.12.17		Heavy fall of snow. Motor transport entirely interrupted. Evacuation of sick carried out with considerable difficulty by horse transport. C.W.S.	
	20.12.17		Capt. H.Y. FITZGERALD, R.A.M.C. returned from temporary duty with 408 C.F.A. C.W.S.	
YAUCOURT-BUSSUS (ABBEVILLE 1/100,000)	21.12.17		Unit moved to YAUCOURT-BUSSUS. Authority 6th Cav. Brigade L567/d/20/12/17 C.W.S.	

Instructions regarding War Diaries and Intelligence Summaries are contained in F. S. Regs., Part II. and the Staff Manual respectively. Title pages will be prepared in manuscript.

WAR DIARY
or
~~INTELLIGENCE~~ SUMMARY. IV

(Erase heading not required.)

Army Form C. 2118.

No. 6 CAVALRY FIELD AMBULANCE No. ___ Date ___ 1st CAVALRY DIVN.

Place	Date	Hour	Summary of Events and Information	Remarks and references to Appendices
YAUCOURT-BUSSUS. (ABBEVILLE 1/100,000)	21.12.17 (contd)		The 2nd Life Guards were left behind in isolation in the 7th Brigade area, owing to an outbreak of Epizootic Lymphangitis. Under instructions from A.D.M.S. d/20/12/17 a light ambulance (with 2 horses & a driver) and a Corporal R.A.M.C. were left behind to evacuate the sick of the 2nd Life Guards. To avoid contagion this party was billeted in the neighbouring village of QUERRIEU. Patients admitted to Hospital during week ending 21st inst. = 11. (1 to scabies + 10 diarrhoea)	
	27.12.17		Medical charge of 2nd Life Guards handed over to M.O. 8 C.F.A. (A.D.M.S. H/1034 d/25/12/17). The two horses for light ambulance at Querrieu (vide above) handed over to 2nd Life Guards, as the 6th Cavalry Brigade would not take the responsibility of allowing them to return to the Brigade. Harness, horse rugs, etc were also handed over to the 2nd Life Guards. A fresh pair of horses, with harness etc was sent out to bring the ambulance back to this unit. The ambulance was thoroughly disinfected under the supervision of an officer before the horses were harnessed in. W.J.	

Instructions regarding War Diaries and Intelligence Summaries are contained in F. S. Regs., Part II. and the Staff Manual respectively. Title pages will be prepared in manuscript.

WAR DIARY
or
~~INTELLIGENCE SUMMARY.~~ V

(Erase heading not required.)

Army Form C. 2118.

Place	Date	Hour	Summary of Events and Information	Remarks and references to Appendices
YAUCOURT–BUSSUS. (Abbeville 1/100,000)	27.12.17		A motor ambulance proceeded to No 8 C.F.A. for temporary duty.	C.W.S.
	until 28.12.17		The two motor ambulances remaining on the strength were sent out on duty today & both failed to return. Held up in snowdrifts.	C.W.S.
	29.12.17		The car which was stuck in the snow near ABBEVILLE yesterday returned this morning. Fortunately this car was returning from evacuation duty when blocked by snowdrifts, so no patients were in the car at the time. A Divisional Wheelers shop having been opened today at DOMART, the wheeler belonging to this unit was sent there today for duty. C.W.S.	
	31.12.17		The other motor ambulance car, held up in snowdrifts near BEAUMETZ on the 28th inst returned this evening. Patients admitted to hospital during period 22nd – 31st 12 (Scabies nil, Diarrhoea nil). C.W.S.	
			During the period 17th – 31st, owing to heavy snow falls & severe frost, the work of this unit was	C.W.S.

2353 Wt. W2544/1454 700,000 5/15 D. D. & L. A.D.S.S./Forms/C. 2118.

Instructions regarding War Diaries and Intelligence Summaries are contained in F. S. Regs., Part II. and the Staff Manual respectively. Title pages will be prepared in manuscript.

WAR DIARY

or

~~INTELLIGENCE SUMMARY.~~ VI

(Erase heading not required.)

Army Form C. 2118.

Place	Date	Hour	Summary of Events and Information	Remarks and references to Appendices
YAUCOURT -BUSSUS (Abbeville 1/100,000)			carried out with the greatest difficulty. During the greater part of the period motor transport was completely immobilized. Extra teams of horses had to be put into light Ambulances & wagons. The frost cogs supplied were of very poor quality & wore down rapidly. A trek of ten miles over ground which was partly soft snow & partly ice, was sufficient to render a large proportion of these frost cogs useless.	
			Total patients admitted to Hospital during month = 68. (Scabies 4. Diarrhoea 1)	
			Patients evacuated during the month:	
			Officers sick 5 wounded 0. = 5	
			O. Ranks " 36 " 0 = 36	
			Total = 41	
			[illegible] Capt. R.A.M.C. O.C. No 6 C. F. Ambulance.	

16

Instructions regarding War Diaries and Intelligence Summaries are contained in F. S. Regs., Part II. and the Staff Manual respectively. Title pages will be prepared in manuscript.

WAR DIARY
or
~~INTELLIGENCE SUMMARY.~~
(Erase heading not required.)

Army Form C. 2118.

6th Cav Fd Amb
37

Place	Date	Hour	Summary of Events and Information	Remarks and references to Appendices
YAUCOURT – BUSSUS (Abbeville 1/100,000)	1.1.18		Take over medical charge of 7th Brigade Headquarters & 14th Mob Vet Section at FRANSU (Author. A.D.M.S. H/1034/2/1, d/1/1/18. C.W.S.	
	3.1.18		One motor ambulance returned from temporary duty with MO & C.F.A. C.W.S.	
	5.1.18		Take over medical charge of 2nd Life Guards at RIBEAUCOURT, also of 3rd Cav. Div School, BERNAVILLE. C.W.S.	
	7.1.18		Take over medical charge of 3rd Dragoon Guards during absence of their Medical Officer. Medical arrangements for outside units were shown in Appendix (I).	vide App. D.
			Patients admitted to Hospital during week ending 7.1.18 – 19. (Scabies, 3 Diarrhoea 1). C.W.S.	
	11.1.18		"Thaw scheme" in force from 6 pm tonight. C.W.S.	
	12.1.18		Officer Commanding Cavalry Field Ambulance, appointed to rank of acting Lieut. Colonel (Authority W.O. letter no/Medical/517/A.M.D.1/d/16/12/17) Authority in accordance with C.D.S. 384 (Sec. III) obtained & the acting rank assumed by me today. C.W.S.	
	13.1.18		"Thaw scheme" postponed. C.W.S.	

Instructions regarding War Diaries and Intelligence Summaries are contained in F. S. Regs., Part II. and the Staff Manual respectively. Title pages will be prepared in manuscript.

WAR DIARY
or
INTELLIGENCE SUMMARY.
(Erase heading not required.)

II

Army Form C. 21

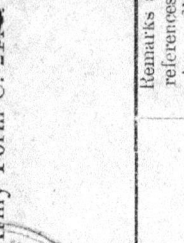

Place	Date	Hour	Summary of Events and Information	Remarks and references to Appendices
YAUCOURT -BUSSUS (Abbeville [illegible])	13.1.18	Contd.	Report sent to A.D.M.S. 3rd Cav. Div. with reference to proposed reduction in personnel, horses, transport + supplies of all kinds in Cavalry Field Ambulances (A.D.M.S. H/1059/d/4/1/18). Report (6 C.F.A. S/534/13/1/18) recommends (1) various reductions in A.F. G1098-62 Add/Dec 1916, + recommends certain additions. (2) no reduction in personnel or horses. (3) no change from heavy H.T. transport to lorry transport. C.W.J.	
	14.1.18		Patients admitted to Hospital for week ending 14.1.18 = 11. (Scabies 4) C.W.J.	
	15.1.18		"Thaw" scheme in force from today. C.W.J.	
	16.1.18		3rd Cav. Dismounted Division returned today from trenches. This unit prepared + distributed hot soup to above Dismounted Division (800 all ranks) at LONPRÉ Station. C.W.J.	
	18.1.18		1.O.R. A.S.C., 1 O.R. R.A.M.C. + 1 water cart returned today from duty with 6th Dismd. Batt. C.W.J.	
	19.1.18		Capt. C.M. Willmott R.A.M.C. returned from duty with 3rd Cav. Div. Inf. Bde. C.W.J.	
	21.1.18		"Thaw scheme" cancelled. Patients admitted to Hospital for week ending Jan 21st = 24 (Scabies 2, Diarrhoea 1). C.W.J.	

Instructions regarding War Diaries and Intelligence Summaries are contained in F. S. Regs., Part II. and the Staff Manual respectively. Title pages will be prepared in manuscript.

WAR DIARY
or
~~INTELLIGENCE SUMMARY.~~ III

(Erase heading not required.)

Army Form C. [illegible]8.

Place	Date	Hour	Summary of Events and Information	Remarks and references to Appendices
YAUCOURT -BUSSUS (Abbeville 1/100000)	24.1.18		Capt. C.M. WILLMOTT R.A.M.C. and six O.Rs. proceeded for temporary duty with 3rd Cav. Pioneer Regt. at TREFCON. 1st Anzac Corps Cav. Regt. attached to 6 Cav. Brig., & to this unit for medical arrangements. No 75607 Cpl. Robb R.A.M.C. returned from temporary duty as clerk to A.D.M.S. Dismounted Divisions. C.M.S.	
	25.1.18		Capt. H.Y. FITZGERALD, R.A.M.C. assumes medical charge of North Somerset Yeomanry during absence on leave of Capt. Clarke, R.A.M.C. C.M.S.	
	27.1.18		7 O.Rs. proceeded by lorry to new area (MONCHY-LAGACHE). All sick remaining in Hospital evacuated to No 3 Australian General Hospital, ABBEVILLE. C.M.S.	
BELLOY-SUR-SOMME. (AMIENS 1/100000)	28.1.18		Unit moved to BELLOY-SUR-SOMME.	C.M.S.
GUILLAUCOURT (Amiens 1/100000)	29.1.18		Unit moved to GUILLAUCOURT.	
MERAUCOURT (62C. V12 b28)	30.1.18		Unit moved to MERAUCOURT.	
~~[illegible]~~	31.1.18		Unit to move to final area, TREFCON, tomorrow 1.2.18. Patients admitted to hospital for period 22–31/1/18 = 42 (Scabies 2. Diarrhoea 3). Total number of patients admitted during January 1918 = 96. C.M.S.	

2353 Wt. W2544/1454 700,000 5/15 D. D. & L. A.D.S.S./Forms/C. 2118.

Instructions regarding War Diaries and Intelligence Summaries are contained in F. S. Regs., Part II. and the Staff Manual respectively. Title pages will be prepared in manuscript.

WAR DIARY
or
INTELLIGENCE SUMMARY.
(Erase heading not required.)

IV

Army Form C. [redacted].

Place	Date	Hour	Summary of Events and Information	Remarks and references to Appendices
MERAUCOURT (62C. V12b2.6.)	31.1.18	cont^d	which 11 were Scabies, + 5 Diarrhoea. Evacuations during Jan. 1918 =	
			Officers, sick 4. wounded nil.	
			O.Rs. " 62 " "	
			Total 66. Returned to duty = 30.	
			Appendix ①.	
			Scheme of medical arrangement for units of 6th & 7th Cavalry Brigades and 3rd Cav. Div. School, dated 7.1.18.	
			Motor ambulance with Medical Officer leaves daily at 9 a.m. on round:- ① DOMLEGER, 1st L. Guards, ~~collect~~ sick ② RIBEAUCOURT, 2nd L. Guards + (3) FRANSU, 7th Brig. Hd Qrs. + 14 M.V.S. collect sick. (4) BERNAVILLE, Divisional School, + ⑤ BERNEUIL 7th M. Gun. Sqdn see sick. ⑥ DOMART, Divisional Hd. Qrs. + ⑦ MOUFFLERS, 1st R. Dragoons, collect sick.	
			Motor ambulance with M.O. leaves daily at 9 a.m. on round:- ① EPAGNE, 6th M.G. Sqdn see sick. ② LONG, N.S. Yeomanry & 6 Brig. Hd Qrs. collect sick. ③ AILLY-LE-HAUT CLOCHER 3rd D. Guards see sick. Light ambulance to GORENFLOS to collect sick of R.H. Guards. Light Ambulance to BUSSUS-BUSSUE to collect sick of 3rd D. Guards.	
			[illegible] Lieut. Colonel RAMC O.C. No 6 C.F.A.	

2353 Wt. W2544/1454 700,000 5/15 D. D. & L. A.D.S.S./Forms/C. 2118.

Feb. 1918.

140/2784

No. 6. Cav. F. A.

Instructions regarding War Diaries and Intelligence Summaries are contained in F. S. Regs., Part II. and the Staff Manual respectively. Title pages will be prepared in manuscript.

16

WAR DIARY
or
~~INTELLIGENCE SUMMARY.~~ I
(*Erase heading not required.*)

Army Form C. [redacted]

Vol 38

Place	Date	Hour	Summary of Events and Information	Remarks and references to Appendices
TREFCON (62 C NE 10a46)	1.2.18		Move to TREFCON. Take over site from "SECUNDERABAD" Cavalry Field Ambulance, including 3 III Army Huts, 1 Adrian Hut, 3 Nissen Huts, & 2 Hospital marquees. In medical charge of 6th & 7th Cavalry Brigades. Weekly baths with exchange of clothing at Brigade baths, lately arranged for the personnel. C.W.S.	
	3.2.18		Capt. C.M. WILLMOTT, RAMC & 1 O.R. RAMC returned from temporary duty with 3rd Cav. Pioneer Regt. Inspection by A.D.M.S. C.W.S.	
	4.2.18		Attend Brigade conference re measures for protection against enemy bombing. 2 other ranks RAMC returned from temporary duty with 3rd Cav. Pioneer Regt. C.W.S.	
	5.2.18		Attend conference at A.D.M.S. Office. Arrange particulars re modified light section for use in event of a German attack. Main features being 5 light ambulances, lighter load of stores & equipment to be carried; pack & mounted section to be in abeyance, but sergeants to be mounted. C.W.S.	
	6.2.18		Capt. A NEILSON RAMC & 7 O.R. RAMC returned from temporary C.W.S.	

Instructions regarding War Diaries and Intelligence Summaries are contained in F. S. Regs., Part II. and the Staff Manual respectively. Title pages will be prepared in manuscript.

WAR DIARY
or
~~INTELLIGENCE SUMMARY.~~ II

(Erase heading not required.)

Army Form C. [redacted]

Place	Date	Hour	Summary of Events and Information	Remarks and references to Appendices
TREFCON (62CW10a46)	6.2.18	contd.	duty with No 5 C.C.S. TINCOURT. Detail Medical Officer in charge of 33 Labour Coy. & "U" Battery, both at CAULINCOURT. A.D.M.S. Concentration orders, H/1202 d/6/2/18 received. [initials]	
	7.2.18		Capt. MACCALLUM RAMC. to No 8 C.F.A. for temporary duty. Patients admitted to Hospital week ending Feb. 7th = 29 (Scabies 1, Diarrhoea 3). [initials]	
	8.2.18		Brigade orders received today re concentration in event of enemy attack. [initials]	
	9.2.18		Capt. MacCallum RAMC from No 8 C.F.A. from temporary duty. [initials]	
	10.2.18		2 A.S.C. drivers & 4 horses to Divisional Potato Farm for ploughing. [initials]	
	11.2.18		Authority obtained for motor ambulances of 6 C.F.A. to travel against the traffic arrows in this area. [initials]	
	12.2.18		One O.R. sent in accordance with A.D.M.S. instructions to 7th Brigade Baths at CAULAINCOURT, with dressings for use in case of enemy bombing. This man to see all men attending baths, & to detect early cases of vermin or scabies. [initials]	

T.2134. Wt. W708-776. 500000. 4/15. Sir J. C. & S.

Instructions regarding War Diaries and Intelligence Summaries are contained in F. S. Regs., Part II. and the Staff Manual respectively. Title pages will be prepared in manuscript.

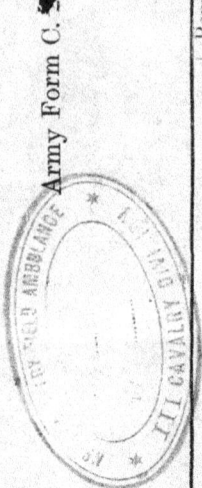

WAR DIARY
or
~~INTELLIGENCE~~ SUMMARY. III

(*Erase heading not required.*)

Army Form C.

Place	Date	Hour	Summary of Events and Information	Remarks and references to Appendices
TREFCON (62C, W10a 46)	13.2.18		Report sent to A.D.M.S. re recent increase in no. of cases of Diarrhoea. No definite cause can be ascribed. C.W.J.	
	14.2.18		Patients admitted to F.A. week ending Feb. 14th = 49. (Scabies 4, Diarrhoea 6). C.W.J.	
	15.2.18		G.O.C. 6th Cav. Brigade inspected camp. C.W.J.	
	16.2.18		3 Motor ambulance cars (all Sunbeams) to 3rd Cav. Div. Sup. Col. for transfer to 5th Cav. Division. C.W.J.	
	18.2.18		3 motor ambulance cars (1 Daimler, 1 4 cylinder Wolsley, 1 6-cylinder Wol.) report for duty from 5th Cav. Division. 3 bombs dropped on Trefcon last night, one man wounded, 14 horses of [illegible] killed. C.W.J.	
	19.2.18		Orders received from D.D.M.S. Cav. Corps. re medical arrangements in event of an enemy attack. C.W.J.	
	21.2.18		"Thaw precautions" in operation. 33 Labour Coy. T/ of medical charge. Patients admitted to F.A. for week ending Feb 21st = 47 (Scabies 8, Diarrhoea 1). C.W.J.	
	22.2.18		2 mounted stretcher bearers R.A.M.C. to be attached daily C.W.J.	

T.134. Wt. W708-776. 500000. 4/15. Sir J. C. & S.

Instructions regarding War Diaries and Intelligence Summaries are contained in F. S. Regs., Part II. and the Staff Manual respectively. Title pages will be prepared in manuscript.

WAR DIARY
or
~~INTELLIGENCE SUMMARY.~~ IV

(*Erase heading not required.*)

Army Form C. 2118.

Place	Date	Hour	Summary of Events and Information	Remarks and references to Appendices
TREFCON (62c, W10a46)				
	22.2.18 contd.		to working party from Brigade digging defensive lines, authority G.O.C. 3rd Cav. Div. per 6 Cav. Brig. L/49/10/d/20/2/18. C.W.S.	
	23.2.18		5 O.R. RAMC to A.D.S. VERMAND for temporary duty (A.D.M.S. H/1288/d/22/2/18. Inspection by A.D.M.S. C.W.S.	
	24.2.18		"Thaw precautions" cancelled. Capt. H.V. FITZGERALD, RAMC & 3 nursing orderlies to RAMC School of Instruction (5th Army), HAM; & 1 O.R. to School of Sanitation, PERONNE, for course of training. C.W.S.	
	25.2.18		3 O.Rs, RAMC returned from temporary duty with 3rd Cav. Pioneer Regt. C.W.S.	
	26.2.18		Further operation orders from A.D.M.S. with special reference to formation of walking wounded Posts. C.W.S.	
	28.2.18		Working party on Defensive Lines cancelled. Two drivers & 4 horses returned from duty at Divisional Potato Farm. Patients admitted to H. for week ending Feb. 28th = 14 (Scabies 3). Total admissions for February 1918 = 139. (Scabies 6. Diar[illegible])	

C.W.S.

Instructions regarding War Diaries and Intelligence Summaries are contained in F. S. Regs., Part II. and the Staff Manual respectively. Title pages will be prepared in manuscript.

WAR DIARY
or
~~INTELLIGENCE SUMMARY.~~ V
(Erase heading not required.)

Army Form C. [redacted]

Place	Date	Hour	Summary of Events and Information	Remarks and references to Appendices
TREFCOM (62C. W10a 4.6)			Evacuations:	
			Officers:— Sick 3 wounded nil } = 75 } = 139	
			O. Rank:— " 71 " 1 }	
			Returned to Duty = 47 Remaining = 17 Total = 64 }	
			Infection cases = Dysentery 2	
			Mumps 3	
			Dipthenia 1	
			Cerebro Spinal Fever 1	
			The month of February has been characterized by —	
			I. Operation orders varying from time to time & dealing with arrangements in event of an attempted German "break through". These orders laid down "Stand To" & "Concentration" Points, & organization of personnel & equipment in event of alarm. There also came into force a 5th Army scheme arranging for a Central Records Office, at BERNES for ~~receiving~~ Cavalry Corps units & med	
			C.W.S.	

T.134. Wt. W708-776. 500000, 4/15. Sir J. C. & S.

Instructions regarding War Diaries and Intelligence Summaries are contained in F. S. Regs., Part II. and the Staff Manual respectively. Title pages will be prepared in manuscript.

WAR DIARY
or
~~INTELLIGENCE SUMMARY.~~ VI
(Erase heading not required.)

Army Form C. [redacted]

NO. 6 CAVALRY FIELD AMBULANCE ... CAVALRY

Place	Date	Hour	Summary of Events and Information	Remarks and references to Appendices
TREFCON (62C W10 a 4.6)			particulars of each case on A.F. W3210 to Central Record Office, whence casualty wires will be sent to D.D.M.S. Corps. Field medical card to accompany soldier.	
			II The amount of construction work done on the present ambulance site. The main work done may be summarized as follows:- (1) Construction of cook houses & ovens for personnel, hospital, sergeants' mess & officers, (2) Re-erecting of Nissen Hut, (3) Bricks paths all over camp, transport stand, & stand for motor ambulances. (4) Digging up unused ground for cultivation (5) Bomb protection for all huts & marquees. (6) New guard room, temporary walls for stables, hut for reserve forage, Quartermaster's store, Pack store, fire stands, lay floor of Hospital huts. (7) Brick incinerator for incineration of faeces. (8) External tarring & internal painting of Hospital huts. (9) Ablution bench & patients' latrines. Repairs & renovation of existing work was also carried out.	
			W. Stringer Lt. Col. RAMC O.C. No 6 C.F.A.	
			Jack Powell Lieut. Col. R.A.M.C. A. D. M. S. 3rd Cav. Div.	

T.134. Wt. W708–776. 500000. 4/15. Sir J. C. & S.

Mar. 1918.

110/2849

No. 6 Cav. F. A.

24 6 C F A

Instructions regarding War Diaries and Intelligence Summaries are contained in F. S. Regs., Part II. and the Staff Manual respectively. Title pages will be prepared in manuscript.

WAR DIARY
or
~~INTELLIGENCE SUMMARY.~~
(Erase heading not required.)

No 6 C F A

I 6 Cav Fd Amb

Vol 39

Army Form C. 2118.

Place	Date	Hour	Summary of Events and Information	Remarks and references to Appendices
TREFCON (62c. W10a.4.6.)	1·3·18		Conference at office of A.D.M.S. re medical arrangements in event of defensive fighting. C.W.J.	
	4·3·18		Capt. P.A. McCALLUM, RAMC returned from leave & proceeded to No 8 C.F.A. for temp. duty. No 7 C.F.A. complete with 3 Officers billeted on this unit today. Cut down Hospital accomodation accordingly to 20 beds. C.W.J.	
	5·3·18		Inspection of cars by D.D. Mechanical Transport. Cars in excellent condition. Inspection of Light Section by A.D.M.S. Everything satisfactory. C.W.J.	
	6·3·18		Capt. Fitzgerald returned from course of Instruction at HAM. C.W.J.	
	7·3·18		Patients admitted to Hospital for week ending March 7th = 1 Off. 43 O.R (Scabies 3. Diarrhoea 3). C.W.J.	
	9·3·18		Capt. H.V. FITZGERALD, RAMC transferred to No 8 C.F.A. Capt. A.W. FORREST RAMC from No 8 C.F.A. taken on the strength of this unit. C.W.J.	
	11·3·18		Capt. Forrest to 1st R. Dragoons for temporary duty. C.W.J.	
	12·3·18		Advance party to ST. CREN to take over Divisional Rest Station from No 4 C.F.A. Advance party from 73rd F. Amb. arrive to take over this site. 4 O. Ranks returned from temp. duty at A.D.S. VERMAND. C.W.J.	

T.2134. Wt. W708—776. 500000. 4/15. Sir J. C. & S.

Instructions regarding War Diaries and Intelligence Summaries are contained in F. S. Regs., Part II. and the Staff Manual respectively. Title pages will be prepared in manuscript.

WAR DIARY
or
~~INTELLIGENCE SUMMARY.~~
(Erase heading not required.)

II

Army Form C. 2118.

Place	Date	Hour	Summary of Events and Information	Remarks and references to Appendices
ST. CREN (62a. P27a)	13.3.18		Move to ST. CREN. Take over 2 Nissen Huts, 2 Adrian Huts & some house accomodation. Take over 25 patients. Open as Divisional Rest Station, also for reception of sick of 6th Cav Brig. & neighbouring units of 3rd Cav. Div. Also the Division is now being administered by XIX Corps. A.T.S.	
	14.3.18		Patients admitted to Hospital for week ending Mar 14th = 2 Off. 88 O. Ranks (Scabies 13. Diarrhoea 5). A.T.S.	
	16.3.18		Arrange for construction of vapour bath for treatment of Scabies of the Division, work well in hand. A.T.S.	
	17.3.18		Capt. McCALLUM returned from temporary duty with No 8 C.F.A. 1 Off. & 15 O.R. arrived for temporary duty from No 1 C.F.A. A.T.S.	
	18.3.18		Inspected by G.O.C. 3rd Cav Div. & A.D.M.S. Later horses were inspected by A.D.V.S. A.T.S.	
	20.3.18		Transport inspected by O.C. A.S.C. 3rd Cav. Div. very pleased with everything	
	21.3.18		1 Off. + 15 O.R. from No 1 C.F.A. returned to their unit. Capt. A. NEILSON to Royal Canadian Dragoons for temporary duty. ~~Heavy~~ section A.T.S.	

T2134. Wt. W708–776. 500000. 4/15. Sir J. C. & S.

Instructions regarding War Diaries and Intelligence Summaries are contained in F. S. Regs., Part II. and the Staff Manual respectively. Title Pages will be prepared in manuscript.

WAR DIARY
or
~~INTELLIGENCE SUMMARY~~

(Erase heading not required.)

III

Army Form C. 2118

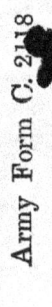

Place	Date	Hour	Summary of Events and Information	Remarks and references to Appendices
BEAUMONT-EN-BEINE. (66d W 6)			remained at ST. CREN to clear cases & hand over site to 73 F. Amb. the following day (22.3.18). Light section left ST. CREN at 4.30 pm, accompanying 6th Cavalry Brigade. Arrived BEAUMONT-EN-BEINE at 9.30 pm. C.T.S. Patients admitted for week ending 21st = 2 Off. 126 O.R. (Scabies 10. Diarrhoea 3).	
VILLEQUIER-AUMONT. (66d X 24 c)	22.3.18		Leave Beaumont-en-Beine at 7.30 am. Arrive at VILLEQUIER-AUMONT at 8.30 am. See Regt. Medical Officers & make medical arrangements. This ambulance is the medical unit for the IIIrd Corps Reserve Cavalry which is comprised of 7th & Canadian Brigades (Cavalry). At 10.30 pm I moved the Headquarters & personnel of the C.F.A. to a point just outside Villequier-Aumont owing to the latter place being bombed. Cavalry still in Reserve. C.T.S.	→ 66d X 24 c 5 9.
	23.3.18		Cavalry dismounted & put into line this morning. I established a bearer & aid post in FRIÈRES wood (66e. S 9 d 9 2) to look after 7th Brigade. The post consisted of Capt. LOVELL RAMC, 8 bearers, 1 mounted Sergt RAMC. Stretchers, blankets & dressings, + 2 light ambulances. I also established a similar post on main road just outside FALLOUEL for the Canadian Brigade. This post was in charge of Capt McCALLUM RAMC. Both posts evacuated to 52 Field Ambulance Main Dressing Station in VILLEQUIER-AUMONT. This worked satisfactorily till the Field Ambulance was shelled out of Villequier & the nearest point of evacuation became GUIVRY (66d W 29 d). The light ambulances actually performed this journey & returned, but wounded could not have been got away if fullest use had not been made of empty	→ 66e S 2 d.

C.T.S.

1875 Wt. W593/826 1,000,000 4/15 J.B.C. & A. A.D.S.S./Forms/C. 2118.

Instructions regarding War Diaries and Intelligence Summaries are contained in F. S. Regs., Part II. and the Staff Manual respectively. Title pages will be prepared in manuscript.

WAR DIARY
or
~~INTELLIGENCE SUMMARY.~~ IV

(*Erase heading not required.*)

Army Form C. 21[illegible]8.

Place	Date	Hour	Summary of Events and Information	Remarks and references to Appendices
VILLEQUIER-AUMONT. (66d X24c59)			lorries + horse transport of every description. A relief of horses was also made as light ambulances passed the Headquarters at Villequier-Aumont (66d X24c59.). Unable to get into communication with D.D.M.S. III Corps + A.D.M.S. 18th Div, ordered to fall back to UGNY. Sent my limbers back but kept up the Horse ambulances till the last moment. Later with Headquarters	
UGNY. (66d X20d)			of C.F.A. at UGNY I established a post a GUYENCOURT under Capt. Lovell in conjunction with 56 F. Amb. Light ambulances now worked from Guivry to Guyencourt. This post was withdrawn to UGNY at 8pm. 56 F.A. returning to Guivry. ^cavalry Brigades now in reserve. C.T.J.	
CHATEAU D'ESTAY (70 2 K18a11)	24.3.18		Had to move unit at 4 a.m. owing to getting splashed by shell bursts. Left UGNY at 6 a.m. + move to CAILLOUËL (70E, E24), remain there till about 1pm. + then move to ~~[illegible]~~ 70E K12d, just outside village of DAMPCOURT. Remain there for 2 hours + get shelled. Ordered to move back to BRETIGNY. Order cancelled when unable on road C.T.J.	

Army Form C. 2118.

WAR DIARY
or
~~INTELLIGENCE SUMMARY.~~

(Erase heading not required.)

Instructions regarding War Diaries and Intelligence Summaries are contained in F. S. Regs., Part II. and the Staff Manual respectively. Title pages will be prepared in manuscript.

Place	Date	Hour	Summary of Events and Information	Remarks and references to Appendices
CHATEAU D'ESTAY			+ Division ordered back to area 70 E K 12 & 18. Establish a dressing station in Chateau ESTAY (70 E K18 a 11). Bearer post in cellar in DAMPCOURT. Division still in reserve. 2 motor ambulances + 12 bearers arrive as reinforcements. E.T.S.	
OLLENCOURT (70 E V 6 b 65)	25.3.18		C.F.A. moved at 5.30 a.m. to road west of APPILLY (Sheet 70 E K 16 c) under Capt. LOVELL. I moved to APPILLY + established a collecting post there with 3 motor ambulance cars. Later had to move cars out of Appilly owing to shelling. Cut off from C.F.A. by enemy shelling. Later I sent cars away by last remaining avenue of escape i.e. bridge over Canal de l'Oise at 70 E K 23 d. Bridge barely holding when cars got over having been hit 3 times by enemy shells. Later (about 12 noon) I left APPILLY, there being no other British troops there, + moved to BRETIGNY (70 E K 28 d). Shelling of this village fairly profuse, some casualties in cavalry, but cars were largely employed in evacuating French wounded. Trek to CUTS where I met the C.F.A. E.T.S.	

2353 Wt. W2544/1454 700,000 5/15 D. D. & L. A.D.S.S./Forms/C. 2118.

Instructions regarding War Diaries and Intelligence Summaries are contained in F. S. Regs., Part II. and the Staff Manual respectively. Title pages will be prepared in manuscript.

WAR DIARY
or
INTELLIGENCE SUMMARY. VI
(Erase heading not required.)

Army Form C. 2118.

Place	Date	Hour	Summary of Events and Information	Remarks and references to Appendices
			at western exit of City (Sheet 70 2 O 14 c). The C.F.A. had moved to this point via BABOEUF, canal crossing at ~~J~~ J 30 c, + VARESNES. Move to CARLEPONT, where unit was relieved by Canadian C.F.A. At 9 p.m. move to OLLENCOURT where night was spent resting. C.W.J.	
CHOISY-AU-BAC. (Ref. map Beauvais 1/100,000)	26.3.18		Move to Choisy-au-bac. Park in field on South side of the river AISNE. C.W.J.	
	27.3.18		Left at 12.10 a.m. move back to CARLEPONT. Object being to reinforce Canadian C.F.A. Whole division moved back this morning so trek back again to CHOISY-AU-BAC. + park in former site. C.W.J.	
	28.3.18		Bombed this morning. 1 horse killed + 5 wounded. One A.S.C. H.T. driver severely wounded. Get 3 more motor ambulances, + one motor lorry for carrying bearers + dressings etc. 5 horses sent from 3rd D. Guards to replace casualties. 10 additional riding horses sent to make bearers + sergeants more mobile. All personnel ~~recalled~~ recalled from Heavy Section except 1 Ramc. Sergt, 1 spare driver + the necessary drivers. Capt WILLMOTT to 1st R. Dragoons for temp. duty. C.W.J.	

Instructions regarding War Diaries and Intelligence Summaries are contained in F. S. Regs., Part II. and the Staff Manual respectively. Title pages will be prepared in manuscript.

WAR DIARY
or
~~INTELLIGENCE~~ SUMMARY. VII
(Erase heading not required.)

Army Form C. 2118.

Place	Date	Hour	Summary of Events and Information	Remarks and references to Appendices
~~29.3.18~~ AIRION (BEAUVAIS 1/100,000)	29.3.18		Move to AIRION via Compiegne, Arsy, Clermont, ~~[illegible]~~. Arrive 4.30 pm. Capt. Forrest RAMC returns from temp. duty with 1st R. Dragoons. C.W.S.	
LA RACINEUSE FME (66E A9 C62)	30.3.18		Trek across country to ESTREES-SUR-NOYE, via St. Just. Bivouac at LA RACINEUSE Farm. C.W.S.	
	31.3.18		Same position of readiness. C.W.S.	
			Under instructions from D.D.M.S. Cav. Corps, no admission and discharge book was opened. So there is no record of cases passing through the hands of this unit. A large no. of French casualties were dealt with in addition to British. Total recorded admissions for the month = 5 Offs. 275 O.Rs (Scabies 26, Diarrhoea 11). As period is not completed & time doesn't permit of separate report, comment & criticism of recent operations will be held over till next month.	
			Evacuations during March – 6 officers, O.Rs. 256. To duty, O.Rs. 44.	

C.W. S[illegible]
Lt. Col. RAMC
O.C. 6 C.F.A.

2353 Wt. W2514/1454 700,000 5/15 D. D. & L. A.D.S.S./Forms/C. 2118.

160/2902

Apr. 1918.

6th Cavalry Field Amb.

24

Instructions regarding War Diaries and Intelligence Summaries are contained in F. S. Regs., Part II. and the Staff Manual respectively. Title pages will be prepared in manuscript.

WAR DIARY
or
~~INTELLIGENCE SUMMARY.~~

(Erase heading not required.)

I

6 Cav Fd Amb.

Army Form C. 2118.

Vol 40

Place	Date	Hour	Summary of Events and Information	Remarks and references to Appendices
BOVES. (Amiens 1/100000 E2)	1·4·18		Move at 6.15 am from La Racineuse Farm to BOVES. C.F.A.s are divisionalized + come directly under orders of A.D.M.S. Reconnoitre forward area. C.W.J.	
	2·4·18		Move at 1.30 pm to BLANGY-TRONVILLE. Men in billets. C.W.J. Send in list of names for recommendation to Hd. Qrs 6th Cav Brig. C.W.J.	
BLANGY-TRONVILLE (Amiens 1/100,000 72)	3·4·18		Resting. Capt. McCALLUM, 4 stretcher bearers + 2 motor ambulances left at 1 am. for duty in BOIS L'ABBÉ (Sheet 62d O26d 56) with elements of 6th Cavalry Brigade, lying there in reserve for 1st Cavalry Division. Relieve this officer + bearers by Capt. LOVELL + 4 other bearers at 8 pm. C.W.J.	
Sheet 62 d O26c94.	4·4·18		BOIS L'ABBÉ shelled. Some casualties. Car post moved back to O26c94. 6th + 7th Brigades moved into line dismounted early this morning. 6 C.F.A. moved up + established a Dressing Station in outbuildings of Chateau in O26c94. Visit 6th Cav. Brig. Hd. Qrs. Joined by Capt Lovell, his 4 stretcher bearers + 2 motor ambulance cars, giving a total of the latter of 5 cars. Capt. LYONS, Ramc (M.O. i/c 1st Roy. Drags.) joined this unit from leave. Establish an Advanced Dressing + Collecting station at VILLERS-BRETONNEUX (Amiens 1/100000)(O29c48). C.W.J.	

2353 Wt. W2544/1454 700,000 5/15 D. D. & L. A.D.S.S./Forms/C. 2118.

Instructions regarding War Diaries and Intelligence Summaries are contained in F. S. Regs., Part II. and the Staff Manual respectively. Title pages will be prepared in manuscript.

WAR DIARY
or
~~INTELLIGENCE SUMMARY.~~ II

(Erase heading not required.)

Army Form C. 2118.

Place	Date	Hour	Summary of Events and Information	Remarks and references to Appendices
Sheet 62d O26 C94	4.4.18	contd.	under Capt. Lyons with one motor ambulance car, 2 mounted orderlies, one wheeled stretcher, & 8 bearers with stretchers. This bearer post was tentative & to clear line O18 b to Villers-Bretonneux & P25 to same place. Later the shelling of VILLERS-BRETONNEUX became so intense that this post had to be moved to O23 c 88, when line of evacuation was through FOUILLOY to AUBIGNY where there was an Infantry Main Dressing Station. The 6 C. F. A. Dressing station at O26 c 94 remained owing to the steady stream of British Infantry & Australian wounded coming through. A small number of Cavalry wounded also came down. I visited the bearer post in Villers-Bretonneux, & tried to get through from there to 6th Brigade Headquarters, but just on the other side of V. Bret. I was finally cut off by a severe & prolonged barrage, & I had to return. Arrangements made that if shelling of Villers-Bretonneux died down, an effort must be made to evacuate Cavalry C.W.S.	

Instructions regarding War Diaries and Intelligence Summaries are contained in F. S. Regs., Part II. and the Staff Manual respectively. Title pages will be prepared in manuscript.

WAR DIARY
or
~~INTELLIGENCE SUMMARY.~~ III

(Erase heading not required.)

Army Form C. 2118.

Place	Date	Hour	Summary of Events and Information	Remarks and references to Appendices
Sheet 62d O26c94	4.4.18 contd		wounded to 6 C.F.A. at O26c94. Shortly after returning to O26c94, a ~~short~~ but hurricane bombardment was put down on the Dressing Station. Casualties = 2 killed (one patient), 9 wounded (5 remaining at duty); 3 horses killed, 6 wounded; lorry for walking wounded & stores was hit, the engine being smashed up; 1 motor bicycle & 1 push bicycle knocked out of action. Remainder of transport was variously holed but fit for the road. I ordered immediate evacuation of site. This was done in a smart & orderly manner, all patients & stores being removed. Shortly after leaving, the site was again heavily shelled thus justifying the move.	
N28d04			Moved unit back to N28d04, & opened up an A.D.S. in an Adrian Hut. I had to move so far back owing to there being no intermediate cover for wounded. It was raining steadily & I had no tentage. Capt. McCALLUM R.A.M.C. to 7th Drag. Guards to replace Med. Off. wounded.	

Instructions regarding War Diaries and Intelligence Summaries are contained in F. S. Regs., Part II. and the Staff Manual respectively. Title pages will be prepared in manuscript.

WAR DIARY
or
~~INTELLIGENCE SUMMARY.~~ V

(Erase heading not required.)

No 6 CAVALRY FIELD AMBULANCE No. ______ Date ______ 1st CAVALRY DIVISION

Army Form C. 2118.

Place	Date	Hour	Summary of Events and Information	Remarks and references to Appendices
CAMON (Amiens 1/100,000)	6.4.18 contd.		from temp. duty with Roy. Canadian Dragoons. Capt. WILLMOTT RAMC returned from temp. duty with 1st Roy. Dragoons. Motor ambulance Convoy car sent to report to 1st Cav. Div. Heavy Section rejoins unit from PONT DE METZ (Amiens 1/100,000). Open up Hospital at Camon, to accommodate about 25. C.W.S.	
	7.4.18		Attend conference at A.D.M.S.'s office. Capt. P.A. McCALLUM RAMC returned from temp. duty with 7th D. Gs. Capt. FORREST RAMC transferred to No 7 C.F.A. Capt. MITCHELL, G.W. RAMC from No 7 C.F.A., taken on the strength of this unit. Patients admitted to H. for week ending April 7th = 61, of whom 26 were wounded + 35 sick (3 scabies, 3 diarrhoea). Permission was obtained on the 5th inst. to open an Admission + Discharge Book. ~~[illegible]~~ written authority A.D.M.S. T/10/8/4/18. C.W.S.	
	8.4.18		Resting. C.W.S.	
	9.4.18		Reinforcements to replace casualties came up today. Unit is now complete in officers + personnel. C.W.S.	

Army Form C. 2118.

Instructions regarding War Diaries and Intelligence Summaries are contained in F. S. Regs., Part II. and the Staff Manual respectively. Title pages will be prepared in manuscript.

WAR DIARY
or
~~INTELLIGENCE SUMMARY.~~ IV
(Erase heading not required.)

No. 6 CAVALRY FIELD AMBULANCE * III CAVALRY DIVISION * No. ______ Date ______

Place	Date	Hour	Summary of Events and Information	Remarks and references to Appendices
Sheet 62 D N28d04.	4.4.18	contd.	Lorry obtained from 3rd Cav. Div. M.T. Coy. in replacement of the one knocked out by shell fire. Car & bearer post established at O26c23 (3 light & 1 motor ambulance). Constant touch maintained with Regt. Med. Officers of 6th Cav. Brig. Re-inforce A.D.S. at O23 c.88 with extra bearers (16). Steady stream of wounded all night. C.H.J.	
	5.4.18.		Visit A.D.M.S., 6th Cav. Brig. Hd. Qrs, & A.D.S. at O23c88. All wounded cleared, & medical arrangements thoroughly satisfactory. Visit VILLERS-BRETONNEUX, shelling there very slight, so return & push up car & bearer post to O28d74. Increase this post to 1 Med. Off. 2 motor amb. cars, 2 light ambulances + 8 bearers. Arrange for Cavalry wounded to come down via VILLERS-BRETONNEUX. Canadian C.F.A. move into N28d04 as a reinforcement. Quiet day. Very few wounded. C.H.J.	
CAMON. (Amiens 1/100,000 22).	5.4.18		Relieved at 8 a.m. by Field Ambulance of 5th Australian Division. March back to CAMON. Go into billets. Capt NEILSON, R.A.M.C. returned C.H.J.	

2353 Wt. W2544/1454 700,000 5/15 D. D. & L. A.D.S.S./Forms/C. 2118.

Army Form C. 2118.

CAVALRY FIELD AMBULANCE
No. ________
Date ________
III CAVALRY DIVISION

WAR DIARY
or
~~INTELLIGENCE SUMMARY.~~ VII

(Erase heading not required.)

Instructions regarding War Diaries and Intelligence Summaries are contained in F. S. Regs., Part II. and the Staff Manual respectively. Title pages will be prepared in manuscript.

Place	Date	Hour	Summary of Events and Information	Remarks and references to Appendices
FERFAY Hazebrook 1/100,000 7.6	13.4.18	Contd.	Remain there, standing by, until 2 pm. when unit moved to FERFAY. Heavy Section to SAINS-LES-PERNES (Lens 1/100,000, 21). (from BOYAVAL). On 3 hours notice. Capt. WILLMOTT R.a.m.c. to command Divisionalized Heavy Sections. C.W.S.	
	14.4.18		Stand to at 7 a.m. On 1 3/4 hours notice. Clean + overhaul transport. Patients admitted to Hospital during week ending April 14th = 1 wounded, 43 sick (7 Scabies, 3 Diarrhoea). C Battery R.H.A. rejoins Brigade + located at SACHIN. Medical Officer detailed by me to see their daily sick. C.W.S.	
	15.4.18		Stand to at 6.30 a.m. On 3 1/2 hours notice. C.W.S.	
	16.4.18		Stand to at 7 a.m. On 3 1/2 hours notice. G.O.C. inspects horses. Very pleased. Gas parade. C.W.S.	
	17.4.18		Stand to at 7 a.m. 3 1/2 hours notice. Capt. Willmott granted leave of absence from 18/4/18 to 2/5/18. No 32668 Cpl. Smith, R.a.m.c. 6 C.F.A. awarded Military Medal as an immediate reward for following act of gallantry. "On March 23rd, when the village C.W.S.	

2353 Wt. W2544/1454 700,000 5/15 D. D. & L. A.D.S.S./Forms/C. 2118.

Instructions regarding War Diaries and Intelligence Summaries are contained in F. S. Regs., Part II. and the Staff Manual respectively. Title pages will be prepared in manuscript.

WAR DIARY
or
~~INTELLIGENCE SUMMARY.~~ VI

(Erase heading not required.)

No 6 CAVALRY FIELD AMBULANCE No.______ Date______ 1st CAVALRY DIVISION

Army Form C. 2118.

Place	Date	Hour	Summary of Events and Information	Remarks and references to Appendices
CAMON	9.4.18	contd.	Forward brief report to A.D.M.S. on lessons learnt in recent fighting, vide Appendix A. Total battle casualties in the unit in men & horses during period March 21st – April 6th = Personnel – Killed 1 Wounded 15 Horses – Killed 3 Wounded 14 Further list of names for recommendations forwarded to A.D.M.S. 3rd Cav. Div. C.W.J.	Appendix A.
	10.4.18		To conference at A.D.M.S.'s Office. Unit on 1/2 hours notice from 10 a.m. Later cancelled. To move tomorrow. Capt. MITCHELL + 40 O.Rs. to M1, Sheet 62D to take over 1st Cav. Div. Collecting Station. Left at 6 p.m. & relieved at 8 p.m. by an Australian Field Ambulance. C.W.J.	
BACHIMONT (LENS 1/100,000 B3)	11.4.18		Leave Camon 7.30 a.m. Arrive BACHIMONT 6 p.m. C.W.J.	
CONTEVILLE (LENS 1/100,000 D1.)	12.4.18		On 3/4 hours notice from 11 a.m. Leave at 2 p.m. Arrive CONTVILLE at 10 p.m. Bombed en route. No casualties. C.W.J.	
	13.4.18		Leave 6.30 a.m. Arrive BAILLEUL-LES-PERNES about 10 a.m. C.W.J.	

Instructions regarding War Diaries and Intelligence Summaries are contained in F. S. Regs., Part II. and the Staff Manual respectively. Title pages will be prepared in manuscript.

WAR DIARY
or
~~INTELLIGENCE SUMMARY.~~ VIII
(Erase heading not required.)

Army Form C. 2118.

Place	Date	Hour	Summary of Events and Information	Remarks and references to Appendices
FERFAY	17.4.18	Contd.	of GUYENCOURT was being heavily shelled & had been evacuated by all British troops, he entered the village to bring out a wounded man. Unfortunately the man had been hit a second time & killed. C.W.S.	
	18.4.18		Stand to at 7 a.m. On 3 1/2 hours notice. C.W.S.	
	19.4.18		Stand to at 7 a.m. On 1 3/4 hours notice. Henry Leaton rejoins unit from SAINS-LES-PERNES (LENS 1/100,000). Capt WILLMOTT, RAMC returned to unit, leave having been cancelled. C.W.S.	
	20.4.18		Stand to 7 a.m. On 1 3/4 hours notice. C.W.S.	
	21.4.18		Stand to 7 a.m. On 1 3/4 hours notice. Interpreter VERNOT arrives for duty. Patients admitted to Hospital for week ending April 21st = 36 of which 3 were Scabies + 3 Diarrhoea. Small Hospital opened for the retention & treatment of slight cases, with a view to reducing sick wastage. Arrangements made to clear this hospital at very short notice. C.W.S.	
	22.4.18		Stand to 7 a.m. On 3 1/2 hours notice. C.W.S.	
	23.4.18		Stand to 8 a.m. On 3 1/2 hours notice. C.W.S.	

Instructions regarding War Diaries and Intelligence Summaries are contained in F. S. Regs., Part II. and the Staff Manual respectively. Title pages will be prepared in manuscript.

WAR DIARY

or

~~INTELLIGENCE SUMMARY.~~

(*Erase heading not required.*)

IX

No. 6 CAVALRY FIELD AMBULANCE
No. ....
Date ....
III CAVALRY DIVISION

Army Form C. 2118.

Place	Date	Hour	Summary of Events and Information	Remarks and references to Appendices
FERFAY	24.4.18		Stand to 8 a.m. On 3½ hours notice. Capt. (a/Lt. Col.) C.H. STRINGER, Ramc. awarded the D.S.O. Move to FONTAINE-LEZ-HERMANS. Transfer patients to new site where improvised Hospital was opened up. C.H.S.	
FONTAINE-LEZ-HERMANS. (Hazebrouck 1/100,000).	25.4.18		On ¾ hours notice from 6 a.m. to 8 a.m., during which time unit was saddled up. Remainder of 24 hours at 3½ hours notice. Orders received re route and area in case of move in support of XI Corps. C.H.S.	
	26.4.18		Same notice & stand to as on 25th. C.H.S.	
	27.4.18		Same notice & stand to as on 26th. C.H.S.	
	28.4.18		At ¾ hours notice from 6 a.m. No. 339024 Sgt. G.L. MAC ARTHUR, Ramc and No 368088 2nd Cpl. WATCHORN, D.C.M. awarded the Military Medal. (A.MMS. Cav. Corps. No. A.M.S./500/304/26/4/18. C.H.S.	
	29.4.18		Same notice as on 28th. No T/20690 Dr. (a/Sgt.) R. HALLAM, M.C. awarded a bar to his Military Medal. (A.M.S. Cav. Corps No. A.M.S./500/32. On reconnaissance to forward area. C.H.S.	
	30.4.18		Same notice as on 29th. Capt. P. McCALLUM Ramc. to 3rd Dragoon Guards for temporary duty, vice Capt. H.A. RONN, Ramc. to this C.H.S.	

T.134. Wt. W708-776. 500000. 4/15. Sir J. C. & S.

Instructions regarding War Diaries and Intelligence Summaries are contained in F. S. Regs., Part II. and the Staff Manual respectively. Title pages will be prepared in manuscript.

WAR DIARY
or
~~INTELLIGENCE SUMMARY.~~ X
(Erase heading not required.)

Army Form C. 2118.

Place	Date	Hour	Summary of Events and Information	Remarks and references to Appendices
FONTAINE -LEZ- HERMANS.	30.4.18	contd	unit for temporary duty. Total no. of patients admitted to Hospital during April 1918 = 172 (Scabies 15, Diarrhoea 12) Total evacuation for the month:–	
			Sick / Wounded / Total	
			Officers 4 / 1 / 5	
			O. Ranks 121 / 25 / 146	
			Total 125 / 26 / 151.	
			[signature] Lt. Col. Ramc O.C. 6 C.F.A.	

Instructions regarding War Diaries and Intelligence Summaries are contained in F. S. Regs., Part II. and the Staff Manual respectively. Title pages will be prepared in manuscript.

WAR DIARY
or
INTELLIGENCE SUMMARY.
(Erase heading not required.)

Appendix "A"

Army Form C. 2118.

No. 6 CAVALRY FIELD AMBULANCE No. .... Date .... III CAVALRY DIVISION

Place	Date	Hour	Summary of Events and Information	Remarks and references to Appendices
A.D.M.S. 3rd Cav. Div.				See Page 6.
			Herewith brief report on lessons learnt in recent fighting + rough suggestions for future changes.	
			(1) Uselessness of Heavy Section as organised + placed. Never available for use.	
			(2) As sequence of (1) the necessity for some other means of transport for essential portion of Heavy Section Equipment. For this purpose a lorry would be best, doing away with one G.S. Wagon.	
			(3) Uselessness of Pack Mounted Section as a whole. Two mounted R.A.M.C. orderlies with Shell Dressing Haversacks + Saddle bags filled with Sh. Dressings are useful. No value was found for other personnel + Equip. of P.M. Section as such. It was useful having orderlies + Sergeants mounted, but the necessity for looking after the horses detracted considerably from their use. Suggest dumping Pack saddle + folding stretchers. The latter are a bad + tiring form of stretcher.	
			(4) Suggest carriage of tentage on a lorry with Light Section. I had to go back too far on one occasion in order to find cover for wounded. Tentage in open is safer than buildings.	
			(5) Difficulty in carrying dismounted bearers. 2nd Lorry very useful for this + could also be used for walking wounded + thus save cars. Repeated trips by motor ambulances when available, meet this difficulty.	
			C.W.S.	

T2134. Wt. W708-776. 500000. 4/15. Sir J. C. & S.

Instructions regarding War Diaries and Intelligence Summaries are contained in F. S. Regs., Part II. and the Staff Manual respectively. Title pages will be prepared in manuscript.

WAR DIARY
or
~~INTELLIGENCE SUMMARY~~.
(Erase heading not required.)

Appendix A Continued

Army Form C. 2118.

Place	Date	Hour	Summary of Events and Information	Remarks and references to Appendices
			(6) Regimental intercommunication orderlies proved valuable.	
			(7) Suggest that Motor ambulances be not divisionalized till necessity for doing so becomes apparent.	
			(8) ~~[illegible]~~ Necessity for some light & rapid means of conveyance for O.C. or his deputy, was very clearly demonstrated in the early days of the retreat. Medical arrangements were in danger by only having a horse available for this purpose. This car to be used for visits to A.D.S., R.A.P. (if possible), B. Hd. Qrs, Div Hd. Qrs. Suggest a Ford car.	
			(9) Light ambulances were useful & fulfill a necessary purpose. But motor ambulances were much more useful. Suggest substituting 2 Mot. ambs (one to be a Ford) for two Horse ambs. Full complement of 4 Mot. ambs, + 2 motor cycles were essential & sometimes hardly sufficient to ensure efficiency.	
			(10) RAMC personnel not large enough to run an efficient Dressing Station and also, at the same time, to provide a sufficient no. of bearers. Absolute necessity for all RAMC to be category A1.	
			(11) Dump lamps, distinguishing & substitute box with light inside. Red X & sign cut in box & covered with red cloth.	
			C.W.S.	

Instructions regarding War Diaries and Intelligence Summaries are contained in F. S. Regs., Part II. and the Staff Manual respectively. Title pages will be prepared in manuscript.

WAR DIARY
or
~~INTELLIGENCE SUMMARY.~~
(Erase heading not required.)

Army Form C. 2118.

Appendix A .. continued

Place	Date	Hour	Summary of Events and Information	Remarks and references to Appendices
	(12)		Suggested modified transport for a C.F.A.:–	
			4 Light ambulances,	
			6 motor " (to include a Ford)	
			2 " cyclists.	
			2 lorries.	
			4 limbered G.S. wagons.	
			2 G.S. wagons.	

The fourth limber to carry reserve dressings, blankets, officers mess kit, ~~Vermo~~ oral spray. Equipment from discarded G.S. wagon to be carried on a lorry, i.e. Soyer stove, medical comforts & pannier, Tentage, flags & complete, Rice soup box, remaining ground sheets, 1 additional office box, 2nd tank operating, stretchers.

W. Stringer
Lt. Col. RAMC
O.C. 6 C.F.A.

Camon.
9/4/18.

May 1918.

140/2983.

No. 6 Cav. F. A.

No 6 C F A

Instructions regarding War Diaries and Intelligence Summaries are contained in F. S. Regs., Part II. and the Staff Manual respectively. Title pages will be prepared in manuscript.

WAR DIARY
or
~~INTELLIGENCE SUMMARY.~~ I
(Erase heading not required.)

Army Form C. 2118.

No 6 CAVALRY FIELD AMBULANCE No. Date May 1918 1st CAVALRY DIVISION

Vol 41

Place	Date	Hour	Summary of Events and Information	Remarks and references to Appendices
FONTAINE-LES-HERMANS (HAZEBROUCK 1/100,000)	1.5.18	6.0am	Horses saddled & harnessed, ready to move ~~on~~ ½ hrs notice till 8.0am when off saddled & at 1¾ hrs	SRR
	2.5.18		Same state of readiness as for 1st 2 O.R. R.A.M.C. att 3rd Cav Div HQ taken on strength & left detached	SRR
			CAPT. E.R. LOVELL, RAMC. SR. awarded the Croix de Guerre (French) of the senior class	SRR
	3.5.18		Same notice as for 2nd	SRR
	4.5.18		Commencing from 6am unit on 3¾ hrs notice (LENS 1/100,000 C3) Unit moves with 6th Cav Bde to VACQUERIE LEBOUCQ. A few dismounted men proceed with dismounted personnel of brigade & join unit later on 7th	SRR
VACQUERIE LE BOUCQ (LENS 1/100,000 C.3)	5.5.18		Notified by Bde that unit would probably not move but about 4.30pm these orders were cancelled & move to FROHEN-LE-GRAND (LENS 1/100,000 C4)	SRR
FROHEN-LE-GRAND (LENS 1/100,000 C4)	6.5.18		CAPT WILLMOTT, RAMC proceeds on 14 days leave (contract) to UK. ~~Heavy~~ Light Sec Section, including all RAMC personnel with exception of 1 sergt	SRR

T2134. Wt. W708–776. 500000. 4/15. Sir J. C. & S.

Army Form C. [illegible]18.

Instructions regarding War Diaries and Intelligence Summaries are contained in F. S. Regs., Part II. and the Staff Manual respectively. Title pages will be prepared in manuscript.

WAR DIARY

or

~~INTELLIGENCE SUMMARY.~~ II

(Erase heading not required.)

No. 6 CAVALRY FIELD AMBULANCE
Date May 1918
III CAVALRY DIVISION

Place	Date	Hour	Summary of Events and Information	Remarks and references to Appendices
FROHEN-LE-GRAND	6.5.18	cont.	RAMC move to bivouac area at CONTAY (LENS 1/100,000 F6). Horses in good dry standings in the open. Few men accomodated in barns, remainder in bivouacs.	
			Heavy Section remains ~~at FROHEN~~ behind SRL & proceeds after midday to BEALCOURT (LENS 1/100,000 C4) 1 RAMC. sergt detached with this section. SRL	
			~~Unit~~ Bde put on two hours notice to move from 6 am daily till further notice. SRL	
CONTAY. (LENS 1/100000 F6)	7.5.18		Unit saddled up at 6.0 am ready to move. Impossible to boil tea for mens breakfast owing to fires before dawn being out of the question on account of E.A. Tea arranged for later	
			One OR RAMC evacuated to FA.	
			Patients admitted to FA for week 35 (includes 1 Scabies + 3 Diarrhoea) SRL	
	8.5.18		All available officers reconnoitre tracks leading from transport lines to concentration area allotted by Bde in the event of a sudden move being necessary	
			At 2.15 pm conference of all CO's at Bde HQ	

SRL

T2134. Wt. W708–776. 500000. 4/15. Sir J. C. & S.

Instructions regarding War Diaries and Intelligence Summaries are contained in F. S. Regs., Part II. and the Staff Manual respectively. Title pages will be prepared in manuscript.

WAR DIARY

or

~~INTELLIGENCE~~ SUMMARY. III

(Erase heading not required.)

Army Form C. 2118.

No 6 CAVALRY FIELD AMBULANCE No. ___ Date May 1918 III CAVALRY DIVISION

Place	Date	Hour	Summary of Events and Information	Remarks and references to Appendices
CONTAY.	8.5.18	Cont.	1 OR ASC HT reinforcement arrives. Programme of digging parties required from 6th Cav Bde received. Three brigades take turns in supplying parties. Under ADMS instructions 1 MO, 4 stretcher ~~parties~~ bearers, 4 stretchers + necessary dressings are to be sent up by affiliated CFA. SRL.	
	9.5.18	10 am	Conference of OC's CFA's at ADMS office SRL. 1 OR ASC HT to H. 2 OR's RAMC arrive from 14th Lancers. Two OR's RAMC (clerks) proceed to III Corps Walking Wounded Collecting Station for ~~[illegible]~~ duty. These OR's are to record + transmit casualties of the 3rd Cav. Div. ~~[illegible]~~ ADMS III Corps + ADMS 3rd Cav. Div. SRL	
	10.5.18	7 pm	Party as laid down by ADMS proceeds with brigade digging party. Unit was saddled up by 5 am this morning. Offsaddled at 5.30 am + then remained at 1 hrs notice till 8 am when came on 2 hrs notice. SRL	
	11.5.18		As brigade found digging party for night of 10th/11th unit remained on two hours notice but did not saddle up. SRL	

SRL.

T2134. Wt. W708–776. 500000. 4/15. Sir J. C. & S.

Instructions regarding War Diaries and Intelligence Summaries are contained in F. S. Regs., Part II. and the Staff Manual respectively. Title pages will be prepared in manuscript.

WAR DIARY
or
~~INTELLIGENCE SUMMARY.~~ IV
(*Erase heading not required.*)

Army Form C. 2118.

CAVALRY FIELD AMBULANCE — May 1918 — CAVALRY DIVISION

Place	Date	Hour	Summary of Events and Information	Remarks and references to Appendices
CONTAY	12.5.18.	9.30am	Usual party proceeds with brigade digging party as for former night digging parties Unit saddled up 5 am Offsaddled 5.30 am 1 hrs notice till 8.am ~~th~~ from then 2 hrs SRK	
	13.5.18		1 OR RAMC reinforcement received CARTER LOVELL RAMC SR. appointed Acting Major (auth AA+QMG 3rd CAV DIV No A/8472 d 12.5.18) Under instruction from ADMS (PA/131/18 d 13.5.18) A+D book was closed. Send cases now as direct admissions to infantry M.D. stations + render a nominal roll of such cases daily to ADMS. On same notice as for 12th SRK	
		7.0pm	Digging party proceed	
	14.5.18		Two hours notice Patients admitted to R for week 29 (twenty nine) SRK.	
	15.5.18		Saddled up 5 am 5.30 am Offsaddle and remain at 1 hrs notice till 8.am from then two hrs. SRK	
		9.45 am	Send off usual party for day working party SRK.	
	16.5.18		Same notice as yesterday Receive 1 OR ASC HT reinforcement SRK	
	17.5.18.	5.30am	Move to BELLOY-SUR-SOMME (ref map AMIENS 1/100,000 B1) with brigade arriving about 1.0pm. Joined by Heavy Section by 4.0 pm. Unit are all accomodated in billets with the exception of Sergts and a few SRK.	

(A7092). Wt. W12839/M1293. 75,0.0. 1/17. D. D. & L., Ltd. Forms/C.2118/14.

Instructions regarding War Diaries and Intelligence Summaries are contained in F. S. Regs., Part II. and the Staff Manual respectively. Title pages will be prepared in manuscript.

WAR DIARY
or
~~INTELLIGENCE SUMMARY.~~ V.

(Erase heading not required.)

Army Form C. 2118.

Place	Date	Hour	Summary of Events and Information	Remarks and references to Appendices
BELLOY-SUR-SOMME (AMIENS 1/100,000 B1)	17.5.18	cont.	corporals who are in two bell tents near the transport. There is stabling for nearly all the horses.	
			No hospital accomodation so far but ECOLE LIBRE is suitable if present unit now billeted there can be moved.	
			Heavy Section of Canadian Cavalry Field Ambulance is attached.	ERL
	18.5.18		ECOLE LIBRE is now free & have taken it over as a Hospital. There is accomodation for 20-25 stretchers. Bell tents pitched on transport field for treatment of Scabies. A+D book reopened	
			CAPT AARONN RAMC proceeds to England on 14 days special leave	ERL
	19.5.18		Corps Commander held parade for presentation of Medal Ribands. Two officers & detachment of ORs attended from this unit.	ERL
	20.5.18		Under ADMS instructions all anti typhoid inoculation stopped	ERL
	21.5.18		Conference of OC CFAs & Sergt. Majors at ADMS's Office to discuss equipment carried & method of loading etc	ERL
			Patients admitted for last week 19 (3 scabies)	ERL
	22+23		Ordinary routine ERL	
	24.5.18		Lt Col CH Stringer DSO RAMC proceeds to ~~Eng~~ ERL Ireland on 14 days special leave	
			At 4 pm. Canadian Cavalry F.A Heavy Section ~~F~~ marched off to rejoin C. CFA. at St OUEN.	ERL

ERL.

(A7092). Wt W12839/M1293. 750,000. 1/17. D. D. & L., Ltd. Forms/C.2118/14.

Instructions regarding War Diaries and Intelligence Summaries are contained in F. S. Regs., Part II. and the Staff Manual respectively. Title pages will be prepared in manuscript.

WAR DIARY
or
~~INTELLIGENCE SUMMARY.~~
(*Erase heading not required.*)

VI

Army Form C. 2118.

Place	Date	Hour	Summary of Events and Information	Remarks and references to Appendices
BELLOY-SUR-SOMME.	25.6.18		Routine work SRL	
	26.6.18		CAPT A NEILSON's name submitted for approval of ADMS for MO i/c 3rd D.G.	SRL
	~~[illegible]~~		CAPT. CM WILLMOTT RAMC under instructions from ADMS proceeds to 3rd CAV. Reserve Park vice CAPT. R. McLEAN RAMC to this unit SRL	
	27.6.18		CAPT. A NEILSON RAMC proceeds to 3rd D.G. in relief of CAPT. HA RONN RAMC taken on strength of this unit. CAPT R.A. McCALLUM at present doing temp duty with 3rd D.G. returns SRL	
	28.6.18		1 OR. (Cpl RAMC) surplus to establishment sent to Cyclist Base Depot SRL	
	29.6.18		CAPT. G.W. MITCHELL RAMC proceeded to 139th F.A. (auth DGMS No B1483/7/11 d 23.5.18) 1 OR ASCMT who arrived from Hospital on 27th & is surplus sent to 7th CFA under ADMS instructions SRL CAPT. A.R. GRANT. RAMC T. joins this unit	
	30.6.18		Sent 1 off 1 sergt & three orderlies trained as clerks in M.A. to take over site, buildings etc from No 7 CFA situated at MONTIGNY (Amiens 1/100,000 F1) Similar party arrive from No 7 CFA to take over billets, including hospital & patients SRL	
	31.6.18	8.45 am	Unit (less heavy section, left behind attached to 7th CFA) moves with 1st Cav Bde to MONTIGNY (Amiens 1/100,000 F1) arriving at 1 pm Unit came at once under 1¾ hrs notice	SRL

(A7092). Wt W12839/M1293. 75,0.0. 1/17. D. D. & L., Ltd. Forms/C.2118/14.

Instructions regarding War Diaries and Intelligence Summaries are contained in F. S. Regs., Part II. and the Staff Manual respectively. Title pages will be prepared in manuscript.

WAR DIARY
or
~~INTELLIGENCE SUMMARY.~~
(*Erase heading not required.*)

VII

Army Form C. 2118.

No 6 CAVALRY FIELD AMBULANCE — Date May 1918 — CAVALRY DIVISION

Place	Date	Hour	Summary of Events and Information	Remarks and references to Appendices
MONTIGNY. (AMIENS 1/100,000 F1)	31.6.18	cont.	Men are in trench cover RRR bivouacs which have already been protected by small parapets. Took over also 4 bell tents two of which are used by officers. Erect two bell tents carried on light section. Small barn used as a M.I. Room with perhaps poor accommodation for detaining three or four patients. Under instructions from ADMS A&D book is closed & cases sent as direct admissions to the infantry M.D. stations. Patients admitted for period 22nd – 31st 42 (4 Scabies) During the month 124 patients have been admitted (3 diarrhoea & 11 Scabies). 47 of the 124 were transfers from 4th CFA & 19 cases were transferred to 4th CFA when unit moved to the forward area. Evacuations were Off Sick 1 Wounded 0 Total 1. ORs " 82 — 0 — 82 83 RRR	

T.2131. Wt. W708–776. 500000. 4/15. Sir J. C. & S.

Instructions regarding War Diaries and Intelligence Summaries are contained in F. S. Regs., Part II. and the Staff Manual respectively. Title pages will be prepared in manuscript.

WAR DIARY

or

~~INTELLIGENCE SUMMARY.~~

(Erase heading not required.)

VIII

Army Form C. 2118.

No 6 CAVALRY FIELD AMBULANCE
No
Date May 1918
III CAVALRY DIVISION

Place	Date	Hour	Summary of Events and Information	Remarks and references to Appendices
MONTIGNY			Dental Cases. Nominal rolls were called for from regiments of men requiring dental treatment. 144 of these were examined by CAPT. SHUTE CADC whilst he was attached with the Heavy Section of the C.CFA. 38 cases were sent to 5 CCS for treatment whilst unit was at BELLOY-SUR-SOMME. SRR.	

SRRowell Major RAMC.
for OC 6 CFA

June 1918

No. 6 Cav Fld Amb

Vol 42

140/3131

War Diary
for June 1918

Instructions regarding War Diaries and Intelligence Summaries are contained in F. S. Regs., Part II. and the Staff Manual respectively. Title pages will be prepared in manuscript.

WAR DIARY
or
~~INTELLIGENCE SUMMARY.~~
(Erase heading not required.)

I

Army Form C. 2118.

No 6 CAVALRY FIELD AMBULANCE No.— Date June 19 III CAVALRY DIVISION

Place	Date	Hour	Summary of Events and Information	Remarks and references to Appendices
MONTIGNY (Amiens 1/100,000 F1)	1-6-18		Capt. A.R. GRANT, Ramc. T to 3rd Drag. Guards for duty as R.M.O. Capt. A NEILSON, Ramc. from 3rd Drag. Guards for duty in C.F.A. Brigade concentration point in event of sudden move arranged for in C13d and C19b. (Ref. map Sheet 62d) working parties detailed daily from Brigade for work on forward defences, medical Officers detailed for this party on combined Regimental & Field Amb. roster. C.W.S.	
	2-6-18		Compulsory wearing of gas masks by all ranks & all horses for 5 mins. from 6 pm today. C.W.S.	
	7-6-18		Patients admitted week ending June 7th = 4 (Mechanical dental Tr.) A & D. book still closed for ordinary sick & wounded C.W.S.	
	8-6-18		Inspection of unit by G.O.C. 6th Cav. Brigade. C.W.S.	
	9-6-18		Orders received from A.D.M.S. re medical arrangements in case of a move into XXXI Corps (French) area. C.W.S.	
BELLOY-SUR-SOMME (Amiens 1/100,000 B1)	14-6-18		Move to BELLOY-SUR-SOMME. Leave 10.15 am. Arrive 3 pm.	
			Patients admitted week ending June 14th = 15 (11 Transfers from 6 C.F.A.) of which 4 were scabies. C.W.S.	

T.134. Wt. W708–776. 500000. 4/15. Sir J. C. & S.

Instructions regarding War Diaries and Intelligence Summaries are contained in F. S. Regs., Part II. and the Staff Manual respectively. Title pages will be prepared in manuscript.

WAR DIARY
or
~~INTELLIGENCE SUMMARY.~~ II
(*Erase heading not required.*)

Army Form C. 2118.

No 6 CAVALRY FIELD AMBULANCE No.____ Date June 1918 III CAVALRY DIVISION

Place	Date	Hour	Summary of Events and Information	Remarks and references to Appendices
BELLOY-SUR-SOMME	16.6.17		Capt McCALLUM, RAMC. +1 O.R. to Cav. Corps Gas School (CAYEUX-SUR-MER) for course of instruction. Capt R. McLEAN RAMC. to No 7 C.F.A. for duty. CWJ	
	17.6.18		Course of instruction in duties of medical orderlies started today, attending are 2 O.Rs attached from 6th M.G. Sqdn, "C" Batt. RHA. + 3rd Cav. Div. M.T. Coy, total of six attending class. when proficient these orderlies go out in replacement of regular RAMC personnel. CWJ	
	18.6.18		"Russian" Chamber taken into use. CWJ	
	21.6.18		Patients admitted to H. week ending June 21st = 35 of which 7 were Influenza + 4 Scabies. CWJ	
	22.6.18		Heavy section, No 7 C.F.A. returned to its own unit today at ST. OUEN. First admissions for the new + highly infectious Influenza. 32 cases in H. Start isolation Hospital of 7 bell tents. 1 Light Horse Ambulance + 2 nursing orderlies to Cav. Corps Hd. Qrs for duty in connection with Influenza outbreak. CWJ	
	23.6.18		Capt. H.A. RONN RAMC. to 3rd Drag. Guards for duty. Major E. R. LOVELL RAMC. assumed medical charge of Hd. Qrs, IV Brig. R.H.A. CWJ	

T2134. Wt. W708-776. 500000. 4/15. Sir J. C. & S.

Instructions regarding War Diaries and Intelligence Summaries are contained in F. S. Regs., Part II. and the Staff Manual respectively. Title pages will be prepared in manuscript.

WAR DIARY
or
~~INTELLIGENCE SUMMARY.~~
(Erase heading not required.)

111

Army Form C. 2118.

No 6 CAVALRY FIELD AMBULANCE No. Date June 1918 III CAVALRY DIVISION

Place	Date	Hour	Summary of Events and Information	Remarks and references to Appendices
BELLOY-SUR-SOMME	23.6.18	cont'd	66 cases of Influenza in Hospital. Isolation H increased to 18 tents. CWJ	
	24.6.18		130 cases of Influenza in H. Capt. McCALLUM RAMC & 1 O.R. return from Gas Course. Orders received to organize a Divisional Convalescent Camp at BELLOY for Influenza cases. This camp to receive (1) all cases of Influenza from 6th Cav. Brig. (2) overflow acute cases from the other Field ambulances of the Division, & (3) all convalescents from the other field Ambulances & from the C.C. Stations. All convalescents to be collected by this unit from C.C. Station. CWJ	
	25.6.18		6th Cav. Brig. less 6th C.F.A. moved to SOUES. C.F.A. remained at BELLOY to carry on Infectious Hospital. This move throws a heavy strain on the transport capacity of the unit, as sick have still to be collected from new brigade area. Two light ambulances detached to Brig. Hd. Qrs. for collection & evacuation of ordinary (non infectious) Brigade sick. 230 cases of Influenza in H. 51 circular tents & 3 marquees now erected in Infectious H. CWJ	

T.134. Wt. W708-776. 500000. 4/15. Sir J. C. & S.

Instructions regarding War Diaries and Intelligence Summaries are contained in F. S. Regs., Part II. and the Staff Manual respectively. Title pages will be prepared in manuscript.

WAR DIARY
or
~~INTELLIGENCE SUMMARY.~~ IV

(*Erase heading not required.*)

Army Form C. 2118.

No 6 CAVALRY FIELD AMBULANCE, III CAVALRY DIVISION

Place	Date	Hour	Summary of Events and Information	Remarks and references to Appendices
BELLOY-SUR-SOMME	26.6.18.		307 cases of Influenza in D. C.W.J.	
	27.6.18		312 cases of Influenza in D. 60 tents erected. Owing to large no of personnel, especially N.C.Os in Hospital with Influenza, the A.D.M.S. sent 2 S/Sgts. of No12 San. Sec. to assist. C.W.J.	
	28.6.18		387 cases of Influenza in D. 75 tents erected. Collection of Brigade sick now arranged for by 37 M.A.C.	
	29.6.18		468 cases of Influenza in D. 87 tents erected. C.W.J.	
	30.6.18		492 cases of Influenza in D. 94 tents erected. One light ambulance + 1 Medical orderly returned from duty with Cav. Corps Hd. Qrs. One Light amb. returned from temp. duty with 6th Cav Brig. Hd. Qrs.	
			Patients adm. to D. 22/6/18 – 30/6/18 = 901 of which 871 were Influenza, 8 Scabies + 1 Diarrhoea.	
			Total patients admitted to D during month = 955, of which 878 were Influenza, 16 Scabies & 1 Diarrhoea.	
			Of this figure 955, 186 were transfers from No 7 C.F.A. (170 of which were Influenza), and 101 were transfers	
			C.W.J.	

T.134. Wt. W708–776. 500000. 4/15. Sir J. C. & S.

Instructions regarding War Diaries and Intelligence Summaries are contained in F. S. Regs., Part II. and the Staff Manual respectively. Title pages will be prepared in manuscript.

WAR DIARY
or
~~INTELLIGENCE SUMMARY.~~
(Erase heading not required.)

Army Form C. 2118.

No 6 CAVALRY FIELD AMBULANCE No. Date June 1918 III CAVALRY DIVISION

V

Place	Date	Hour	Summary of Events and Information	Remarks and references to Appendices
BELLOY-SUR-SOMME.	30.6.18 Contd.		from Canadian C.F.A. (all Influenza)	
			Evacuations: Offrs 21. O.Rs 76. Total = 97. all sick.	
			Discharged to duty during June = 381.	
			Appendices	
		I	A Russian Chamber built according to plan was built & operated during the month. Up to now it has not proved sufficiently satisfactory. It is very wasteful in fuel. It is difficult to regulate the draught. In this particular chamber it is difficult to obtain the regd temp. It only deals with a small quantity of clothing at a time. There is no satisfactory method of recording the temperature in the chamber.	
		II	Attached are 2 charts showing Influenza incidence, "A" for 6th Cav. Brig. incidence, & "B" for 6 C.F.A. incidence.	
			[signature] Lt. Col. Rame. O.C. 6 C.F.A.	

T.2134. Wt. W708-776. 500000. 4/15. Sir J. C. & S.

19

July 1918

July 1918

Vol. ~~43~~

War Diary

No. 6 Cav Fd Amb

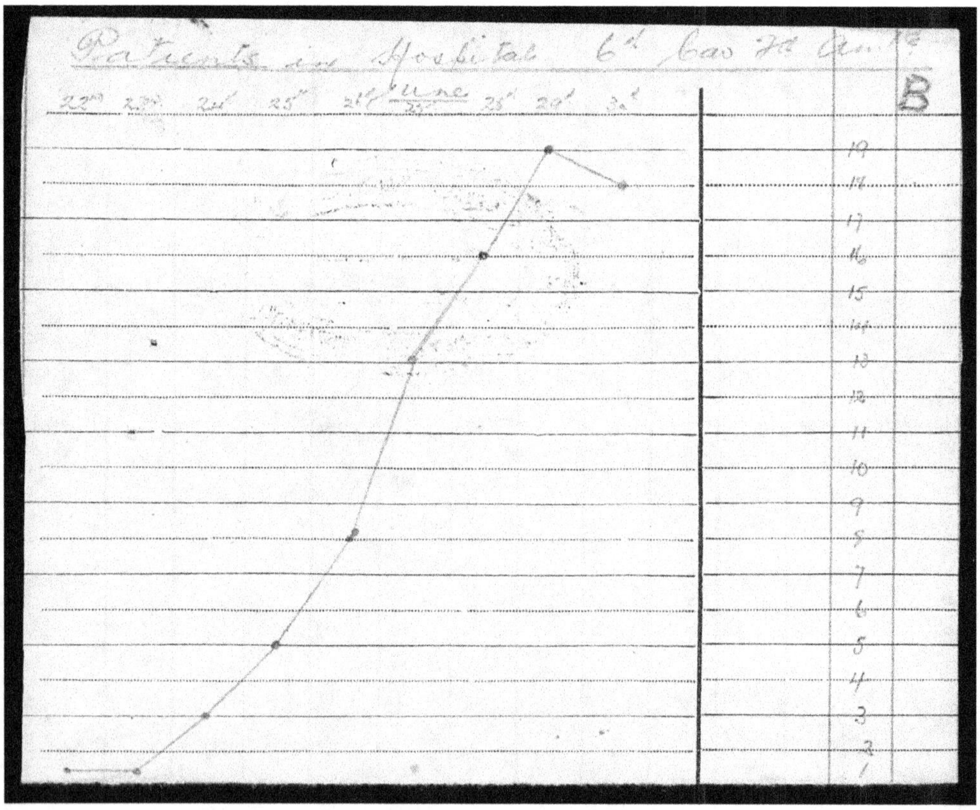

Patients in Hospital
June
B
19
18
17
16
15
14
13
12
11
10
9
8
7
6
5
4
3
2
1

6th Cav Bde Patients in Hospital A

June 1918

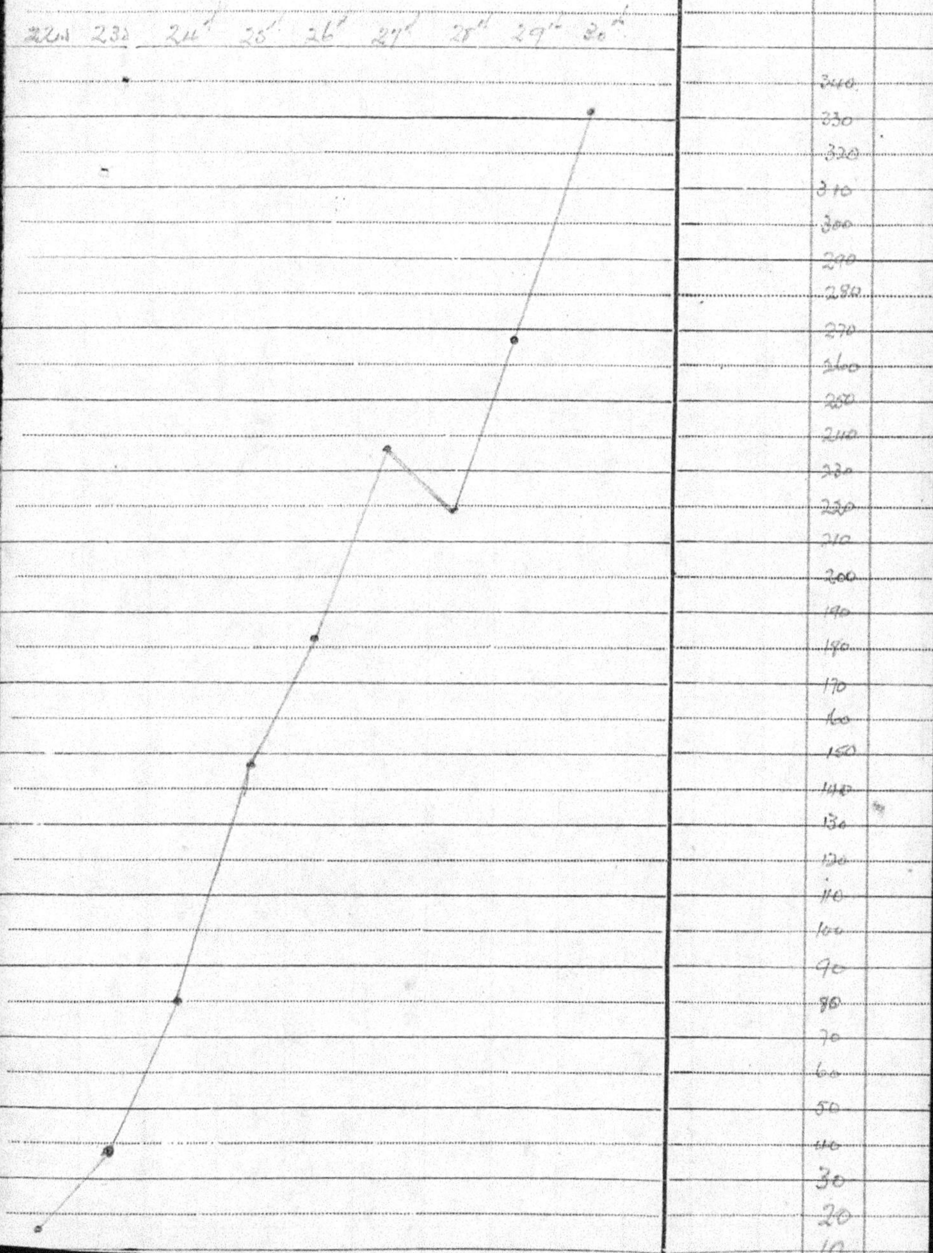

Instructions regarding War Diaries and Intelligence Summaries are contained in F. S. Regs., Part II. and the Staff Manual respectively. Title pages will be prepared in manuscript.

WAR DIARY
or
~~INTELLIGENCE SUMMARY.~~
(Erase heading not required.)

I

Army Form C. 2118.

Place	Date	Hour	Summary of Events and Information	Remarks and references to Appendices
BELLOY-SUR-SOMME (Amiens 1/1000 B11)	1.7.18		Over 500 patients in H. with Influenza. Of these 353 are from 6th Cav. Brigade. C.W.S.	
	2.7.18		400 patients in H., visited by D.M.S. ~~4th Army~~, D.D.M.S. Cav. Corps, + A.D.M.S. 3rd Cav. Division. Two Military Policemen taken on the strength today for the purpose of policing the village + vicinity of the Hospital. C.W.S.	
	3.7.18		363 patients in H. C.W.S.	
	4.7.18		299 patients in H. Influenza incidence dropping. All such cases from the Canadian Cav. Brigade to be admitted to this Hospital. C.W.S.	
	5.7.18		~~[illegible]~~ 301 C.W.S. patients in H. Some tents struck today. C.W.S.	
	6.7.18		301 patients in H. C.W.S.	
	7.7.18		Continued drop in admissions. 15 tents struck today. Patients admitted to H. week ending July 7th = 339 of whom 324 were Influenza, 2 Scabies + no diarrhoea. C.W.S.	
	8.7.18		Continued abatement of Influenza epidemic. More tents struck. C.W.S.	
	9.7.18		Continued abatement. First rain today after a long C.W.S.	

T2134. Wt. W708–776. 500000. 4/15. Sir J. C. & S.

Instructions regarding War Diaries and Intelligence Summaries are contained in F. S. Regs., Part II. and the Staff Manual respectively. Title pages will be prepared in manuscript.

WAR DIARY
or
~~INTELLIGENCE SUMMARY.~~
(Erase heading not required.)

II

Army Form C. 2118.

No. 6 CAVALRY FIELD AMBULANCE No. .... Date .... III CAVALRY DIVISION

Place	Date	Hour	Summary of Events and Information	Remarks and references to Appendices
BELLOY-SUR-SOMME	9.7.18	contd.	period of drought. The Influenza epidemic has been steadily dropping for the last 8 days. Course of instruction for medical duties for Regimental orderlies which commenced 17.6.18, completed today & men returned to their units as fit to replace the Ramc orderlies.	[initials]
	10.7.18		Influenza cases from 6th Cav. Brig. remaining in F.A. dropped to below 100 today for the first time since 26.6.18. G.O.C. 3rd Cav. Div. visited F.A. Capt. J. S. KINROSS, Ramc. T.C. joined this unit for duty. [initials] All Influenza cases from No. 7 Cav. Fd. Amb. to be admitted to this F.A.	[initials]
	11.7.18		More tents struck. Up to date 350 stretchers & 510 blankets received on loan from C.C.S.s have been returned. [initials]	
	14.7.18		Uninterrupted drop in admissions for Influenza. Only 28 such cases from 6th Cav. Brig. remaining in F.A. Patients adm. to F.A. for week ending 14.7.18 = 110, of which 77 were Influenza. Scabies & Diarrhoea nil. [initials]	
	16.7.18		From today all admissions for Influenza are to be evacuated to [initials]	

T.2134. Wt. W708-776. 500000. 4/15. Sir J. C. & S.

Instructions regarding War Diaries and Intelligence Summaries are contained in F. S. Regs., Part II. and the Staff Manual respectively. Title pages will be prepared in manuscript.

WAR DIARY
or
~~INTELLIGENCE SUMMARY.~~ III
(Erase heading not required.)

Army Form C. 2118.

No. 6 CAVALRY FIELD AMBULANCE No. ____ Date ____ III CAVALRY DIVISION

Place	Date	Hour	Summary of Events and Information	Remarks and references to Appendices
BELLOY-SUR-SOMME			C.C.S. & not to be detained. C.H.J.	
	17.7.18		37 M.A.C. cease to collect Brigade sick. This unit to arrange transport in future. Stop collection of 3rd Cav. Div. Convalescents from C.C.S.s. C.H.J.	
	20.7.18		Influenza Hospital finally closed. Remaining Tents, blankets & stretchers on loan returned. C.H.J.	
RIENCOURT (Amiens 1/100,000 A1)	21.7.18		Move to Riencourt. Patients admitted to H for week ending 21.7.18 = 43, of which 16 were Influenza, Scabies 6, Diarrhoea 1. C.H.J.	
	22.7.18		1 Light Ambulance returned from temporary duty with Hd. Qrs 6 Cav. Brig. C.H.J.	
	29.7.18		Conference at Brigade Headquarters, re possible future movements. C.H.J.	
	30.7.18		This unit takes 1st & 2nd prizes in the Class for pairs at the Brigade Horse Show held today. C.H.J.	
	31.7.18		Admissions to H. for period ~~21~~ 31.7.18 = 46. Influenza 8, Scabies 5, Diarrhoea nil. C.H.J.	
			Total admissions for July = 538 of which 425 were Influenza, 13 Scabies & 1 Diarrhoea. C.H.J.	

T.134. Wt. W708–776. 500000. 4/15. Sir J. C. & S.

Instructions regarding War Diaries and Intelligence Summaries are contained in F. S. Regs., Part II. and the Staff Manual respectively. Title pages will be prepared in manuscript.

WAR DIARY
or
~~INTELLIGENCE~~ SUMMARY. IV.

(*Erase heading not required.*)

Army Form C. 2118.

Place	Date	Hour	Summary of Events and Information	Remarks and references to Appendices
RIENCOURT	July 1918.		<u>Evacuations</u> during July 1918 =	
			Sick / wounded / Total	
			Officers 7 / nil / 7	
			O. Ranks 118 / nil / 118.	
			<u>Dental cases</u> treated at C.C.S. during July = 247.	
			<u>Influenza Epidemic.</u>	
			A report on this Epidemic was sent to the A.D.M.S. 3rd Cav. Div. on 23/7/18.	
			Total no. admitted = 1331	
			This includes 3rd Cav. Div. & other formations.	
			No. admitted from 6th Cav. Brigade = 770.	
			Of this no. the 3 Regiments contributed as below:-	
			X R. Hussars = 165	
			3rd D. Guards = 213	
			1st R. Dragoons = 205	
			A.W.J.	

2353 Wt. W2514/1454 700,000 5/15 D. D. & L. A.D.S.S./Forms/C. 2118.

Instructions regarding War Diaries and Intelligence Summaries are contained in F. S. Regs., Part II. and the Staff Manual respectively. Title pages will be prepared in manuscript.

WAR DIARY
or
~~INTELLIGENCE SUMMARY.~~ V

(*Erase heading not required.*)

Army Form C. 2118.

Place	Date	Hour	Summary of Events and Information	Remarks and references to Appendices
RIENCOURT	July 1918		Influenza Epidemic contd: No. of cases of Relapse in Hospital = 13 " " " " after return to duty = 9 No. of cases of Re-infection = 5. Following figures give an accurate chart of the Influenza Epidemic. The figures represent the highest number of cases from 6 Cav. Brig. only remaining in Hospital each day from & including June 24th to & including July 19th. 105. 186. 187. 231. 290. 302. 334. 353. highest figure July 1st. 346. 339. 317. 281. 253. 213. 173. 126 – first rain after a period of drought. 100. 81. 76. 70. 47. 28. 17. 11. 7. 3. 50% of the personnel of No 6 C.F.A. contracted the disease. During the Epidemic period there was a marked fall in the admissions for ordinary sickness. After the Epidemic there was a marked rise in ordinary sick admissions. C.W. Stringer Lt. Col. Rame O.C. 6 C.F.A.	

2353 Wt. W2544/1454 700,000 5/15 D. D. & L. A.D.S.S./Forms/C. 2118.

Aug. 1918.

140/3700.

No. 6 Cav. F. A.

16

Instructions regarding War Diaries and Intelligence Summaries are contained in F. S. Regs., Part II. and the Staff Manual respectively. Title pages will be prepared in manuscript.

WAR DIARY
or
~~INTELLIGENCE SUMMARY.~~
(Erase heading not required.)

Army Form C. 2118.

No 6 CAVALRY FIELD AMBULANCE No. Date III CAVALRY DIVISION

6 C Da

Vol 44

Place	Date	Hour	Summary of Events and Information	Remarks and references to Appendices
RIENCOURT (Amiens 1/100,000 A1)	1.8.18		In billets at RIENCOURT. Horses + transport in lines just outside village. C.W.J.	
LE MESGE (Amiens 1/100,000 A1)	5.8.18		Night march to LE MESGE. Brigade conference earlier in day re coming operations. 3 stretcher bearers from each Regiment detailed for duty as a "Medical Mounted Patrol", to be under orders of an officer detailed by this unit. This M.M.P. to be with Brigade Headquarters + to act as a link between Regimental Medical Officers + the C.F.A. C.W.J.	
	6.8.18		Night march to RENANCOURT (nr. PONT DE METZ, nr. AMIENS). Leave at 11 pm. arrive 4 am. 7th. C.W.J.	
RENANCOURT (AMIENS 1/100,000 D2)	7.8.18		Heavy section move from LE MESGE to SOUES. Patients admitted to hospital week ending 7th = 33 of whom 1 was Diarrhoea + 1 Scabies. Leave RENANCOURT at 9 pm. for concentration in N31d (Ref. map 62d 1/40,000). C.W.J.	
N31d (Sheet 62d 1/40,000)	8.8.18		Arrive concentration area 3.30 am. Attack at 4.20 am. Moved C.W.J.	

2353 Wt. W2544/1454 700,000 5/15 D. D. & L. A.D.S.S./Forms/C. 2118.

Army Form C. 2118.

Instructions regarding War Diaries and Intelligence Summaries are contained in F. S. Regs., Part II. and the Staff Manual respectively. Title pages will be prepared in manuscript.

WAR DIARY
or
~~INTELLIGENCE~~ SUMMARY.
(Erase heading not required.)

No 6 CAVALRY FIELD AMBULANCE
No.........
Date.........
III CAVALRY DIVISION

Place	Date	Hour	Summary of Events and Information	Remarks and references to Appendices
T10 d 4 2 (62d)	8.8.18	Contd.	at 6.30 am. to western edge of BOIS DE GENTELLES at T10 d 4 2 (62d). Parked off road + reinforced by 5 light ambulances, 2 motor ambulances + 1 motor lorry from the Canadian C.F.A.	
			At 7 am. a party of bearers with two motor ambulances + 4 light ambulances under Capt. NEILSON Rouse was sent out to patrol the roads from T10 a 00 to GENTELLES + CACHY. At same time a clerking post was established at X Road T10 a 00, to check all Cavalry wounded passing down.	
			I made a reconnaissance of the roads leading forward from CACHY and found them blocked. I therefore sent a patrol of the same strength as above under Capt. P.A. McCALLUM to X Roads at U15 b 88 (62d), to clear BOIS DE HANGARD area + to evacuate through DOMART-SUR-LA-LUCE on to main AMIENS-ROYE road. Owing to the rapid advance only a comparatively small number of cases were dealt with in this way + evacuated to the M.D.S. at M.36 c (62d). During the stay of the C.F.A. H.Q. in	
			Contd.	

2353 Wt. W2544/1454 700,000 5/15 D. D. & L. A.D.S.S./Forms/C. 2118.

Instructions regarding War Diaries and Intelligence Summaries are contained in F. S. Regs., Part II. and the Staff Manual respectively. Title pages will be prepared in manuscript.

WAR DIARY
or
~~INTELLIGENCE SUMMARY.~~
(Erase heading not required.)

111

NO. 6 CAVALRY FIELD AMBULANCE — No. ...... Date ...... — III CAVALRY DIVISION

Army Form C. 2118.

Place	Date	Hour	Summary of Events and Information	Remarks and references to Appendices
T10d42 (62D)	8.8.18 Contd		at BOIS de GENTELLES. Considerable assistance was rendered by walking wounded 'Lorries' to the Canadian Infantry Ambulance located near by.	
			At 3 p.m. Capt. Neilson + party + Capt. McCallum + party were withdrawn.	
C11d (66E).			At 5 p.m. the Entire unit was moved forward to X Roads at C11d (66E). From there Capt. KINROSS with 1 motor ambulance + 2 light ambulances to patrol road to DEMUIN, but as no wounded were to be found he was soon withdrawn.	
			Horse ambulances + motor transport from Canadian C.F.A. were returned to that unit.	
MAISON BLANCHE (D20b 66E)			At 6.30 p.m. the unit was moved forward to X Roads at MAISON BLANCHE (D20b, 66E).	
			Capt. Neilson was sent out with a party of bearers and succeeded in Establishing a Collecting post in a cutting at the X tracks in D16d (66E). From this point contact was Established with	
			C.E.W.	

2353 Wt. W2544/1454 700,000 5/15 D. D. & L. A.D.S.S./Forms/C. 2118.

Instructions regarding War Diaries and Intelligence Summaries are contained in F. S. Regs., Part II. and the Staff Manual respectively. Title pages will be prepared in manuscript.

WAR DIARY
or
~~INTELLIGENCE SUMMARY.~~
(Erase heading not required.)

IV

Army Form C. 2118.

Place	Date	Hour	Summary of Events and Information	Remarks and references to Appendices
MAISON BLANCHE	8.8.18 contd		with the Canadian Cavalry Brigade and wounded were evacuated by horse ambulances across country to MAISON BLANCHE. The tracks used by these ambulances were persistently shelled but there were no casualties. At 9 p.m. the Canadian Cavalry Brigade having been taken out of action & all the wounded having been cleared, the post at D16d was withdrawn. At 10 p.m. the Hd. Qrs. of the C.F.A. was moved back to the transport lines which had previously been established at D13c99. C.T.J.	
	9.8.18		At 7 a.m. entire unit, transport included, moved up to MAISON BLANCHE. Bearers were sent out to post in D16d and from thence they went forward in wake of 6th Cav. Brigade to a point at D23b88 (66E). This brigade was then in a position of readiness in wood in E15a (66E). Casualties were collected & brought to quarry in E3c64, where they were evacuated by transport of No 5 C.F.A. C.T.J.	

2353 Wt. W2544/1454 700,000 5/15 D. D. & L. A.D.S.S./Forms/C. 2118.

Instructions regarding War Diaries and Intelligence Summaries are contained in F. S. Regs., Part II. and the Staff Manual respectively. Title pages will be prepared in manuscript.

WAR DIARY
or
~~INTELLIGENCE SUMMARY.~~
(*Erase heading not required.*)

Army Form C. 2118.

No. 6 CAVALRY FIELD AMBULANCE · III CAVALRY DIVISION · No. .... Date ....

Place	Date	Hour	Summary of Events and Information	Remarks and references to Appendices
MAISON BLANCHE	9.8.18	contd.	I got into touch with Div. H.Q. G.M. in D12a + later in E13 (66?), & also with Medical Mounted Patrol of 6th Cav. Brigade at D6a43. During the day the motor lorries (1 C.F.A. + 1 No 12 San. Sec.) + 2 motor ambulances (one having broken down on evening of 8th) worked backwards from MAISON BLANCHE in conjunction with Cav. Inf. Dr. Stn. Quite a large no. of infantry cases were evacuated + a few cavalry cases which were brought down were dressed + fed. The main Amiens – Roye road towards LE QUESNEL was patrolled by horse ambulances but only a few cavalry wounded were found. The night was spent at Maison Blanche. For several hours the immediate area was heavily bombed but no casualties incurred. [initials]	
	10.8.18		In touch with A.D.M.S. + 6th Cav. Brig. Med. Mounted Patrol. A move to area K9c was ordered but situation having	

T2134. Wt. W708–776. 500000. 4/15. Sir J. C. & S.

Instructions regarding War Diaries and Intelligence Summaries are contained in F. S. Regs., Part II. and the Staff Manual respectively. Title pages will be prepared in manuscript.

WAR DIARY
or
~~INTELLIGENCE SUMMARY.~~
(Erase heading not required.)

VI

No. 6 CAVALRY FIELD AMBULANCE No. ______ Date ______ III CAVALRY DIVISION

Army Form C. 2118.

Place	Date	Hour	Summary of Events and Information	Remarks and references to Appendices
BOUCHOIR (K23c61)	10.8.18	Contd.	developed further I took the whole unit forward to BOUCHOIR (K23c.61 (66E)). Shortly afterwards information was received that the 6th Cav. Brig. was moving forwards between limits, BOUCHOIR – ROUVROY-EN-SANTERRE.	
			Three patrols (each consisting of bearer squad despatch rider, + light horse ambulance) were sent forward to keep in touch with the Brigade.	
			Patrol No1 proceeded along main Amiens – Roye Road to L31 central. Patrol No2 :- Bouchoir – ROUVROY Rd to Rouvroy. Patrol No3 :- Bouchoir – LE QUESNOY to Le Quesnoy.	
			No2 Patrol was found to be of little value + was shortly withdrawn. No1 Patrol on the Amiens – Roye Road got into touch with the Royal Can. Dragoons + Fort Garry Horse. No3 Patrol established liaison with the 3rd Dragoon Guards at Le Quesnoy.	
			Meanwhile the C.F.A. opened up as an Advanced	
			C.G.S.	

Instructions regarding War Diaries and Intelligence Summaries are contained in F. S. Regs., Part II. and the Staff Manual respectively. Title pages will be prepared in manuscript.

WAR DIARY
or
~~INTELLIGENCE SUMMARY.~~
(Erase heading not required.)

VII

No. G CAVALRY FIELD AMBULANCE No. ____ Date ____ III CAVALRY DIVISION

Army Form C. 2118.

Place	Date	Hour	Summary of Events and Information	Remarks and references to Appendices
BOUCHOIR	10.8.18 (contd)		Dressing Station at K23C61 (Bouchoir). Abandoned German huts provided dressing rooms & kitchen accommodation. A considerable number of Infantry cases were received here prior to the arrival of the 92nd Fd. Amb. advance party. In the afternoon the Canadian Cavalry Brigade made a charge at Hill 100 astride the Amiens - Roye Road. Bearer parties were sent forward and the wounded removed by hand carriage to L31 central thence by horse ambulance to A.D.S. Bouchoir where they were dressed & fed. Evacuation from this point was by motor ambulance & lorry to Dr. HANGEST & Maison Blanche. It was not possible to clear all the wounded during daylight & some men of the Fort Garry Horse lying close to the front line had to be left for a few hours. Under cover of darkness a bearer party under Capt. Mailson, Ramc went forward & succeeded in completely clearing	

P.T.O.

Instructions regarding War Diaries and Intelligence Summaries are contained in F. S. Regs., Part II. and the Staff Manual respectively. Title pages will be prepared in manuscript.

WAR DIARY
or
~~INTELLIGENCE SUMMARY.~~ VIII
(Erase heading not required.)

No. 6 CAVALRY FIELD AMBULANCE · No. ...... Date ...... · 3RD CAVALRY DIVISION

Army Form C. 2118.

Place	Date	Hour	Summary of Events and Information	Remarks and references to Appendices
BOUCHOIR	10.8.18 (contd)		The ground bringing back 5 men of the Fort Garry Horse. This party was subjected to a considerable amount of machine gun fire. All cavalry wounded had been collected, & the A.D.S. cleared by 12 midnight. Enemy aircraft were very active over the immediate area during the night. A considerable number of [illegible] casualties (not cavalry) were collected & dealt with. O.W.J.	
	11.8.18		Desultory shelling of Bouchoir with H.E. & gas. No casualties. The cavalry Brigades were now west of Bouchoir. Assistance was rendered to 32nd Div. A.D.S. during the day & lorries + cars were loaned to them for transport of wounded. At 6.30 pm. the A.D.S. was closed & the whole unit moved back along the Amiens – Roye Road to ST. NICHOLAS, & thence to FOUENCAMPS. Heavy bombing en route. No casualties. O.W.J.	
FOUENCAMPS	12.8.18		Arrive Fouencamps 3 am. In billets. O.W.J.	
(Amiens 1/100,000 23)	13.8.18		Refitting. Visited by G.O.C. of Division who complimented O.W.J.	

T2134. Wt. W708–776. 500000. 4/15. Sir J. C. & S.

Instructions regarding War Diaries and Intelligence Summaries are contained in F. S. Regs., Part II. and the Staff Manual respectively. Title pages will be prepared in manuscript.

WAR DIARY
or
~~INTELLIGENCE SUMMARY.~~
(Erase heading not required.)

~~IX~~

No. 6 CAVALRY FIELD AMBULANCE
No. ______
Date ______
III CAVALRY DIVISION

Army Form C. 2118.

Place	Date	Hour	Summary of Events and Information	Remarks and references to Appendices
FOUENCAMPS	13.8.18	contd.	the unit on its good work during recent operations.	
			Heavy section rejoins unit from Somes.	
	14.8.18		Patients adm. to Hospital week ending 14th = 15 of whom 4 were Diarrhoea & 1 Scabies. During period of active operation A & D book was closed. No 6762 Pte Tomlin T. Ramc awarded 5 years Penal Servitude for sleeping at his post while on guard. C.W.S.	
	15.8.18		March at 9 pm. to RIENCOURT. C.W.S.	
RIENCOURT	16.8.18		Arrive Riencourt 4.30 am. C.W.S.	
Amiens 1/100 000 A1	19.8.18		Capt. A.R. GRANT Ramc posted to unit & goes on leave today. Capt. J. S. KINROSS Ramc posted to 3rd Field Squadron for duty. C.W.S.	
	20.8.18		No T/32801 Dr. H.G. WEST, A.S.C.H.T. & No T4/250081 Dr F.W. LARRETT A.S.C.H.T. awarded Military Medal (Cav. Corps. 500/346) as immediate reward for behaviour during recent operations. At 8.15 pm orders received re being on 3/4 hours notice from reveille 21st cancelled at 10.30 pm. To be on 3 hours notice from 5 am. 21st. C.W.S.	

T.2134. Wt. W708-776. 500000. 4/15. Sir J. C. & S.

Instructions regarding War Diaries and Intelligence Summaries are contained in F. S. Regs., Part II. and the Staff Manual respectively. Title pages will be prepared in manuscript.

WAR DIARY
or
INTELLIGENCE SUMMARY.
(*Erase heading not required.*)

Army Form C. 2118.

X

Place	Date	Hour	Summary of Events and Information	Remarks and references to Appendices
RIENCOURT	20.8.18	(contd)	to take part in operations by 3rd Army. C.W.J.	
	21.8.18		On 3 hours notice from 5 am. Conference at Brigade Hd. Qrs. Orders to march at 12 midnight. Heavy section to march to BETHENCOURT ST OUEN. C.W.J. Admissions for week = 8 Diarrhoea 6. Scabies 2. C.W.J.	
MONTRELET (LENS 1/100,000 C5)	22.8.18		Arrive MONTRELET 5 am. On 3 hours notice. C.W.J.	
	23.8.18		On 3 hours notice. C.W.J.	
	24.8.18		On 3 hours notice. C.W.J.	
	25.8.18		Marched at 10.20 pm. for CUMONVILLE. C.W.J.	
CUMONVILLE (Lens 1/100,000 A4.)	26.8.18		Arrive CUMONVILLE 4 am. Heavy section rejoined unit at 6 am. from Bethencourt St Ouen. On 3 hours notice. C.W.J.	
	[illegible]		Leave at 6.15 pm. Arrive NUNCQ 10.30 pm. C.W.J.	
NUNCQ (Lens 1/100,000 D3.)	27.8.18		On 3 hours notice. On 1 hours notice from 10 am. On 2 1/2 hours notice from 12 noon. C.W.J.	
	28.8.18		On 2 1/2 hours notice. Capt. A NEILSON Ramc. awarded the Military Cross for behaviour during recent operations (M.S. G. 71.Q4/1049). C.W.J.	
	29.8.18		On 2 1/2 hours notice. Later warned to move at 8 pm. tonight to forward concentration area in WAILLY. Move cancelled later. On 3 hours notice. Capt. C.B. CRUIKSHANK M.C. Ramc. joins unit for duty. C.W.J.	

Instructions regarding War Diaries and Intelligence Summaries are contained in F. S. Regs., Part II. and the Staff Manual respectively. Title pages will be prepared in manuscript.

WAR DIARY
or
~~INTELLIGENCE SUMMARY.~~ XI
(*Erase heading not required.*)

Army Form C. 2118.

Place	Date	Hour	Summary of Events and Information	Remarks and references to Appendices
NUNCQ	30.8.18		On 2½ hours notice, under orders again to move up to forward concentration area tonight. Cancelled later. On 3 hours notice. C.W.S.	
	31.8.18		On 3 hours notice up to 12 noon. On 6 hours notice from 12 noon. Heavy section rejoins. Open up Hospital. M.O. to see daily sick of M.T. Coy. (3rd Cav. Div) at AVERDOINGT. Patients admitted to H 21/8/18 – 31/8/18 = 56 of which 14 were Diarrhoea, Scabies, etc. C.W.S.	
			Total admissions August = 155. (Diarrhoea 25. Scabies 4).	
			Evacuations August:– W. S.	
			Officers – 7	
			O.Rs – 137 includes 23 cases for mechanical dental tr.	
			Wounded treated & cleared during period 8.8.18 – 11.8.18:– British = 301. French 3. Germans 7. Large nos. in addition were cleared but no record was kept – they were not detained but merely passed through.	
			C.W. Fleming Lt Col. RAMC.	

T.2134. Wt. W708–776. 500000. 4/15. Sir J. C. & S.

Sept 1918

140/3059

6 Cav Field Ambce.

27

Nob CFA

WAR DIARY
or
~~INTELLIGENCE SUMMARY.~~ I
(Erase heading not required.)

Army Form C. 2118.

Instructions regarding War Diaries and Intelligence Summaries are contained in F. S. Regs., Part II. and the Staff Manual respectively. Title pages will be prepared in manuscript.

Place	Date	Hour	Summary of Events and Information	Remarks and references to Appendices
NUNCQ (Lens 1/100,000) D.3	1.9.18		On 6 hours notice to move. C.W.J.	
	2.9.18	7am.	On 3½ hours notice, later on 1 hours notice 4.55pm. on 3 hours notice	
		8.15pm	On 6 hours notice C.W.J.	
	3.9.18	9.50pm	On 2 hours notice. 11pm. on 6 hours notice. C.W.J.	
	4.9.18		2 clerks to Corps Walking Wounded Collecting Post at ARRAS for clerking of Cav. Corps wounded. C.W.J.	
LE PARCQ (Lens 1/100,000)	5.9.18		Move to LE PARCQ. Open Hospital for Brigade sick. On 24 hours notice as G.H.Q. Reserve. C.W.J.	
	7.9.18		Patients adm. to Hospital for week ending Sept 7th = 33 of which 5 were Diarrhoea + 1 Scabies. C.W.J.	
	17.9.18		Light section under 2nd in command, marched out at 5 a.m. to take part in divisional manoeuvres. Heavy section + Hospital as before. Light section billeted nights of 17th–18th at AUTHEUX. C.W.J.	
	18.9.18		Light section rejoin at LE PARCQ. Patients admitted to Hospital for week ending Sept 14th = 37 (Diarrhoea 4, Scabies 6). C.W.J.	
REBREUVE (Lens 1/100,000)	19.9.18		Move to REBREUVE. Open Hospital for Brigade sick. C.W.J.	
	21.9.18		Patients adm. to Hospital for week ending Sept 21 = 29 (Diarrhoea 5, Scabies 2) C.W.J. Continental time system adopted	
BUS-LES-ARTOIS. (Lens 1/100,000)	25.9.18		March at 10pm. to BUS-LES-ARTOIS. C.W.J.	
	26.9.18		Arrive 2 am. March at 9pm to MEAULTE area. C.W.J.	
MEAULTE (Amiens 1/100,000)	27.9.18		In bivouac at roadside ~~between~~ MEAULTE + ALBERT. [illegible] [illegible]. March at 8 pm. to HEM C.W.J.	

(A7092). Wt. W12839/M1293. 75,0 0. 1/17. D. D. & L., Ltd. Forms/C.2118/14.

Instructions regarding War Diaries and Intelligence Summaries are contained in F. S. Regs., Part II. and the Staff Manual respectively. Title pages will be prepared in manuscript.

WAR DIARY
or
~~INTELLIGENCE SUMMARY.~~ II
(Erase heading not required.)

Army Form C. 2118.

Place	Date	Hour	Summary of Events and Information	Remarks and references to Appendices
HEM (Amiens 1/100,000)	28.9.18		Arrive 1 a.m. Billeted in shelters at Station. CWF	
	29.9.18		5 cars from No 11 M.A.C. arrive for temporary duty. On 3 hours notice to move from 12.10 pm. March at 3 pm. Heavy section plus 1 light ambulance divisionalised & remain in present area. One motor cyclist to A.D.M.S. CWF	
VERMAND (St. Quentin 1/100,000)			Arrive Vermand 8.30 pm. In houses & cellars. CWF	
	30.9.18		Mounted Ramc sent to A.D.M.S. for temporary duty. Conference A.D.M.S. at 2.30 pm. On 2½ hours notice. Patients adm. to Hospital 21/9/18 – 30/9/18 = 63 (Diarrhoea 6, Scabies 4). CWF	
			Total admissions for month of September = 162. (Diarrhoea 20, Scabies 13).	
			Total evacuations during September:-	
			sick Offs. 1 O.Rs. 119	
			wounded nil nil	
			C.W. Fleming Lt Col. RAMC O.C. 6 C.F.A.	

(A7092). Wt. W12839/M1293- 75,0.0. 1/17. D. D. & L., Ltd. Forms/C.2118/14.

Oct. 1918

140/3327

No 6 Cav. Field Ambce.

Instructions regarding War Diaries and Intelligence Summaries are contained in F. S. Regs., Part II. and the Staff Manual respectively. Title pages will be prepared in manuscript.

24 6 CDA

WAR DIARY
or
~~INTELLIGENCE SUMMARY.~~
(Erase heading not required.)

Army Form C. 2118.

Vol 46

Place	Date	Hour	Summary of Events and Information	Remarks and references to Appendices
VERMAND (St. Quentin 1/100,000).	1.10.18		Capt. Neilson M.C. to 107 C.F.A., for temporary duty. Capt. J.U. Cruikshank M.C. to 6th Brig. Hd. Qrs. as O.C. Pack Mounted Section. At 1 hours notice from 7 am. CWS	
	2.10.18		Leave at 8.15 am. & march to Sugar Factory, PONTRU. Wait there till 12.00. Cavalry not used. March back to VERMAND. CWS	
STE HELENE (St. Quentin 1/100,000).	3.10.18		Stand to at 8.30 am. March at 9.30 am. to Sugar Factory, PONTRU (St. Quentin 1/100,000). Remain there closed till 4.30 pm. & then move up across St. Quentin Canal at BELLENGLISE to the T Roads N.W. of MAGNY-LA-FOSSE (St. Quentin 1/100,000). Open a dressing station in a ruined farm A & D. book closed. Cavalry moved back at 8 pm. except 1 squadron. Leave 2 motor ambulances, 1 medical officer & a stretcher bearer party behind with the squadron (Joncourt) & return with C.F.A. to STE. HELENE, 1 mile W of BELLENGLISE. Arrive 10.30 pm. Bivouac for night. CWS	
	4.10.18		Relieve M.O. & bearer party at JONCOURT. Send up fresh party & 1 motor ambulance. 3 M.A.C. cars to 107 C.F.A. Capt. Neilson returned from temporary duty with 107 C.F.A. CWS	
TREFCON (St. Quentin 1/100,000)	5.10.18		Move to TREFCON. A & D. Book opened. Capt. McCallum to 3rd Field Squadron, R.E. for temp. duty. Party at JONCOURT withdrawn. M.A.C. cars return from 107 C.F.A. CWS	

(A7092). Wt. W12839/M1293. 75,0.0. 1/17. D. D. & L., Ltd. Forms/C.2118/14.

Instructions regarding War Diaries and Intelligence Summaries are contained in F. S. Regs., Part II. and the Staff Manual respectively. Title pages will be prepared in manuscript.

WAR DIARY
or
~~INTELLIGENCE SUMMARY.~~ II

(Erase heading not required.)

Army Form C. 2118.

No 6 CAVALRY FIELD AMBULANCE No. ... Date ... III CAVALRY DIVISION

Place	Date	Hour	Summary of Events and Information	Remarks and references to Appendices
~~TREFCON~~ BELLENGLISE (St Quentin 1/100,000)	7.10.18		Conferenced at A.D.M.S. 11 am. Leave Trefcon 2.15 pm. Arrive Bellenglise 5 pm. Divisionalised C.F.A. parked on west bank of Canal. Patients admitted to Hospital for week ending 7th = 20 (Diarrhoea & Scabies - nil). Two clerks to M.D.S. VADENCOURT (No 2 F.A.) for purpose of recording Cav. Corps casualties. C.W.J.	
	8.10.18		Move at 6.30 am. to X Rds N. of Magny-la-Fosse. Remain closed. Move on at 12 noon to ESTREES — LE CATEAU Rd, & park off road about 1 mile N.E. of ESTREES. Move back at 5 pm to last nights bivouac area. C.W.J. A. & D. Book closed. C.W.J.	
MARETZ (Valenciennes 1/100,000)	9.10.18		March at 4.15 am. to GENEVE (St Quentin 1/100,000) (B18 a Sheet 62 b). Move again at 9.40 a.m. to western outskirts of MARETZ. Open up A.D.S. in a house with sufficient accommodation & good approach for cars. Very busy up to 2 am. Capt. Grant to 17th Lancers in relief of Capt. Hardy wounded. C.W.J.	
BERTRY (Valenciennes 1/100,000)	10.10.18		Move at 6 am. to form on main Maretz — Le Cateau Rd about halfway between Maretz & Maurois. Leave at 10 am. & move to BERTRY. Open A.D.S. very busy up to 5 pm. when A.D.S. was closed & cavalry withdrawn. C.W.J.	
ELINCOURT (Valenciennes)	11.10.18		~~Move~~ at 3 pm. to ELINCOURT. C.F.A. is ingaded on 3 hours notice. C.W.J.	

(A7092). Wt. W12839/M1293. 750,000. 1/17. D. D. & L., Ltd. Forms/C.2118/14.

Instructions regarding War Diaries and Intelligence Summaries are contained in F. S. Regs., Part II. and the Staff Manual respectively. Title pages will be prepared in manuscript.

WAR DIARY

or

~~INTELLIGENCE SUMMARY.~~ III

(*Erase heading not required.*)

Army Form C. 2118.

Place	Date	Hour	Summary of Events and Information	Remarks and references to Appendices
ELINCOURT	12.10.18		Capt. McCallum returned from temporary duty with 3rd Field Squadron. A & D. book opened. C.W.J.	
BANTEUX (Valenciennes C6)	13.10.18		March at 8 a.m. to BANTEUX. C.W.J.	
BOIS-de-HENNOIS (~~Lens~~ 1/100,000)	14.10.18		March at 7.45 a.m. to MANANCOURT & are billetted in Nissen huts in the BOIS de HENNOIS. Open a divisional Hospital. O.C. Pack mounted section returns from duty with 6th Cav. Brig. Heavy section rejoins. 5 M.A.C. cars returned to M.A.C. Patients adm. to Hospital for week ending 14th = 5 (Diarrhoea one.	
			Patients dressed, fed & evacuated on 9th & 10th, but not shown on A & D. book:-	
			9th Cavalry:- Offs. = 12. O. Rs. = 68.	
			Infantry:- Offs. = 2. O. Rs. = 93. (includes 5 P. of W.)	
			10th Cavalry:- Offs. = 19. O. Rs. = 108	
			Infantry:- Offs. = 7. O. Rs. = 195 (includes 9 P. of W.)	
			In addition light ambulance & cars were loaned to other medical units. C.W.J.	
	18.10.18		Transport inspected by O.C. A.S.C. 3rd Cav. Div. Report — "Excellent as usual". No 8916 Pte. Archer C.W. Rance awarded the Military Medal for services during recent operations. C.W.J.	

(A7092). Wt. W12839/M1293. 75,000. 1/17. D. D. & L., Ltd. Forms/C.2118/14.

Instructions regarding War Diaries and Intelligence Summaries are contained in F. S. Regs., Part II. and the Staff Manual respectively. Title pages will be prepared in manuscript.

WAR DIARY
or
~~INTELLIGENCE~~ SUMMARY.
(Erase heading not required.)

IV

Army Form C. 2118.

Place	Date	Hour	Summary of Events and Information	Remarks and references to Appendices
BOIS-de-HENNOIS. (Lens 1/100,000)	21.10.18		Patients admitted to Hospital during week ending 21st = 113 [Influenza (Epidemic) = 60, Scabies 14, Diarrhoea 8], of the 60 cases of Epidemic Influenza, 8 were from the 6th Cavalry Brigade. C.H.S.	
	22.10.18		Capt. J. W. CRUIKSHANK, M.C. temporarily assumed the duties of M.O. i/c 3rd Field Squadron. C.H.S.	
	29.10.18		Delousing chamber in good working order. C.H.S.	
	31.10.18		Take over Nissen Hut for Scabies cases. Hospital now consists of 5 single + one double Nissen Huts.	
			Patients admitted to Hospital for period ending 31st = 167 (Influenza 103, Scabies 14, Diarrhoea 4).	
			Total admissions for month of October = 305 (Influenza 164, Scabies 28, Diarrhoea 13)	
			Total evacuations during month { O/Rs. W. 5, A+D. 3, O.Rs. book not opened 104	
			Dental cases treated during October = 75. (Ordinary = 70. Mechanical 5). Out of a total admission of 163 Influenza cases 25 or 15.3% had suffered from the disease during the summer influenza epidemic.	
			C.H.S. [signature] Lt. Col. R.A.M.C. O.C. 6 C.F.A.	

2353 Wt. W2514/1454 700,000 5/15 D. D. & L. A.D.S.S./Forms/C. 2118.

Nov. 1918

No. 6 C. F. Amb:

Army Form C. 2118.

Instructions regarding War Diaries and Intelligence Summaries are contained in F. S. Regs., Part II. and the Staff Manual respectively. Title pages will be prepared in manuscript.

WAR DIARY
or
~~INTELLIGENCE SUMMARY.~~ I

(Erase heading not required.)

V 8 47

Place	Date	Hour	Summary of Events and Information	Remarks and references to Appendices
BOIS de HENNOIS (Lens 1/100,000)	1.11.18		Armistice terms with Turkey received. C.W.S.	
	3.11.18		One O. Rank to Div. Hd. Qrs for temp. duty as Medical orderly 3rd Cav. Div. Hd. Qrs. C.W.S.	
	4.11.18		Inspection of horses by G.O.C. 6th Cav. Brig. Classed 2nd of list of Brigade units. Warning order (6th Cav. Brig. B.M. 21/3/11/18) re move tomorrow night. Armistice with Austria from today. C.W.S.	
	5.11.18		On 3 hours notice (6th C.B. L/668). Start clearing hospital. C.W.S.	
MARQUOIN (Valenciennes 1/100,000)	6.11.18		Complete clearing of hospital. Dump Red X Stores. Move at 8 a.m. via GOUZEAUCOURT – TRESCAULT – HAVRINCOURT WOOD to MARQUOIN.	
ESQUERCHIN (Valenciennes 1/100,000)	7.11.18		Move at 8 a.m. via DOUAI to ESQUERCHIN. C.W.S.	
PERONNE (Tournai 8 6 1/100,000)	8.11.18		Move at 8.15 a.m. via DOUAI – TEMPLEUVE to PERONNE. C.W.S.	
RAMECROIX (Tournai 1/100,000)	10.11.18		Move at 10 a.m. to BACHY (Tournai 1/100,000). Heavy section moves to MARTINSART (Tournai 1/100,000). Lie outside Bachy for 3 hours awaiting orders & then via outskirts of Tournai to RAMECROIX. Warning order to be saddled up ready to move at 08.00 tomorrow. C.W.S.	

2353 Wt. W2544/1454 700,000 5/15 D. D. & L. A.D.S.S./Forms/C. 2118.

Instructions regarding War Diaries and Intelligence Summaries are contained in F. S. Regs., Part II. and the Staff Manual respectively. Title pages will be prepared in manuscript.

WAR DIARY
or
~~INTELLIGENCE SUMMARY.~~ II

(Erase heading not required.)

Army Form C. 2118.

No 6 CAVALRY FIELD AMBULANCE
No. —
Date Nov 1918
III CAVALRY DIV.

Place	Date	Hour	Summary of Events and Information	Remarks and references to Appendices
RAMECROIX (Tournai 1/100,000)	11·11·18		Battle orders received at 1 a.m. Objective for 6th Cavalry Brigade was SILLY (Tournai 1/100,000). Move at 7.30 a.m. Arrive outskirts of LEUZE & column was then halted. Big ceremony in Square of Leuze. At 11 a.m. trumpets of 6th Cav. Brigade sounded the "Cease Fire". Band of 55th Div. played English, French & Belgian National anthems. Speech by Mayor of Leuze. 6th C.F.A. was represented by Lt. Col. Stringer, Capts. Neilson & McCallum. March back to previous billets in Ramecroix. C.W.J.	
PONENCHE (Tournai 1/100,000)	12·11·18		Move to better billets in PONNECHE (Tournai 1/100,000). C.W.J.	
	13·11·18		Heavy section rejoins.	
			Patients admitted for week ending Nov. 7th = 79 of which 49 were Influenza, 3 Scabies + 1 Diarrhoea. Of the 79 38 were transfers from 7th C.F.A.	
			Patients admitted for week ending Nov. 14th = 22 of which 3 were Influenza. C.W.J.	

2353 Wt. W2544/1454 700,000 5/15 D. D. & L. A.D.S.S./Forms/C. 2118.

Instructions regarding War Diaries and Intelligence Summaries are contained in F. S. Regs., Part II. and the Staff Manual respectively. Title pages will be prepared in manuscript.

WAR DIARY
or
~~INTELLIGENCE SUMMARY.~~ III

(*Erase heading not required.*)

Army Form C. 2118.

Place	Date	Hour	Summary of Events and Information	Remarks and references to Appendices
PONENCHE (TOURNAI 1/100,000 96.)	14.11.18 to 16.11.18		Resting. Time spent in cleaning + burnishing harness, transport etc + refitting personnel preparatory to the forward move into enemy territory SRL	
	17.11.18		Bde moves on a two regiment front. Unit moves with main body of Bde by main LEUZE - ATH - GISLINGHEM road to billets at RONTANT (TOURNAI 1/100,000 L4) SRL	
RONTANT (TOURNAI 1/100,000 L4)	18.11.18		Move with main body of Bde to Billets in BIERGHES (BRUSSELS 1/100,000 B.4) via ENGHIEN SRL	
BIERGHES (BRUSSELS 1/100,000 B.4)	19.11.18		Capt A. NEILSON MC RAMC. proceeds to X Royal Hussars for temporary duty SRL	
	20.11.18		Capt H.H. MACKENZIE CAMC arrives from 7th CAN CAV. F A for temporary duty SRL Lt Col STRINGER DSO RAMC granted leave to IRELAND 25/11/18 to 9/12/18 SRL	
	21.11.18		Move with main body of Bde to billets in MOUSTY (BRUSSELS 1/100,000 L.5?) passing via BRAINE-LE-CHATEAU + just north of the LION of WATERLOO SRL	
			Patients admitted for week ending 21st 72 of which 28 were British repatriated prisoners of War + 6 French R.P. of W. There were 8 cases of diarrhoea + ten influenza SRL	

D. D. & L., London, E.C. (A10266) Wt W5300/P713 750,000 2/18 Sch. 52 Forms/C2118/16.

Instructions regarding War Diaries and Intelligence Summaries are contained in F. S. Regs., Part II. and the Staff Manual respectively. Title pages will be prepared in manuscript.

WAR DIARY
or
~~INTELLIGENCE SUMMARY.~~
(Erase heading not required.)

IV

Army Form C. 2118.

6 CAVALRY FIELD AMBULANCE Nov 1918 CAVALRY DIVISION

Place	Date	Hour	Summary of Events and Information	Remarks and references to Appendices
MOUSTY (BRUSSELS 1/100,000 G5)	22.11.18		Move with main body of Bde to LONGCHAMPS (BRUSSELS 1/100,000 K5) Enemy had left this village in a very dirty & unsanitary condition SRL	
LONGCHAMPS (BRUSSELS 1/100,000 K6)	24.11.18		Move independently to DHUY (BRUSSELS 1/100,000 K6) Whole unit situated in chateau & chateau farm SRL	
DHUY (BRUSSELS 1/100,000)	30.11.18		Remain here for remainder of month. Patients admitted to H from 22nd - 30th - 53 of which 14 were British R.P of W + 2 French R.P. of W. There were eight cases of diarrhoea, ten of Influenza + one of Scabies Total admitted for November 226 of which 72 were influenza 4 scabies + 14 diarrhoea. Included in the total of 226 are 45 British Ref. P of W + 8 French Ref. P of W. During the march forward through BELGIUM, met with a very warm reception from all the inhabitants. At the various halts amusements (football, whist drives etc) were organised for the men. SRL SRRowell Major RAMC SR.	

D. D. & L., London, E.C.
(A10266) Wt W5300/P713 750,000 2/18 Sch. 52 Forms/C2118/16.

Dec 1918

140/3481

No. 6 Cav. F.A.

17

Instructions regarding War Diaries and Intelligence Summaries are contained in F. S. Regs., Part II. and the Staff Manual respectively. Title pages will be prepared in manuscript.

WAR DIARY
or
~~INTELLIGENCE SUMMARY.~~
(Erase heading not required.)

I

Army Form C. 2118.

988 4

Place	Date	Hour	Summary of Events and Information	Remarks and references to Appendices
DHUY (Brussels 1/100,000)	1-2.12.18		No change. C.H.S.	
	3.12.18		3 N.C.Os & 7 Privates, Ramc to No. Canadian C.C.S. for temp. duty. C.H.S.	
	7.12.18		Patients admitted to Hospital for week ending Dec. 7th = 19. (Scabies 3, + Influenza 5). C.H.S.	
			Warning order to move on 10th. C.H.S.	
	8.12.18		3 N.C.Os + 7 Pts, Ramc returned from temp duty with 1st C.C.S. C.H.S.	
ABBÉ (LIEGE 1/100,000) Cb.	10.12.18		Move to ABBÉ – ½ mile W of ANTHEIT.	
			Capt. P. A. McCallum + 1 O.R. to 3rd Drag. Guards for temp. duty. C.H.S.	
	11.12.18		Capt. A. E. Grant, Ramc from 17th Lancers to office of A.D.M.S. 3rd Cav. Div. for temp duty. C.H.S.	
LA MALLIEUE HALTE (Liege 1/100,000)	12.12.18		Move to LA MALLIEUE HALTE (Author. 6th Cav. Bde. order No. ... d/11/12/18).	
			Patients adm. to Hospital for week ending Dec. 14th = 16 (Diarrhoea – 1, Scabies – 1, Influenza 14). C.H.S.	
	15.12.18		Capt. A. Neilson M.C. rejoined from temporary duty with 10th Roy. Hussars. C.H.S.	
	16.12.18		Assumed medical care of 3rd Cav. Div. M.T. Coy. C.H.S.	
	18.12.18		Capt. H. H. M. Mackenzie C.A.M.C. returned to Canadian No. 7 Can. C.F.A. One O.R. returned from temporary duty with the 3rd Drag. Guards. C.H.S. Lectured to the men yesterday on demobilization + resettlement problems. C.H.S.	

D. D. & L., London, E.C.
(A10266) Wt W5300/P713 750,000 2/18 Sch. 52 Forms/C2118/16.

Instructions regarding War Diaries and Intelligence Summaries are contained in F. S. Regs., Part II. and the Staff Manual respectively. Title pages will be prepared in manuscript.

WAR DIARY
or
~~INTELLIGENCE SUMMARY.~~
(*Erase heading not required.*)

11

Army Form C. 2118.

Place	Date	Hour	Summary of Events and Information	Remarks and references to Appendices
LA MALLIEUE HALTE (Liege 1/100,000).	19.12.18		One corporal, Ramc. to Cav. Corps Concentration Camp, SERAING for temp. duty. C.W.S.	
	20.12.18		One O.R. from temp. duty with A.D.M.S. 3rd Cav. Div. C.W.S.	
	21.12.18		Patients admitted to H. for week ending Dec. 21st = 19. (Diarrhoea — 1; Scabies — 2; Influenza 1). C.W.S.	
	22.12.18		First lot of demobilized men leave the unit (one Demobilyzer — policeman + 4 coal miners). C.W.S.	
	23.12.18		One O.R. from temp. duty with A.D.M.S. 3rd Cav. Div. C.W.S.	
	24.12.18		Capt. J. M. Cruikshank M.C. returns from temp. duty with 1st Royal Dragoons. C.W.S.	
	30.12.18		Confidential reports on all officers in this unit sent in in accordance with instructions. Three motor ambulances with drivers arrived from No 11 M.A.C. for temp. duty. C.W.S.	
	31.12.18		No 6 C.F.A. is now in charge of, in addition to all Brigade units, the following units:- 146 A.T. Coy R.E. — SERAING. Cav. Corps Con. Camp. — " 198 Lab. Coy — ENGIS. 114 " — AMAY. 3rd Fd. Squadr. R.E. — SCLESSIN. 3rd Cav. Div. M.T. Coy. — ENGIS. C.W.S.	

D. D. & L., London, E.C.
(A10266) Wt W5300/P713 750,000 2/18 Sch. 52 Forms/C2118/16.

Instructions regarding War Diaries and Intelligence Summaries are contained in F. S. Regs., Part II. and the Staff Manual respectively. Title pages will be prepared in manuscript.

WAR DIARY
or
~~INTELLIGENCE SUMMARY~~.
(*Erase heading not required.*)

111

Army Form C. 2118.

Place	Date	Hour	Summary of Events and Information	Remarks and references to Appendices
LA MALLIEUE HALTE. (Liege 1/100,000).	31.12.18 Contd		Patients admitted to H. for period Dec. 21st to 31st = 24 (Influenza – 2). Total no. of patients admitted during December = 78 (Diarrhoea – 2; Scabies – 6; Influenza – 13). Total evacuations during December: W. Sick. Officers — 2 Other Ranks — 49 CWJ. Appendix During the month lectures were given to the men on Demobilization, Re-settlement + Education. Every man in the unit was then examined separately, questioned about his future prospects, given advice or help where necessary. Men were advised to utilize the time prior to their demobilization in improving their general knowledge, + where possible in improving themselves at their old trades. It was found that the men who had ~~trades were~~ not anxious to leave the unit to go CWJ.	

D. D. & L., London, E.C.
(A10265) Wt W5300/P713 750,000 2/18 Sch. 52 Forms/C2118/16.

Instructions regarding War Diaries and Intelligence Summaries are contained in F. S. Regs., Part II. and the Staff Manual respectively. Title pages will be prepared in manuscript.

WAR DIARY
or
~~INTELLIGENCE~~ SUMMARY. IV

(*Erase heading not required.*)

Army Form C. 2118.

Place	Date	Hour	Summary of Events and Information	Remarks and references to Appendices
Appendix Contd.			go to school of instruction in works before etc. they probably thought that this might cause them to lose opportunities for being demobilized. A certain no. of men expressed a desire for an improved general education & education in special subjects such as French, book keeping etc. Some men desired further & better training in nursing than could be obtained in a C.F.A. & names were submitted with a view to transfer to a General Hospital. This was not approved by D.D.M.S. Cav. Corps who was of opinion that sufficient knowledge could be obtained in a C.F.A. Having obtained all the information ~~necessary~~, an Education Officer (Capt. Neilson, RAMC) was appointed, & he is arranging, as far as possible, instruction for those who desire it. A derelict German motor ambulance car has been retrieved & is being used for instructional purposes. A total of 1 Demobilizer, 1 long service soldier, & 8 coalminers were demobilized	

C.W.S.

D. D. & L., London, E.C.
(A10266) Wt W5300/P713 750,000 2/18 Sch. 52 Forms/C2118/16.

Instructions regarding War Diaries and Intelligence Summaries are contained in F. S. Regs., Part II. and the Staff Manual respectively. Title pages will be prepared in manuscript.

WAR DIARY
or
~~INTELLIGENCE~~ SUMMARY.
(Erase heading not required.)

V

Army Form C. 2118.

Place	Date	Hour	Summary of Events and Information	Remarks and references to Appendices
Appendix cont'd			during December. In addition, under the scheme for demobilizing men on leave 8 other Ranks were not wired for or did not use the return half of their tickets, marked to return to unit.	
			A brief report was sent in to A.D.M.S. 3rd Cav. Division reference medical aid rendered by this unit to French civilians + French military services.	
			The outstanding feature of the month has been the absolute break down in the system for returning men to their units on completion of leave. A gradually increasing number of men since Dec 6th have been accumulating at a so-called camp in LOOS (near LILLE). The authorities have been unable to send these men from the camp to their units. One such soldier was evacuated sick from this camp, + having subsequently recovered was discharged from Hospital + made his own way back to this unit. Owing to these men not being returned demobilization of Long Service men in the unit + the sending away on leave of men due for leave have been largely stopped. There are now 33 men absent on leave.	
			C H Turner [?] Lt. Col. Rame. O.C. 6 C.F.A. [?]	

D.D. & L., London, E.C. (A10266) Wt W5300/P713 750,000 2/18 Sch. 52 Forms/C2118/16.

Jan 1919

3RD CAV DIV

140/3490

Box 853

No. 6 Cav. F A.

Box 853

19

Instructions regarding War Diaries and Intelligence Summaries are contained in F. S. Regs., Part II. and the Staff Manual respectively. Title pages will be prepared in manuscript.

WAR DIARY
or
~~INTELLIGENCE SUMMARY.~~
(Erase heading not required.)

6 Cav Fd Amb I

Army Form C. 2118.

No. 6 Cavalry Field Ambulance, XIII Cavalry Brigade

18/49

Place	Date	Hour	Summary of Events and Information	Remarks and references to Appendices
LA MALLIEUE HALTE. (Liege proper)	1.1.19		Capt P. McCALLUM returned from temporary duty with the 3rd Dragoon Guards. C.W.T.	
	4.1.19		One O. Rank to Cav. Corps Concentration Camp for demobilization C.W.T.	
	5.1.19		Capt. A. NEILSON to LIEGE on temporary duty as Med. Off. in charge of Returning Prisoners of War Camp. C.W.T.	
	7.1.19		Patients admitted to Hospital for week ending 7.1.19 = 2 Officers + 47 O. Ranks (Influenza = 25, Scabies 2, Diarrhoea 1, Venereal Disease = 8). C.W.T.	
	8.1.19		Inspection of Hospital by D.D.M.S. Cavalry Corps. C.W.T.	
	10.1.19		One orderly (Corporal) to Medical Inspection Room of Cav. Corps Conc. Camp as Med. orderly. C.W.T.	
	11.1.19		2 N.C.O.s + 2 privates to Cav. Corps Conc. Camp for demobilization C.W.T.	
	13.1.19		1 N.C.O. + 1 private to C.C.C. Camp for demobilization. C.W.T.	
			2 O. Ranks to C.C.C. Camp for demobilization.	
	14.1.19		Patients admitted to H. for week ending 14th = 31. (Influenza = 13, Scabies 1, Venereal 12). C.W.T.	
	15.1.19		2 N.C.Os to C.C.C. Camp for demobilization C.W.T.	
	18.1.19		Capt. Neilson returned from temporary duty in Liege. C.W.T.	
	20.1.19		Beat "B" Squadron, Xth Hussars in final of Brigade football competition by 1 - nil. C.W.T.	
	21.1.19		Patients admitted to H. for week ending 21st. 3 Officers + 44 O. Ranks (Influenza - 15, Scabies 1, Venereal - 13). C.W.T.	

D. D. & L., London, E.C.
(A10266) Wt W5300/P713 750,000 2/18 Sch. 52 Forms/C2118/16.

Instructions regarding War Diaries and Intelligence Summaries are contained in F. S. Regs., Part II. and the Staff Manual respectively. Title pages will be prepared in manuscript.

WAR DIARY
or
~~INTELLIGENCE~~ SUMMARY. II

(*Erase heading not required.*)

Army Form C. 2118.

Place	Date	Hour	Summary of Events and Information	Remarks and references to Appendices
LA MALLIEUE HALTE	31.1.19		Patients admitted to Hospital for period Jan 22nd to 31st = 1 Off. & 40 Other Ranks (Influenza 11. Scabies 3. Diarrhoea = 4 venereal = 8).	
			Total no. of patients admitted during January 1919 = 168. (Influenza = 63. Venereal = 41. Scabies 7. Diarrhoea = 8).	
			Total no. of patients evacuated during January 1919:- = Officers 6. other ranks 89.	
			In addition to the sick from 6th Cavalry Brigade & from 3rd Cav. Divisional Headquarters, the following units remain under medical charge of this unit.	
			749 Area Employment Coy — Engis	
			146 A.T. Coy. R.E. — Seraing	
			Cav. Corps Rest Camp —	
			193 Labour Coy. — Engis	
			114 — Amay	
			~~[illegible]~~ 3rd Cav. Div. M.T. Coy — Engis	
			66 Aux. Steam & Petrol Coy. — Amay	
			15th G.H.Q. M.T. Coy —	
			Animal Collecting Camp — Engis.	
			The main medical feature of the month was the large increase in the number of cases of Influenza & of Venereal Disease.	
			[illegible]	

D. D. & L., London, E.C.
(A10265) Wt W5300/P713 750,000 2/18 Sch. 52 Forms/C2118/16.

Instructions regarding War Diaries and Intelligence Summaries are contained in F. S. Regs., Part II. and the Staff Manual respectively. Title pages will be prepared in manuscript.

WAR DIARY
or
~~INTELLIGENCE~~ SUMMARY.

(*Erase heading not required.*)

Army Form C. 2118.

Place	Date	Hour	Summary of Events and Information	Remarks and references to Appendices
LA MALLIEUE HALTE	31.1.19.		The former, in so far as it could be called an epidemic was entirely confined to Divisional Hd. Qrs, & amongst men who had been untouched by previous outbreaks. This type of Influenza was much more severe than formerly. All cases ~~suffered~~ suffered from Bronchitis, a number developed Broncho-pneumonia & 2 developed Pneumonia. The uncomplicated cases had a persistent high temperature & a prolonged convalescence.	
			Venereal disease assumed serious proportions. Many lectures were given to the men, & Early treatment rooms were established in all units. These rooms have become relatively popular, & the end of the month saw a decided decrease in the number of cases. Early identification & removal of the infecting women was carried out. The incidence of the disease was almost entirely confined to units living in villages in the Meuse valley, the towns of SERAING & JEMAPPE being the most notorious.	
			From an administrative point of view the outstanding feature of the month was the complete failure of men on leave to return from leave	
			a.e.s.	

D. D. & L., London, E.C.
(A10266) Wt W5300/P713 750,000 2/18 Sch. 52 Forms/C2118/16.

WAR DIARY
or
~~INTELLIGENCE SUMMARY.~~

(Erase heading not required.)

Army Form C. 2118.

Instructions regarding War Diaries and Intelligence Summaries are contained in F. S. Regs., Part II. and the Staff Manual respectively. Title pages will be prepared in manuscript.

IV

Place	Date	Hour	Summary of Events and Information	Remarks and references to Appendices
LA MALLIEUE HALTE (Liège 1/100,000)	31.1.19.		not, as was the case in December, because they were being held up in a camp near Loos (these men were returned by train on 5.1.19), but because the kindly authorities at home are trying to demobilise them. Wires continue to be sent to this unit asking for the release of these men, who are not entitled to release on grounds of age, service, occupation or any other reason, except that of happening to be at home on leave. Wires continue to be sent by this unit to the Home authorities demanding the return of these men. The men continue to remain on leave. The matter has been taken up by the Division & a letter sent to the Corps. [illegible] Lt. Col. RAMC O.C. 60 F.A.	

D. D. & L., London, E.C. (A10266) Wt W5300/P713 750,000 2/18 Sch. 52 Forms/C2118/16.

Feb. 1919

140/332 K

No. 6 Cav. F.A.

31

Instructions regarding War Diaries and Intelligence Summaries are contained in F. S. Regs., Part II. and the Staff Manual respectively. Title pages will be prepared in manuscript.

WAR DIARY
or
~~INTELLIGENCE SUMMARY.~~
(Erase heading not required.)

I

Vol 50

Army Form C. 2118.

No 6 CAVALRY FIELD AMBULANCE

Place	Date	Hour	Summary of Events and Information	Remarks and references to Appendices
LA MALLIEUE HALTE Liege 1/100,000	1.2.19		Nothing to note. C.W.S.	
	2.2.19		Capt. J. K. Cruikshank M.C. to 48 C.C.S. for temporary duty. C.W.S.	
	5.2.19		Details arranged re composite Brigade for use in any emergency. C.W.S.	
	7.2.19		Patients admitted for week ending 7th = 20 (Scabies 2, Influenza 2, Diarrhoea 1, Venereal 5) C.W.S.	
	14.2.19		Patients admitted for week ending 14th = 34. (Scabies 2 Influenza 15, Venereal 4). C.W.S.	
	18.2.19		Arrange an "Early Treatment" Room in Liege, with two orderlies in charge. C.W.S.	
	21.2.19		Capt. A R GRANT (on temporary duty with A.D.M.S. 2nd Cav. Div.) to 37 M.A.C. & struck off the strength of this unit. Patients admitted for week ending 21st = 46. (Influenza 30) Venereal 6). C.W.S.	
	26.2.19		Make out fresh list of names of personnel to constitute cadre in accordance with new establishment of 30 Rank & 13 A.S.C. C.W.S.	
	27.2.19		5 other Ranks (Rame) to 53 C.C.S. for temporary duty. C.W.S.	

D. D. & L., London, E.C.
(A10266) Wt W5300/P713 750,000 2/18 Sch. 52 Forms/C2118/16.

Instructions regarding War Diaries and Intelligence Summaries are contained in F. S. Regs., Part II. and the Staff Manual respectively. Title pages will be prepared in manuscript.

WAR DIARY
or
~~INTELLIGENCE SUMMARY.~~ II

(*Erase heading not required.*)

Army Form C. 2118.

Place	Date	Hour	Summary of Events and Information	Remarks and references to Appendices
LA MALLIEUE HALTE	28-2-19		Patients admitted for week ending 28th = 26 (Influenza 12, Venereal 7). Total no. of patients admitted during February 1919 = 132. of which 6 were German P. of W. (Influenza = 73 include 4 P. of W. Venereal = 22). In addition to the sick from 6th Cav. Brigade & from 3rd Cav. Div. Hd. Qrs. the following units remain under medical charge of this unit.— 6th Machine Gun Squadron — Amay. "C" Battery R.H.A. — Awirs. 3rd Cav. Div. M.T. Coy. Engis. Animal Collecting Camp — Engis. 749 Area Employ. Coy — " 104 Labour Coy — " 347 Rd. Constr. Coy. R.E. — Amay 66 Aux. Steam & Petrol Coy. — " There was an increase in the Influenza epidemic, but not a marked increase. The type of Influenza was the same as that noted in last month's Diary. Those previously	

D. D. & L., London, E.C.
(A10266) Wt W5300/P713 750,000 2/18 Sch. 52 Forms/C2118/16.

Instructions regarding War Diaries and Intelligence Summaries are contained in F. S. Regs., Part II. and the Staff Manual respectively. Title pages will be prepared in manuscript.

WAR DIARY
or
~~INTELLIGENCE SUMMARY.~~ III

(Erase heading not required.)

Army Form C. 2118.

Place	Date	Hour	Summary of Events and Information	Remarks and references to Appendices
LA MALLIEUE HALTE.			immune still continue to be most affected by this epidemic. The venereal incidence continues to be serious in spite of the large nos. of men demobilized. The newly organized E.T. room in Liege is dealing with an increasingly large number of men. A scheme for the abortive treatment of gonorrhoea has been started, but it is too early to give an opinion. Only cases in the first day of the disease are being dealt with. During the month 6 R.A.M.C. O.Rs + 2 A.S.C. O.Rs were demobilized. W. Tonge Lt. Col. R.A.M.C. O.C. 6 C.F.A.	

Dias. 1919.

160/3551

No. 6 Cav. F. A.

Instructions regarding War Diaries and Intelligence Summaries are contained in F. S. Regs., Part II. and the Staff Manual respectively. Title pages will be prepared in manuscript.

WAR DIARY
or
~~INTELLIGENCE SUMMARY.~~
(Erase heading not required.)

Army Form C. 2118.

Place	Date	Hour	Summary of Events and Information	Remarks and references to Appendices
LA MALLIEUE HALTE (Liege 1/100,000)	1.3.19		1 OR RAMC transferred to DDMS Cav. Corps. SRL	
	2.3.19		1 OR RAMC evacuated to 50 CCS SRL	
			Capt A NEILSON MC proceeds on leave to the UK SRL	
	5.3.19		1 OR RASC HT to C.C. Concentration Camp for demobilization SRL	
	6.3.19		Lt Col C H STRINGER DSO proceeds on leave to the U.K from 7.3.19 – 21.3.19 SRL	
	7.3.19		Capt ~~H A~~ RONN MC RAMC arrives for duty from 3rd Dragoon Guards SRL	
			Patients admitted for week 34 (Scabies 1 Influenza 20 Venereal 8) SRL	
	8.3.19		1 OR RASC AT to C.C. Concentration Camp for demobilization SRL	
	11.3.19		Major J R LOVELL to No 4 CFA for temp. duty	
			Belgian red cross stores returned to Belgian Red Cross Spa SRL	
	12.3.19		Capt A NEILSON MC RAMC returned from leave to the U.K having been wired to return for demobilization SRL	
	13.3.19		Capt A NEILSON MC RAMC to C.C. Concentration Camp for demobilization SRL	
			5 OR's RAMC return from temp duty with 53 CCS	
	14.3.19		No 17 patients admitted for week 34 (2 Scabies, 2 influenza, 1 Diarrhoea + 9 venereal) SRL	
			Capt J LYONS RAMC arrives for temp duty. SRL	
	16.3.19		5 OR's RASC HT sent to C.C. Concentration Camp for demobilisation SRL	
			1 OR RASC HT evacuated to 50 CCS	

D. D. & L., London, E.C.
(A10266) Wt W5300/P713 750,000 2/18 Sch. 52 Forms/C2118/16.

Instructions regarding War Diaries and Intelligence Summaries are contained in F. S. Regs., Part II. and the Staff Manual respectively. Title pages will be prepared in manuscript.

WAR DIARY
or
~~INTELLIGENCE~~ SUMMARY. II

(Erase heading not required.)

Army Form C. 2118.

Place	Date	Hour	Summary of Events and Information	Remarks and references to Appendices
LA MALLIEUE	17.3.19		Cpl Wheeler returns from temp duty with 3rd Cav Div Reserve Park SRL	
HALTE			Capt J LYONS RAMC to 1st Royal Dragoons for duty SRL	
(LIEGE			Patients admitted for week 28 (1 Scabies 3 Influenza, 3 Venereal) SRL	
1/100,000)	21.3.19		Capt J.N. CRUICKSHANK MC RAMC transferred to 48 CCS SRL	
	22.3.19		MAJOR G.R LOVELL RAMC from temp duty with No 4 CFA	
			4 OR's RASC MT to 81 Coy RASC 3rd Cav Div SRL	
	27.3.19		Capt P.A. McCALLUM RAMC proceeds to CCC Camp for demobilisation	
	29.3.19		1 OR (RASC MT) with motor cycle D10 to 3rd Cav Div MT Coy SRL	
	31.3.19		1 OR (RASC MT) to 3rd Cav Div MT Coy for demobilisation SRL	
			Patients admitted period 22nd - 31st 47 (Scabies 3, Influenza 11 and Venereal 13). Capt J S KINROSS RAMC arrives for duty from 3rd Field Squad RE.	
			There were 136 admissions to hospital for the month of which 4 were Scabies 1 Diarrhoea 36 Influenza + 35 Venereal.	
			In addition there were 36 German P of W admitted (29) these were influenza.	
			~~[illegible]~~ SRL In addition to the brigade units the following units are visited daily.	
			4 Cav Bde HQ, 3rd Cav Div MT Coy, Animal Collecting Camp Engrs, 3rd P of W Coy Engrs, HQ 4th Bde RHA CHOKIER, Cadre of Div HQrs, certain details of regiments awaiting demobilization at Awans 1st, 2nd + 3rd Cavalry Reserve Parks, Cav Corps troops Reserve Park	

D. D. & L., London, E.C.
(A10266) Wt W5300/P713 750,000 2/18 Sch. 52 Forms/C2118/16.

Instructions regarding War Diaries and Intelligence Summaries are contained in F. S. Regs., Part II. and the Staff Manual respectively. Title pages will be prepared in manuscript.

WAR DIARY
or
~~INTELLIGENCE~~ SUMMARY. III

(*Erase heading not required.*)

Army Form C. 2118.

Place	Date	Hour	Summary of Events and Information	Remarks and references to Appendices
LA MALLIEVE HALTE LIEGE 1/100,000			3rd Field Squadron, Cav Corps Concentration Camp, X Horse Depot 114 + 102 Lab Coys, 146 + 574 A.T. Coys R.E. + 169 P of W Coy SRL	
			SRLowell Major RAMC	

D. D. & L., London, E.C.
(A10266) Wt W5300/P713 750,000 2/18 Sch. 52 Forms/C2118/16.

140/3550.

Apl 1919

No. 6 Cav. F.A.

Instructions regarding War Diaries and Intelligence Summaries are contained in F. S. Regs., Part II. and the Staff Manual respectively. Title pages will be prepared in manuscript.

12

WAR DIARY
or
~~INTELLIGENCE SUMMARY.~~ I
(Erase heading not required.)

Army Form C. 2118.

NL 52

Place	Date	Hour	Summary of Events and Information	Remarks and references to Appendices
LA MALLIEVE HALTE (Liege 1/100,000)	1.4.19		1 OR RAMC evacuated to 50 CCS	SRL
	3.4.19		1 OR RASC MT being retainable transferred to 1st Cav Div 1 OR RASC MT with one motor ambulance transferred to 3rd C.D. MT Coy	SRL
	4.4.19		3 OR's RASC MT. to Concentration Camp for demobilization	SRL
	7.4.19		Patients admitted to hosp for week ending 7th 6 (six) including 1 scabies + 2 Venereal.	SRL
	8.4.19		Capt (A/Lt Col) C.H. STRINGER DSO to DMS IV area for temp duty Capt J.S KINROSS to 55 CCS for duty	SRL
	9.4.19		Capt A.A. RONN MC to 7th CFA to assume command	SRL
	10.4.19		1 OR (RAMC) evacuated to 50 CCS	SRL
	12.4.19		2 OR. RASC MT. + 2 motor ambulances to 3rd Cav Div MT Coy	SRL
	14.4.19		1 OR RAMC (retainable) to No 1 CFA for duty Patients admitted to hosp during week 14 (fourteen) including 3 (three) venereal	SRL
	15.4.19		2 OR's RASC MT. to concentration camp for demobilisation	SRL
	21.4.19		Patients admitted to hosp. for week 14 (fourteen) including 3 (three) Influenza + 6 (six) Venereal	SRL
	25.4.19		Capt A.A RONN MC and 2 OR's RAMC + 1 OR RASC MT taken on the strength from No 7 CFA	SRL

D. D. & L., London, E.C.
(A10266) Wt W5300/P713 750,000 2/18 Sch. 52 Forms/C2118/16.

Instructions regarding War Diaries and Intelligence Summaries are contained in F. S. Regs., Part II. and the Staff Manual respectively. Title pages will be prepared in manuscript.

WAR DIARY
or
~~INTELLIGENCE SUMMARY.~~
(*Erase heading not required.*)

Army Form C. 2118.

II

Place	Date	Hour	Summary of Events and Information	Remarks and references to Appendices
LA MALLIEVE HALTE (Liege 1/100,000)	26.4.19		Capt AA RONN M.C. granted special leave to the UK from 24.4.19 – 11.5.19	
	30.4.19		Patients admitted to hosp for period 22nd – 30th 17 (seventeen) including 1 (one) Scabies + 7 (seven) Venereal	
			Total sick admissions for the month was 51 British and 10 German P. of War.	
			During the month it has been expected that the cadre would proceed home. The dates of cadres to leave before this unit however has been postponed continually + there is not yet any definite sign of the actual time of departure. It has been very difficult to keep up the morale of the personnel. They have now been reduced to cadre for more than a month with nothing to do + expecting all the while to be sent home. Passes have been given to COLOGNE also to neighbouring towns + other amusements in the form of football matches, dances etc organised.	
			J R Rowell Major RAMC	

D. D. & L., London, E.C.
(A10266) Wt W5300/P713 750,000 2/18 Sch. 52 Forms/C2118/16.

May. 1919

140/35760

No. 6 Cav. Field Amb.

12

6 CFA

May 1919

Vol 53

Instructions regarding War Diaries and Intelligence Summaries are contained in F. S. Regs., Part II. and the Staff Manual respectively. Title pages will be prepared in manuscript.

WAR DIARY
or
~~INTELLIGENCE SUMMARY.~~

(*Erase heading not required.*)

Army Form C. 2118.

Place	Date	Hour	Summary of Events and Information	Remarks and references to Appendices
LA MALLIEUE HALTE LIEGE 1/100,000	1.5.19		Capt (A/Lt Col) C.H. Stringer assumed duties of DADMS IV Area, relinquishing the acting rank of Lt. Col. SRK	
	2.5.19		Under instructions from ADMS IV Area 3 O.R.s withdrawn from E.T. room LIEGE + room closed. Chart showing numbers using room for period Feb 19th – May 2nd attached. As it is impossible to follow the history of these men it is not possible to ascertain if any have contracted venereal disease after the early treatment but cases admitted to the ambulance have been men who have either not used the E.T. room, have carried out inefficient early treatment of their own or have delayed several hours before treatment SRK	
	4.5.19		4 O.R.s to concentration camp (one Z 56 + 3 who were taken on the strength from No 4 CFA pending their return from the base SRK	
	10.5.19		Warning order received that unit will probably entrain at FLEMALLE HALTE (LIEGE 1/100,000) for ANTWERP on 12th inst SRK	

D. D. & L., London, E.C.
(A10266) Wt W5300/P713 750,000 2/18 Sch. 52 Forms/C2118/16.

Instructions regarding War Diaries and Intelligence Summaries are contained in F. S. Regs., Part II. and the Staff Manual respectively. Title pages will be prepared in manuscript.

WAR DIARY
or
~~INTELLIGENCE SUMMARY~~. II

(Erase heading not required.)

Army Form C. 2118.

6 Cav F. Amb
May 1919.

Place	Date	Hour	Summary of Events and Information	Remarks and references to Appendices
LA MALLIEUE HALTE. (LIEGE 1/100,000)	11.V.19		Receive definite orders from cadre brigade to entrain at FLEMALLE on 12th	
			2 O.R.s with remaining motor ambulance and motor cycle sent into 3rd CAV DIV M.T Coy SPA. 1 Pte RAMC was sent in on the car to return by train the same day with receipts. These could not be obtained that day so he was forced to return without them	
			Messenger sent by train to IV Area NAMUR to ascertain 1 If any officer was available to proceed with the cadre 2 Disposal of 1 Pte RAMC retainable 3 Disposal of CAPT RARONN MC on leave due to cross today	
			This was necessary as owing to the shortage of time no answer could be obtained through signals	
		1400	Visited OC No 50 CCS HUY who is taking over medical charge of this area after departure of 6 CFA. Described the situation of the troops remaining & arranged that I should notify all units where a M.O from No 50 CCS would call	

D. D. & L., London, E.C.
(A10266) Wt W5300/P713 750,000 2/18 Sch. 52 Forms/C2118/16.

Instructions regarding War Diaries and Intelligence Summaries are contained in F. S. Regs., Part II. and the Staff Manual respectively. Title pages will be prepared in manuscript.

WAR DIARY or ~~INTELLIGENCE SUMMARY.~~

(Erase heading not required.)

III

6 Cav. F. Amb.
May 1919.

Army Form C. 2118.

Place	Date	Hour	Summary of Events and Information	Remarks and references to Appendices
LA MALLIEUE HALTE			each morning to see sick. All units not situated in the valley of the MEUSE to send their sick down to the nearest unit on the main road or in case of sick in billets a message. Also arranged to visit units on the morning of 12th myself if possible & if I could not send my M.A.C. car into No 50 CCS early enough for a M.O. to come out from there. SRL	
	12.5.19		Capt HARONN to IVth Area.	
			1. OR RAMC to No 48 CCS	
			one MAC car returned to 11 MAC other sent to OC No 50 CCS for duty	
		14.30	Mules arrive from Aux A T Coy & move transport to station	
		15.30	Remaining personnel & loose stores proceed on two motor lorries to FLEMALLE.	
		17.30	Train arrives, one hour late, at FLEMALLE one coach derailed & completely overturned as it was being shunted into the siding This delayed the entrainment	
		20.00	Train left FLEMALLE, one hour behind the scheduled time An uneventful journey to ANTWERP. SRL	

D. D. & L., London, E.C.
(A10266) Wt W5300/P713 750,000 2/18 Sch. 52 Forms/C2118/16.

Instructions regarding War Diaries and Intelligence Summaries are contained in F. S. Regs., Part II. and the Staff Manual respectively. Title pages will be prepared in manuscript.

WAR DIARY IV
or
~~INTELLIGENCE SUMMARY.~~
(Erase heading not required.)

6 Cas. F. Amb.
May 1919

Army Form C. 2118.

Place	Date	Hour	Summary of Events and Information	Remarks and references to Appendices
ANTWERP	12.5.19	6.00	Arrived. Two trains already waiting to unload. Men marched to camp for breakfast returning at 09.30 to proceed with disentrainment	
		10.30	Transport unloaded & parked under a guard in Hangar	
	14.5.19		Patients admitted to hosp for week ending 14th 5 (five) of which two were venereal.	
	19.5.19		Receive orders to embark on S.S. SICILIAN on the 20th. Censor stamp returned by registered post to Army Stationery & Printing department — CALAIS	

J R Howell Major
RAMC SR

D. D. & L., London, E.C.
(A10266) Wt W5300/P713 750,000 2/18 Sch. 52 Forms/C2118/16.

Early Treatment Chart 6th Cav: Fd: Amb E.T. Room Lieu from 19-2-1919 to 2-5-1919.

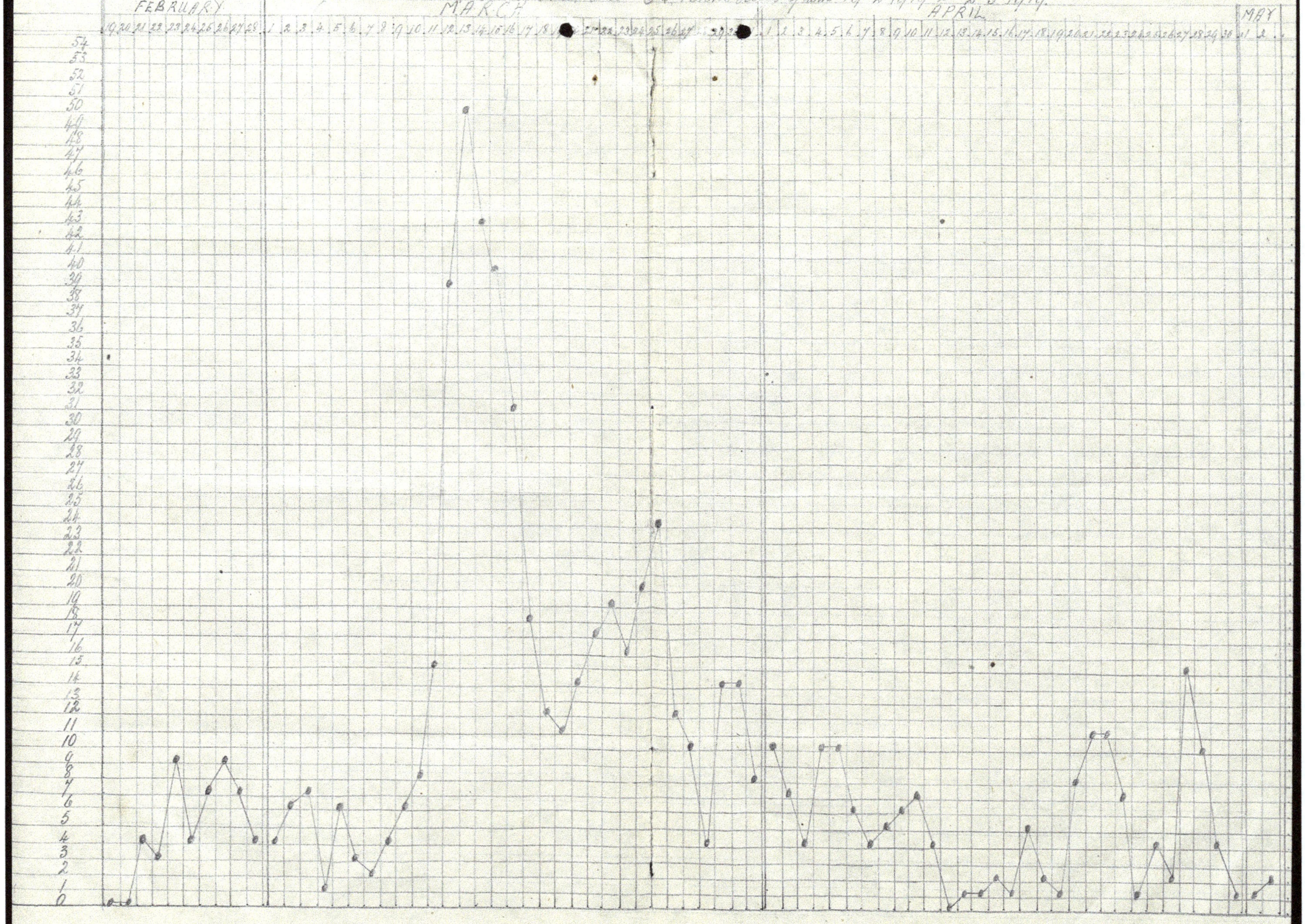